ECHAD

JEWISH WRITING

from

DOWN UNDER:

Australia and New Zealand

general editors ▬

ROBERT *&* **KALECHOFSKY**
ROBERTA

PR
9614.5
.J48
J48

Jewish Writing From Down Under: An Anthology of Australian and New Zealand Jewish Literature. Copyright © 1984 by Micah Publications, 255 Humphrey Street, Marblehead, Ma 01945, U.S.A.

Apart from fair dealing as permitted under the Copyright Act, this book, or parts thereof, may not be reproduced in any form without permission from publisher.

Library of Congress Cataloging in Publication Data
Main entry under title:

Jewish writing from down under.

1. Australian literature--Jewish authors.
2. Australian literature--20th century. 3. New Zealand literature--Jewish authors. 4. New Zealand literature--20th century. 5. Jews--Australia--Literary collections.
6. Jews--New Zealand--Literary collections.
I. Kalechofsky, Robert. II. Kalechofsky, Roberta.
PR9614.5.J48J48   1984   820'.9'8924   84-1098
ISBN 0-916288-16-1

Printed by McNaughton & Gunn, Ann Arbor, Michigan 48106

This volume was made possible through the generous support of the National Endowment for the Arts in Washington, D.C., a Federal Agency.

Acknowledgements: "The Chosen," Fay Zwicky; Voices Within the Ark:The Modern Jewish Poets, ed. Schwartz and Rudolf (Avon Books, 1980), reprinted by permission of author; "Hostages," Fay Zwicky; Coast to Coast, ed Frank Moorhouse, Angus & Robertson, Sydney, 1973, reprinted by permission of author and publisher.
    excerpts from "Founding of the Wellington Community," by Maurice Pitt, published by permission of author.
    "The Trouble With Felix," (excerpt) Alan Collins; from Troubles: *Tsorres, 21 short stories, Kingfisher Books Pty. Ltd, in conjunction with Alros Pty.Ltd, 1983, republished by permission of author.

"Well, What Do You Say To My Boy?" Judah Waten Love And Rebellion; Hodja Educational Resources Co-operative Ltd., 1978; republished by permission of author.

"Seventy Years of Yiddish Theatre," Dr. Serge Liberman, Part One Melbourne Chronicle no. 3(23), June-July, 1980; Part Two Melbourne Chronicle, no 1(25), January, 1981, excerpted; "Two Years in Exile," On Firmer Shores, Globe Press Pty Ltd. 1981; "Drifting," A Universe of Clowns, Phoenix Publications Brisbane, republished by permission of author.

"The House On Lafayette Street," Michele Nayman, faces you can't find again, Neptune Press Pty. Ltd., 1980. Republished by permission of author.

Garden Island People, Nancy Keesing, Wentworth Books, Sydney, 1975. Excerpts reprinted by permission of author.

"Africa Wall," and "Bobbeh," Morris Lurie, Dirty Friends, stories by Morris Lurie, Penquin Books, Australia Ltd., republished by permission of author.

"Jews and Maoris," excerpts from "Interfaces Between Jews and Maoris," and from Tangiwai: A Medical History of 19Century New Zealand, Dr. Laurie Gluckman, published by permission of author.

Dunedin, Charles Brasch, excerpt from Indirections: A Memoir, 1909-1947, Charles Brasch, Oxford University Press, Wellington, 1980.

"The Actor," Herz Bergner, trans. from the Yiddish by Judah Waten, Southerly, no. 2, 1957.

"How Come The Truckloads," "Water A Thousand Feet Deep," published in Poetry Australia, republished by permission of author; "Halley's Comet," published inThe Melbourne Chronicle, republished by permission of editor, Serge Liberman, and author

"The Golden Flight," "I Am Ready," "On The Nature of Fear," How Many Times?" Shmuel Gorr, from Selected Poems and Essays, published by Ben Uri Literary Group; "The Nocturnal Citadel," republished by permission of author.

"God's Word Is More Eternal Than Eternity," "Lord, Do Not Turn From Me," "The Voice Speaks To Israel On Yom Hakippurim," "I, Tongue Of All," Karl Wolfskehl, from 1933, A Poem Sequence, trans. by Carol North Valhorpe and Ernst

Morwitz, Schocken Book, New York, 1947.

"Early Morning And A Poem of Kim Yuk," "To Tu Fu in 'To Wei Pa, A Retired Scholar," "In the Cycle of Recurrence," by Allen Afterman published by permission of author.

"You Who Started All Our Craving," "In The Beginning," "A Kind Of Accord," by Marc Radyzner, published by permission of author.

"The Wheat Mirror," "Waking To Big Stones," "Jerusalem," "Tel Aviv Outskirts," by Susan Whiting, published by permission of author.

"On Mt. Iron," "Poland, October (from Nineteen Thirty-nine)" Charles Brasch, published in An Anthology of New Zealand Verse, selected by Robert Chapman and Jonathan Bennett, Oxford Univ. Press, London & Wellington, 1956; "Ambulando," "By That Sea," "Bred In The Bone," Charles Brasch, published in Ambulando, The Caxton Press, 1964.

"Rumkovsky Was Right," Yvonne Fein, published in Australian Short Stories, Pascoe Publishing, 1983; republished by permission of author.

"My Grandfather," Lilian Barnea, published in Shalom, hardback ed. Collins, 1978, compiled by Nancy Keesing; Penquin, paperback, 1983; republished by permission of author.

"All The Storms and Sun-sets," Maria Lewitt, published in the Melbourne Chronicle, no. 4(24), August-September, 1980; republished by permission of author and editor, Serge Liberman.

Every effort has been made to trace copyright owners and acknowledge previous publication and credit. Any additional information will be incorporated in future editions of this book.

CONTENTS

Jewish Writing From Down Under is the fourth in a series of anthologies intended to discover and to express themes and experiences common to Jews everywhere; hence, they are both literary and sociological. The excessive clamor one hears so frequently regarding the distinction between "politics" and "literature," or content and form are distinctions without a cause. It is the business of literature to leave records of human life, and for every era to find the literary form in which to do it. These anthologies intentionally and hopefully record the Jewish experience in the modern world. That experience differentiates itself from the past not through the existence of the diaspora--- not only a modern condition--but through the global borders of the diaspora--from Africa to Tierra del Fuego, from the Hebrides to New Zealand; and in the global nature of the Jew's intellectual interests.

Jews relate with a totality of responsiveness to the land and climate, people and language they find themselves in. Which is not to say that this is true of every Jew, but that in a given community, be it in the Amazon or in South Africa, one will find a comprehensive number of Jewish writers and intellectuals for whom the country in which they find themselves absorbs their intellectual and moral energies, without conflict with their identities as Jews. In this volume, Dr. Gluckman is one example among several. In the introduction to his richly informative book, Tangwai, A Medical History of 19th Century New Zealand, he writes that he could not "remember a time in his life when he did not have an intimate and educational contact with Maori intellectuals." Born in Auckland in 1920, both he and his wife share an interest in the education of Polynesian children, and his eldest son is a pediatrician who specializes in the health problems of Polynesian children. Though the selection from his book for this volume deals with aspects of similar religious themes between Jews and Maoris--aspects which would naturally attract his attention--his book and his lifelong interests in the Maori go beyond this.

In quite a different discipline from Dr. Gluckman's, New Zealand literature received a cohering influence from the work of Charles Brasch, as a writer and as the editor of Landfalls. Born into an assimilated family that had been settled in New Zealand for a century, cultivated in English themes and prosody, after 1935--like Karl Wolfskehl who came from the other side of the globe--Charles Brasch began to express a sense of himself that had been latent, as his poem, "Bred In The Bone" suggests.

Similarities and differences in the poetic developments of Charles Brasch and Karl Wolfskehl are worth some comments. As the one influenced New Zealand poetry, so the latter influenced modern German poetry. In 1900-1903, Karl Wolfskehl, with Stephan George, edited the 3 volume edition of Deutsche Dichtung, as well as an anthology of Old German Poetry. But the events of the 1930s altered these poetic interests, and his first major work to express this change, 1933 became, like his own life, a symbol of Jewish history in this century. Copies of 1933 were carried out of Germany by fleeing Jews, and carried to the four corners of the earth. While he retained the poetic voice of German lyricism, Karl Wolfskehl's poetry became the liturgical expression of Jewish religion and history. That deeply personal lyricism is missing from the poetry of Charles Brasch, which is often both more introspective and more objective; yet both modalities and lives met in New Zealand, where Brasch wrote,

The songs of Zion are sung on every coast

Jewish emigration to New Zealand and Australia had different social origins, though both began with the emigration of English Jews. Maurice Pitt's work, The Founding of the Wellington Community has a kinship in tone and content with other such documents as, for example, the founding of colonies in the United States. Beginnings begin like this: a few people set out in a boat for the purpose of exploration, trade, adventure, or refuge. Moreover, his work is a reminder that for the restless Jewish historical energy, there is no obscure Jewish history. In the spirit of Klal Israel, every record has its place.

Jewish emigration to Australia, however, began with the arrival of nine Jewish convicts from England in 1788. One arrival of nine Jewish convicts from England in 1788. One John Harris was the father of the first native born Australian-Jewish writer of fiction, John Lang (1816-1864), who published two books about Australian life: The Forger's Wife, 1855, and a collection of short stories, Botany Bay, 1859. This first handful of convict-emigrants settled in Sydney; in 1817 there began a burial society which soon developed into the Great Synagogue of Sydney. Moreover, John Harris, convict-emigrant, was also the grandfather of Lord Casey, who was Governor General, 1965-1969, as well as a writer.

After the twentieth century, Jews began to arrive from eastern European countries, and today many arrive from Arab countries. This pattern of emigration reflects the sociological patterning and alternation between "established" families who came into frontier settlements and bush country, whose values and memories were shaped by pioneer conditions, and those who came during the 1930s, whose memories were shaped by the prevalence of destruction in Europe. Serge Liberman's stories, "Two Years in Exile," and "Drifting" express two phases of the pattern. John Lang's story, "Music A Blast," in Shalom is a romping blast at European cultural pretensions against frontier conditions, as is Judah Waten's more gentle version of the same theme in, "Well, What Do You Say To My Boy."

I have learned much from Nancy Keesing's anthology, Shalom and hope that those who read this anthology will be moved to read hers, to reach out and further to Jewish writers in Australia. In addition to the stimulus which her book provided, I owe many words of gratitude to Shmuel Gorr--who went from Australia to Israel--and who provoked--and provided me with the first necessary steps for this volume--steps which led to Serge Liberman, whose unfailing responsiveness to my requests for more books, more material, more information--and whose guidance and suggestions made this volume possible.

Of Jewish writing in Australia and New Zealand, it must be said, as Dr. Gluckman wrote of the Maori, "Every subject has a specific history and for that matter so does every segment of that subject." The Jews, as elsewhere, are among many migrants into this part of the world: Scots, Italians, Irish. Australia is a large, hospitable country with a growing self awareness; but from the point of view of the Australian aboriginal and the Maori, we speak unhistorically of such places as Australia and New Zealand as being "new" countries. They are new only to us, new in the terms of our history. No place is new. What is new is our awareness.

The twentieth century--it does not have to be said--is the most dramatic and the most revolutionary for Jews in two millennia. As with the fall of the Second Temple, it reckons with both an ending and a beginning, bringing together the consciousness of the extremities of historical life: a concussion of past and present. Jews everywhere know this, and their writings in these anthologies demonstrate that they combine with inimitable balance the poles of their human existence.

Roberta Kalechofsky

Marblehead, 1984.

this volume is dedicated to Karl Wolfskehl

"Exul Poeta"

born in Germany, 1869

buried in Waikumete Cemetery, New Zealand, 1948

"I bid you journey home."

Section 1

FOUNDING THE COMMUNITY

Fay Zwicky

The Chosen — Kalgoorlie, 1894

I The Escape

His father said: Marry her. She's had a hard life—
With you lighter it can't get. She cooks,
Breathes, a little ankle, eyes not bad . . . what
More do you want? For mother's sake . . .
Her heart won't beat for ever . . . a grandchild, a family!
And he ran away. He ran and ran from that
Abrasive calico breast, virgin ankle, awkward
Menial hands, his heart burdened with crimson sunsets.
(Grandmother-mother, hands that moulded love in me but
Passive lay in his impatient palms). Thin spectacled,
Sixteen he fled the fatherland across the Nullarbor.
His mother had her heart-attack and Yahweh,
Rhadamanthine Yahweh (blest be He!) galloped
Snorting after the little puffer, Bobtails blinked,
Smiling among grey stones to see
God go off His Head.

II Retribution Plotted

And Yahweh the Extravagant,
Prodigal Yahweh swore revenge,
Stamped in a desert way off His patch:
A Desert-Dweller all My life!
Don't they know of Me? The trumpet-tones
Shatter on flat stones; ant-hills heave,
Turn over in a dreamless sleep:
My Chosen do not stray far! My ways are wondrous,
Perilous; I am the One (no other shalt thou have)
Who does the choosing here!
Braying maniac brewing cataclysms.
Antediluvian mouths yawn
Under the unshriven sun.

III The Plague

They handed him a key:
This is your house. A sagging box,
Smoke-licked pane webbed by
Sleepy crab-spiders. He'd read
In the old country, Talmud-ridden
Fly, 'In hot climates Spiders
Are able to produce a certain amount of
Local pain.' His skin bristled with small
Spiked crowns. Pain's antidote in peeled
Tub—a pink geranium, stationmaster's ward,
Barren season's suckling.
Weekly his charge gnawed the track to the
Flat horizon, covered a hemisphere in his
Kindled sight, gabbling caterpillar.
But came the Day of the Scorpion.
Clanking, thundering scales, buckling linkages,
From its final poisoned segment issued Yahweh,
Mighty polyphemal ruby eye to sear the spider,
Flower and stripling stationmaster, belching
Plague through flaring nostrils, scattering
Dybbuks through the land.
I CHOOSE, HEIR TO ASHES! Squeaking demons,
Metal-winged, buzz and swoop, pegged within
The confines of His breath.
Ten days he lay reflected in his death, his
Bowels curled limps beside his shoes.
Next train his grieving father
Brought him home.

IV Retribution Achieved

She said: This is the station key.
Your grandfather watched trains as a young man.
I waited.

3

FOUNDING THE COMMUNITY

Early Jewish Colonists: 1840-1843

The association of Jews with Wellington has been continuous since 1840. There were a number of Jewish shareholders in the New Zealand Company but only one director, Sir Isaac Lyon Goldsmid, Baronet. Perhaps some Jews in England became interested in New Zealand through the reports of Joseph Barrow Montefiore who visited New Zealand in 1830, and through the books of Joel Samuel Polack, profusely illustrated by the author, dealing with his New Zealand adventures between 1831 and 1837. Both were Jews. J.B. Montefiore was the originator of the phrase describing New Zealand as "The Britain of the South."

The passenger lists of the New Zealand Company's first four ships which landed their passengers between 22 January and 28 February, 1840 at Pito-one, reveal the names of Jews in the passenger lists of one ship only, the barque Oriental, which sailed from London on 15 September 1839 and arrived at Pito-one on 31 January 1840. These included both cabin passengers and emigrant steerage passengers. Those definitely Jewish were as follows: [1] Abraham Hort, (single) [2] Solomon Levy (single) and Benjamin Levy (single). It is believed that Solomon and Benjamin Levy, carpenters, came out under engagement to Abraham Hort, who preceded his brother Alfred Hort (1842) and his father Abraham Hort, Senior (1843).

From the time of his arrival in 1840 Abraham Hort known after 1843 as Abraham Hort, Junior took a prominent position

----

1. Early Settlers' Journal, vol. 2, no 1, p.9

2. Louis E. Ward, Early Wellington, p.26

4

in the settlement. In the second number of the New Zealand Gazette published at Britannia (Pito-one) on 18 April 1840 it is recorded that at a Committee of Colonists it was resolved that Mr A. Hort be elected to fill the vacancy caused on the Committee by the retirement of Captain Smith. A keen oarsman, Abraham Hort, Junior, featured in a boating incident on Wellington harbour in 1840. Together with Charles Heaphy he launched a boat at Thorndon to beat up Lambton Harbour. The boat capsized but both Heaphy and Hort were rescued.

In October 1842 the election of the first Council of the Borough of Wellington was held and Abraham Hort, Junior polled 155 votes and was thus elected an Alderman of the Borough. This was indeed a notable achievement particularly as Abraham Hort, Junior was then only a young man of twenty-two years of age.

From 1840 to 1843 a very small number of Jews arrived in Wellington individually or in small family groups in the various ships. They came of their own choice and without assistance from the New Zealand Company or any other source. Amongst the passengers who arrived by the packet New York in 1842 was A.W. Hort. He was Alfred Hort, brother to Abraham Hort, Junior. Both their names together with that of their father, Abraham Hort, Senior appear in the Burgess roll of the Borough of Wellington 1843. Alfred Hort [3] and Abraham Hort, Junior in the early fifties of last century became leading merchants and ship-owners in Apia, Samoa and Tahiti. They were the owners of a flourishing island business with a fleet of large and small island schooners trading between Tahiti, Fiji and Samoa with headquarters at Apia, Samoa. (Hort brothers after 1854 suffered severe competition in the Pacific Islands from the Hamburg firm of Godeffroy. In 1860 their business premises were destroyed by a disastrous fire and they liquidated their Islands' business. Abraham Hort, Junior died at Ovalau, Fiji, on 7 June 1862

----

3. Alfred's Hort's wife published in 1866 Henna or Life in Tahiti

and was buried at Sydney.)

Amongst the arrival by the Burma in February 1842 was Miss Esther Solomon aged 18. Four months later the marriage took place on 1 June 1842 of Benjamin Levy to Esther Solomon. This was the first marriage of a Jewish couple in Wellington. Just over a year earlier on 30 May 1841 the marriage is recorded of Hort--Northwood. This Hort would be Abraham Hort, Junior.

By the beginning of 1843 there was a handful of Jews in Wellington and the stage was set for the arrival of the grand patriarch and recognized founder of the Wellington Jewish Community, Abraham Hort, Senior. Together with his wife and five daughters he arrived on 3 January 1843 in the Prince of Wales from London via Nelson. Included in the cabin passengers were Messrs Joseph and Mocatta, the latter being Solomon Mocatta the husband of Abraham Hort, Senior's eldest daughter. The Hort family was a remarkable one as was to expected from the character and personality of A. Hort, Senior who, besides leading the Wellington Jewish Community until 1859, was one of the foremost citizens of Wellington, in those years being associated prominently with every public endeavor.

A. Hort, Senior brought with him in a religious capacity a young man David Isaacs who travelled as an emigrant steerage passenger. This young man because of his Hebraic knowledge and his ability as a shochet, mohel, and chazan was destined to play an important part in the religious life of three Jewish communities, Wellington, Nelson and Dunedin. But in 1843 young David Isaacs worked at his trade, for his name later appears among the list of persons qualified to serve as Jurors for the district of Wellington for the year, 1845. The name of Wellington's and indeed New Zealand's first shochet and mohel and chazan was briefly inscribed in the Jurors' list as Isaacs, David, Lambton Quay, Shoemaker.

Founding the Community

Before leaving England in September 1842 Abraham Hort, Senior, received from the Chief Rabbi of the Great Synagogue, London, Dr. Solomon Herschell, a letter bearing his signature and official seal giving sanction to the formation of a Hebrew Congregation and to other matters in connection with Jewish laws.

A Jewish fortnightly periodical, The Voice of Jacob, printed in English by the Anglo-Jewish Periodical Press referred to the departure of Mr. Abraham Hort and family and Mr. David Isaacs in September 1842 for Port Nicholson. Tribute was paid to Mr. Hort, Senior's devotion to his faith; to his services to The Great Synagogue, Duke's Palace, London; to his philanthropy and contributions to charities. Above all his competence and fitness to found and superintend a Hebrew congregation were extolled.

The Voice of Jacob referred to the suitability of New Zealand as a sphere for Jewish colonization, mentioning its excellent climate, soil and commercial position. A suggestion was made that a body of Jews might even apply to the New Zealand Company for help on emigration. Abraham Hort, Senior's interest in their subject of emigration was stressed and the principle object of his proceeding to New Zealand was stated to be the facilitating of an extensive scheme of Jewish emigration. In the 1840s Jews were subject not only to widespread persecution in various parts of the continent of Europe including Germany, but also to the conversionist zeal of many Christian churches.

On the 3 January 1843 Mr. Abraham Hort, Senior and his family arrived on the Prince of Wales at Port Nicholson. On 21 January 1843 Mr. Hort, Senior wrote from Wellington to the editor of The Voice of Jacob giving his impressions of the voyage, the country and the climate, the Maoris, and prospects for emigrants. In addition he described the holding on 7 January 1843 of the first Jewish service by a Hebrew congregation in Wellington and also in New Zealand.

On the long journey to New Zealand, Abraham Hort, Senior, a devout and orthodox Jew, did not diverge in the slightest degree from the observance of his faith. He had made suitable provision for a supply of kosher meat and food for the journey. In his letter of 21 January 1843 to The Voice of Jacob, the first of a series, he suggested that in the event of extensive Jewish emigration, proper application should be made to the New Zealand Company by influential persons to

7

have meat supplied by Hebrew butchers. As regards Jewish emigration, Mr. Hort, Senior, advised caution recommending the emigration of only "fair" mechanics in the useful branches of the trade, or prospective cultivators of the soil with some small means. He recommended that those who wished to engage in commercial enterprise should be well supported financially in England.

Evidently the conduct of many of the steerage emigrants on board the Prince of Wales during the voyage was disgusting and reprehensible. As a contrast the behaviour of David Isaacs was exemplary and beyond reproach. David Isaacs had been reared in a public institution, Jews' Hospital, London, and was an emigrant steerage passenger on the Prince of Wales under the protection of A. Hort, Senior. A testimonial to his conduct on the voyage was forwarded to London and printed in The Voice of Jacob, and is reprinted here below:

"To his Royal Highness, the Duke of Sussex, Patron of the Jews' Hospital, Mile End, for the education and apprenticeship of youth; and for the support of the aged poor; and to Sir Isaac Lyon Goldsmid, Bart., and the rest of the Directors of the New Zealand Company: --We, the undersigned, captain, chief mate, doctor, and cabin passengers, of the ship Prince of Wales, bound to New Zealand, testify that David Isaacs an emigrant steerage passenger hereby, under the protection of Mr. Hort, has conducted himself in an exemplary manner throughout the voyage, and is of that class of useful mechanics, calculated to benefit the colony and himself." [Here follow the signatures]

The Prince of Wales arrived on 3 January 1843 and on 7 January 1843 the first Jewish service was held. Independently of the whole Hort family there were nine males present who rejoiced at the opportunity offered them for the performance of divine service according to Jewish ritual. (The whole Hort family numbered nine, three males and six

8

females. If every member of the Hort family was present at this service, the first Hebrew congregation of worshippers would number eighteen.) The reading of the law was Parshath Bo, and the Gomel was recited in Hebrew by Abraham Hort, Senior. In addition he offered up a prayer in English which he composed himself, thanking Almighty God for preserving them through the perils of the journey and the fatal malady prevalent on their ship, the Prince of Wales. This first Jewish service was a remarkable one and surely must rank historically as interesting and as noteworthy as other first services in New Zealand by various denominations.

The services of David Isaacs as a shochet were immediately used and mention of this is made by A. Hort, Senior, in his letter of 21 January 1843. Two oxen, a calf, a sheep and a lamb were killed according to Jewish law. The meat was found to be excellent, but A. Hort, Senior, noticed that with some small exceptions, meat was dearer than in England. He hoped that as stock multiplied prices would gradually decline.

Thus with Sabbath observance established by the holding of Sabbath services, and the provision of kosher meat for those who desired it, the Wellington Jewish community commenced under happy circumstances. It is true that there was no paid minister or leader, but David Isaacs, who worked at his trade, was competent to render most religious services. In Abraham Hort, Senior, the community had an outstanding leader and personality, who while attending to the present needs of the community looked to the future with an unswerving aim---extensive Jewish emigration. His aim was not to be realized.

Maurice Pitt

Alan Collins

The Trouble with Felix

During the Depression years we lived in what was formerly a very swish seaside guest house called The Balconies. It was sited on the highest point of land overlooking the grand sweep of Bondi Beach so that any guest entitled to special treatment would be given the first floor corner suite which had a verandah on two sides. From this vantage point one could take in the entire panorama from the Bondi sewerage vent pipe above the north headland, to the sprawling graves of the cemetery that swept down to the very cliff edge of Bronte. Two massive gold leafed glass doors with 'B' on each guarded the entrance. You couldn't see much through the doors because of the intricate sandblasted waves and seagulls, but a little piece of the plush red hall carpet protruded beyond the doors giving a foretaste of the luxury that lay beyond. The first floor verandahs covered the wide footpaths and were held up by elegant fluted iron stanchions, two of which had iron rings bolted to them to tether horses.

When our family came to The Balconies in 1935, I was ten years old and knew nothing of its past sophistication. We arrived toward the end of summer — father, stepmother, my brother and me. The Chevrolet had snorted steam all the way on the short trip from Bellevue Hill, quite rightly objecting to its reduced status. Portmanteaus were roped to its luggage carrier and to the footboards; the bonnet sides were tied back to cool the motor, giving the whole ensemble a most idiotic appearance. Even after father had turned off the ignition, the engine continued to sputter on independently, like an aged person to whom no one listens.

My brother and I sat in the back, only our heads showing above the miscellany of clothing and household effects; father's irritable call to get out and help was, under the circumstances, unheeded until Carmel, our step-mother, removed the overburden of rugs and carpets. Only then were her 'two little mannikins' able to scramble out smelling strongly of newly stirred dust. Father, fully laden, backed himself through the glass doors, beckoning us to follow him into that dim interior, the colour of an Angelina plum. Carmel, her make-up sweat-ruined and a temper to match, carried only her hat box and a majolica vase through the doorway, letting it swing closed on my brother who took the full force of it on his nose which obligingly spouted blood. He dripped onto his shirt, then preserved that from further staining by burying his face in the rolled-up curtains under his arms. I followed him closely, not wishing to meet the same fate. Once inside, I felt a chill of apprehension, not quite fear, more a presentiment that this new era in my life was not going to be an enjoyable one.

My gloomy thoughts were halted by father belligerently ringing a brass handbell and calling up the stair-case, "Mrs Stone, ah there Mrs. Stone, it's me, Mr. Kaiser." The clapper of the bell had barely come to rest when two patent-leather shod feet appeared descending the stairs. From my lowly line of sight I watched as the rest of Mrs. Stone appeared as though a shutter was being raised — first the shoes, then a crushed purple velvet dress, a long glass necklace that swung to and fro on giant pendulous breasts, two chins, two jowls, long thin nose with pince-nez, and a mass of tightly rolled hair that sat on her head like a horse's collar. She bared her teeth in a rictus smile and swept past father to the brass jardiniere which one of us had dislodged from its Chinese black base. Only after it had been adjusted to her satisfaction did she acknowledge him.

In a voice that seemed to be forced out of her by hard pumped bellows she announced, "No need to ring Mr. Kaiser, the dead at Bronte could have heard you." She re-stoked her lungs and, "Your rooms are ready, what about the rent now, two pounds in advance, get your own firewood for the copper and five shillings if you want to put your car round the back."

Carmel started to say, "Did you get the lavatory fixed . . ." but Mrs. Stone, her lungs emptied, had already stormed the stairs leaving us an island of domestic detritus in a red carpeted sea.

"The cholera on you," my father swore softly in Yiddish, then over his shoulder, "This way Carmel, down the passage — Carmel, come away from the mirror for a minute — watch the kids don't knock anything over." He grabbed the two largest trunks and was swallowed up in the gloom of the dank, dark hallway. Carmel called after him, "Felix, if you're going to swear, do it in English; that Yiddish, it embarrasses me so."

He stopped in front of a four panelled ochre coloured door, dropped his load and inserted a huge key in the lock. It made a sound like a meat grinder on bones, but functioned enough for Father to kick the door open and lead the way into our new home. Bringing up the rear, I noticed the painted number '4' on the door and decided then and there I didn't like it at all. Nothing I saw as I entered caused me to weaken in this resolve. Smell — cold despite the dying days of summer; shadows — bizarre colours as a thin ray of sunlight was bisected by the leadlighted fanlight above the only window shrouded in full length drapes. The beam caught the suspended dust particles before it hit a wall mirror and dissipated its feeble strength. Father killed the beam by pulling on the light cord and a tulip shaped candelabra high above us turned the dark into a pale yellow.

"The old devil's taken out the settee," father yelled. "I know it was there when I came last week. Well, can you beat that?" He pointed to the wall and there, even in that weak light, I could see the light patch on the wallpaper. Carmel said, "I begged you not to sell ours." Father rounded angrily on her, reminding her that her settee, together with every other stick of furniture, had gone to settle tradesmen's debts.

I was more interested in the totality of the so-called flat. The floor plan resembled those card houses we built where we constructed numerous cubicle like boxes that had common walls and on top of which we would endeavour to lay more cards to roof them over. Only these cubicles had no roofs of their own — only the high plastered ceiling of the huge room we had entered. Little rooms with thin plywood doors seemed to open off in all directions. The partitioned walls reached up about seven feet, leaving a good eight feet more of height to reach the ceiling. We were, in fact, as father explained later, living in the main dining room of The Balconies. The serving pantry had become our kitchen by closing it off from the main kitchen and installing a stove which had no vent, so that the cooking fumes pervaded every corner of the flat. No matter what Carmel cooked, the smell was always of something else, long gone.

By the evening, we had sorted ourselves out. Father and Carmel had the largest cubicle, my brother and I shared the smaller one, and the remaining box father grandiloquently called his office. From a mansion in Birriga Road, Bellevue Hill to the diningroom of The Balconies was a much greater distance than the hills that physically separated them.

Whoever called this period between wars a Depression was more than just economically correct. Our depression started within days of moving into The Balconies. Father's job as a commercial traveller in hotel supplies had ended months before, leaving him with a sample case of useless goods and a car that had left its vitality on the dusty roads of western New South Wales. It stood outside The Balconies for months with a sale sign on it until one day a farmer bought it, so he said, to "put in me hay shed and hitch the chaff cutter to it."

Uncle Sid came round shortly after that on his first visit to us. Flashy Siddy — unscathed by the Depression except that the scale of his vaguely illicit, varied operations was scaled down, but never sufficient to actually force him to offer himself for Susso. How could he, whilst wearing a gold ring with a star-cut diamond sitting high in a claw that wore away the stitching in his trouser pocket?

"Felix, me son," he wagged his finger at Father, "Here's what we are going to do, you and me. We're going on the road. Now sit down you silly bugger," he said as Father rose in anticipation of another of Sid's law-bending schemes, "this is dead straight and might just get you all out of this dump."

What he proposed was this. All round Sydney and in the country towns, people were desperate for cash. If they only knew it, they had a fortune lying around in drawers. Old jewellery, gold — gold in rings, pocket watches, spectacle rims, mounted sovereigns, even picture frames and lockets. The two of them would go door to door and buy for cash, break it down and sell it to the government assayer. And so they did. When they worked the suburbs they came back to our flat in the evening and emptied out the chamois bags on the kitchen table. My brother and I stood wide eyed at their elbow as the two of them took the dropper from a tiny bottle of nitric acid, touched the gold and watched to see what colour stain it left. If it was a dull green, the gold content was over 18 carat. Next, they took

14

all that little mound of treasure and with a pair of pliers smashed up lockets to remove glass photograph covers; the floor would be strewn carelessly with pictures of soldiers, grandparents and wisps of curly hair. After the rings and necklaces would come the watch cases. Heavy gold hunters with Waltham and Rolex movements were attacked ferociously, the intricate mechanisms thrown aside as one would when gutting a rabbit. They were our part of the spoils. The beautiful balance and escapement wheels beat on like a heart outside a body.

Carmel was torn between desire and contempt for their enterprise. She would run her fingers through the sad remains of the lives of the poor, reading aloud the inscriptions on watch cases until Father snatched them away from her. Cameos in gold frames rested briefly on her neck only to join the twisted pile of gold before she could mouth a plea for saving them for herself. Once she said, "The Jews never seem to sell their family jewels, do they Felix?" Father dropped his magnifying glass in fright, but Uncle Sid said, "They're not drinking away their savings either Carmel, so shut up." She swung round on him and in a controlled fury spat at him, "And I suppose they don't bet S.P. with you Sid ... much too clever by half, aren't they, eh?" Standing quite close to him, I heard him swear in Yiddish, but the only word he allowed her to hear was the derogatory expression for a Gentile woman — 'shikse'. It's funny, I thought, of all the lovely, gentle, warm and comforting Yiddish words used to my brother and me, it was the hate words that remained longest in the memory.

For something over a year, Father and Uncle Sid worked the industrial suburbs of Sydney, but by then many others were also mining the same lode. Some of them were despicable cheats, telling the women at the door whose husbands were away on the track in the country that what they had treasured as gold was, in fact, only rolled gold or even brass. In that year though, we lived a little better than most. Carmel's attitude to my brother and me changed in

15

that time too. We could do nothing right in her eyes. First she would nag us incessantly about our appearance, table manners and laziness, perhaps with some justification. In moments of frustration, she mumbled about "caring for somebody else's bastards". Then we became pawns in a ferocious ongoing feud about money. Carmel started to buy furniture on time payment from a door to door salesman. The flat rapidly filled up with shiny veneered pieces until there was scarcely room to navigate a path among them. Father said very little except to occasionally criticise the quality and compare it with what we had in the Bellevue Hill home. Only when the food on the highly polished table became scarcer and the standard of it appalling did he stand up to Carmel. They blazed away at each other, he calling her a Paddington tart and she retorting that she was too young to be tied for the rest of her life to an old Yid.

At this time, I was, in a small way, an independent business-man myself. Uncle Sid employed me to collect the S.P. bets. On Saturdays I sat bored through the Sabbath morning service at the synagogue, but straight after, changed my clothes and went on my rounds. With a billy-can I covered the surrounding Bondi streets collecting bets. A shilling here, two shillings there, the name of the horse and the punter wrapped around the coins. Then back to Uncle Sid at the rear of the barber shop where he wrote them down in an exercise book. The race would then crackle over the wireless, Sid wrapping up the pitifully few payouts and me back on the round, kidding myself that the police knew nothing of this.

Sid had tired anyway of the gold buying, and without his drive and impudence my Father showed little enthusiasm for fronting the shrivelled women, old before their time, who came to the door offering the spectacles of their dead husbands in return for a few more weeks of living. But Carmel held different views. "You don't need Sid, he's a shyster Felix. Why don't you go to the country? You know the towns well." Oh yes, he knew them well enough;

travelled them for twenty years, known as a good spender to all the publicans west of the Blue Mountains, drank with the police sergeants and been guest at most of the Rotary clubs. And now? Go back as a hawker — no better than some of those Jewish new-comers with their battered suit-cases with dress lengths and thin towels? Carmel quite plainly wanted Father out of town, out of sight and out of her bed as the squabbles through the cardboard walls clearly showed.

And the door to door salesman increased his calls to three times weekly.

He gave us threepence every time he called. A stocky, cocky, tight suited, patented shoed with straight black hair parted dead centre mongrel whose calling card was his pay-ments book left on the hall stand. We took his threepence and went upstairs to our diversion. Mrs. Stone in the bath. Mrs. Stone seen naked in the full length cheval mirror that reflected back in the hall mirror. Mrs. Stone who never locked her door for fear of being found dead days later. The door to her suite stood open a few inches and we flattened ourselves against the wall and watched enthralled as three afternoons a week at around four o'clock she filled the bath tub in her living room with buckets of hot water from the copper in the backyard. Then undressed in time to a Galli Curci record on the gramophone. The ritual had to be completed before the record ended and the machine needed re-winding. Would she make it? Her gigantic whale-like body was finally unsheathed as the first trills sounded, then she lowered herself into the tub like a suet pudding, the water coming within inches of the tub top. We clutched our groins half in fear and half in an effort to subdue the strange tingling in our crutch.

Father came home from the country early one day. His clothes were torn and a bandage was around one hand. Angry, dispirited and smelling strangely of liquor, he brushed aside our breathless questions meant in some way to stall him and ward off the inevitable. He pushed past

17

us and slouched into the flat straight into the bedroom. Within seconds he reappeared, his ruddy face as colourless and formless as Mrs. Stone's flaccid belly.

"The bloody bitch, the whore, oh the slut . . ." Saliva trickled from the corner of his mouth. He turned to me as I tried to escape. "Look, look my son, look at me hand — they put the dogs onto me in Mudgee, and I was only trying to make a living for us all — and she's doing that while me back's turned. Oh Alice, Alice, why did you have to die?" He collapsed like a winded colt and sobbed deep retching sobs into his dirty coat.

I backed away from this different father to the one I loved. At the door I hesitated a moment then fled down the passage. As I got to the hall stand I saw the salesman's payments book. I grabbed it and ran into the street. This evidence of my father's misery I stuffed down the storm water drain. The salesman came out seconds later, saw me and growled, "Seen me order book young shaver?" I shook my head. "If y'find it Moey, I'll give ya a zac if y'bring it to me office." And he sauntered off as though he hadn't a care in the world.

The weeks that followed were unbearably tense. Father stayed in the flat, unshaven and wearing his dressing gown almost continuously. Until now, he had never hit my brother or me, but with every new outburst of fighting between him and Carmel, the predictable result was a vicious swipe at one or both of us, sometimes taking his leather razor strop and flailing us about the legs. We took to staying out on the streets until exhaustion forced us to go home and try to get to bed unseen. We ate on the pay from Uncle Sid's S.P. round. Carmel, on the other hand, became our protector, taunting Father with sneers of "That's right Felix, take it out on the kids why doncha?" As long as the rent was paid, Mrs. Stone ignored the brawling of her tenants. After all, ours was not the only family to show the tenseness of the times by scrapping. The police had come to The Balconies before in response to a wife rushing into the street screaming she was being murdered.

Toward the end of that summer, a sort of peace came to our household. Exhaustion of invective and the approaching end of Father's savings forced him to take the last irrevocable step. He would go on Susso. Putting on his oldest clothes, he went down to the Council and applied for work or a handout. To his surprise they offered him a pick and shovel and told him to join a gang building a walkway around the Bondi cliff tops. Two days a week. The job would last as long as the Council had funds to spin it out. He joined the other defeated men and put in his ten hours a day. The beatings and quarrels stopped. Father had other enemies. The men to whom labouring had been an accepted way of earning a living, resented this soft handed middle aged Jew who had no right to be taking a job from their mates. With that fear of tomorrow that binds desperate men together, they conspired to make Father's work as hateful as possible. The gang foreman saw that he was positioned at the very edge of the cliff, picking away at the crumbling sandstone while the sea roared and crashed hundreds of feet below.

Father came home, his face grey with fatigue and fright. His relations with Carmel were distant and even old fashioned formal. If he spoke to her it was in a stilted, clipped economic tone, not wasting a word and dealing only in topics needed to keep the household functioning. Toward us, he spoke more and more as in the past, referring distressingly often to happier days when our mother was alive. We hadn't the heart to tell him that the door-to-door man had resumed his calls on those days when Father was on relief work.

For nearly a year the job went on, Father getting more maudlin, given to sudden outbursts of tears and constantly looking at his broken fingernails and calloused hands. When the job inevitably ended for Father, his breakdown was nearly complete. One day my brother and I followed him on one of his walks. He would shuffle down to the

19

beach promenade then turn up the cliff walk that he had helped build until he reached a rotunda of rock jutting out over the highest point of the cliff top. There he sat and stared out over the grey sea while the wind tried to whisk the old panama hat from his head. No matter what the weather, he followed the same course every day of the week, returning to the flat at sunset like the wheeling seagulls to their cliff top nooks.

For my brother and me, had we known it, the end of a chapter was about to be written also. In mid-winter of the next year, we came home from school, thinking only of the thick slice of bread and plum jam we would cut for ourselves. Pushing open the door of number four of The Balconies, we entered to see it as bare as the day we moved in three years before. The weak sun showed us the emptiness of our home. My brother scuffed the carpet with his toe where the indentations of the dining table showed freshly. I rushed from cubicle to cubicle to find the same vista of nothingness. Our clothes lay in a heap on the floor. In the kitchen the loaf of bread was lying on the stove, an open tin of plum jam alongside it. But no knife, no plate. "No bloody nothin" I said softly to myself. My brother called plaintively, "Carmel, Carmel where are you?" His reedy voice bounced around the walls.

I took his hand and we went outside The Balconies and sat on the step watching the sun go down and straining our eyes into its rays to be the first to catch sight of Father.

The sun finally sank reluctantly behind the buildings down the road and we drew close together. Two men, big men with sharp blue eyes and dark hats came up to us. One bent down and said to me, "What's your name sonny?" I told him. "And is this your brother?" I nodded. He took a damp envelope out of another brown envelope and showed it to his mate. The other squatted down beside me and said softly, "We're policemen sonny, our car is just up the street a bit, we'd like you to come with us, OK?" He put his arm under mine and the other man did the same to my brother. Together, unresisting, we shuffled to the car. My brother shook himself free as they opened the car door and screamed, "Where's Daddy, we've got to wait for Daddy, he's coming up the hill soon." He sat down on the running board of the car, a compact little parcel of misery. The two policemen talked softly a few feet off then one said, "Sonny, is your mother's name Alice?" My brother sprang up and shouted that her name was Carmel, do you hear me, Carmel, *Carmel, CARMEL!*

"Oh, damn," the policeman said to his mate, "what do we do now? Tell 'em Bob, for Christ's sake, I want to get home for me tea."

"Look sonny, there's been an accident like. Your Dad's fallen off the cliff and he's ... he's ... dead. But the part I can't figure out is in this letter we found on him, he's put down his wife's name as Alice."

When the police car drove away from The Balconies, my brother and I sat in the back, a slab-sided, blue suited policeman between us. I could feel the hard shape of his truncheon against my leg and once when he leaned forward was surprised to see that where his shirt gaped he wore no singlet and his chest was a mass of dark curling hair. He took off his hat and his head was almost bald. His mate steered the car in a stiff, formal regulation style so unlike the happy-go-lucky approach our father had used — weaving in and out of the traffic, waving to ladies and generally behaving like a lair of the thirties — which he was when the going was good before the Depression.

My brother was still whimpering and once when his little body heaved with an enormous shudder of grief I tried to reach across the mountainous barrier of the policeman to comfort him. The policeman said, "He'll settle down soon sonny, don't worry. Now, what's his name?"

21

"Solly," I mumbled from the depth, "and he's nine. And I'm thirteen and me name's . . ." But the policeman interrupted me. "Jack, it's Jack isn't it?" I wondered how he knew but sat up a bit straighter and said defiantly, "No it isn't. It's Jacob." I was astounded at what I had said because I really disliked being known as Jacob and vowed to say no more. I looked out the window at the people on the passing tram with the superiority of a boy actually travelling in a police car.

The driver lit a cigarette, let it droop from the corner of his mouth then half turned to his mate, "Can't remember ever having Yids in this situation before, Bob." He scratched his chin and went on, "excepting that is, when Steeny the tailor ran himself through with his shears."

Bob thumped him hard on the back with his fist. "Shut your mouth and just get us to the Shelter quick as you can." He dug his hand deep in his side pocket and pulled out a tobacco flecked packet of peppermints and offered one to each of us. Solly took one but I was frightened to open my mouth in case I either cried out loud or revealed a bit more about myself. With my eyes half shut and peering through my lashes I could think back on all that had happened, at the same time, with the occasional sneak look, keep a watch on our progress as the car growled up the Sydney hills and skeltered down the steep inclines toward the harbour front.

Except when a tram rattled past, it was quiet and dark in the car — just a glow of the driver's cigarette and the pretty dashboard lights. Solly had flopped back like a broken doll, his mouth open, his sobs escaping through his sleep. The car skirted the quay and turned up beside the south pylon of the Harbour Bridge. It nosed its way through the sandstone cuttings where water dripped down the rock faces until it halted in front of a building with a blue light outside and a brass plate that read, simply and chillingly, Children's Shelter.

The stilted official voice Bob had used when he ordered us into the car was now softened. Leaning across me

22

to open the car door, he said, "Righto Jack, here we are; you just go on in and I'll wake whatsisname, Solly." I shook myself alert and stepped into the road while Bob went to the other door and put his huge arms around my brother, depositing him gently on the pavement. I edged around to Solly and whispered to him, "Let's run Solly, OK?" He felt for my hand and together we took off down the hill toward the waterfront, felt the old cobblestones solid beneath our feet and even while running like hares I wondered why, with years of childhood training to be obedient to authority, we did not stop or hesitate for one second to the bellows of Bob to "stop there you little buggers."

Three pennies jingled like alarm bells in my pocket as our downhill flight gathered momentum. I took them out and threw them behind me catching a glimpse of Bob as he pounded after us. The oily harbour front loomed up in front of us, not like a barrier but as a welcoming friend. The cold night air bit into my lungs and as we got nearer the water I could smell the diesel fumes of the ferry boats. Solly no longer held my hand but ran pace for pace alongside me, his fine hair streaming out behind him; the tears had dried in streaks on his face, his eyes fairly danced and I knew I loved him deeply.

As we reached the water's edge a ferry sounded its horn. I heard the rattle of the gang plank being withdrawn. Now it was Solly who took the lead. Grabbing my hand he pulled me and dragged us to the ferryside. The ferryman put his arm across the gang plank but we crashed through sprawling full length on the deck, watching with childish happiness the ever widening gap as the boat with a great churning of water, set us on a new course. It is just possible that the heavy figure of Bob with his hand raised in a suggestion of a half wave was the last thing I saw before going below to stand shivering beside the beautiful, steaming brass boilers of the ferry, their massive shafts and rods pounding renewed life into Solly and me.

There was brass everywhere. It shone and distorted our reflections, reflected back the dancing harbour lights and vibrated minutely to the throb of the engines. Even the duller copper fittings though pitted with age and endless polishing, gleamed a welcome. Solly, watching me gaping, said, "Remember Jack, how we used to look at ourselves in the backs of the watch-cases?" I was jolted, not by the innocent remark in itself but by the realisation that Solly at nine years was already reminiscing like a man half way through his life. Tonight was surely a cut-off point for both of us; forever more the demarcation would always be 'the night we ran away'. I nodded in reply and a crazy elongated head in a flue pipe did likewise.

Now, as we cleared the docks a cool breeze blew away the diesel fumes and to our right we could see the giant's teeth of Luna Park framed in the span of the Harbour Bridge. I stole a side look at Solly half expecting him to exclaim "... remember when we ..." But he said nothing, his chin was on his chest and he swayed gently to the motion of the boat. I was angry at his silence. One of the few personal treasures we had managed to hide from Carmel's destructive swathe was a picture of Father and Mother photographed at Luna Park on a mock rear platform of the Melbourne Express. Solly was in her arms, I stood beside Father waving ... waving, not at a farewelling crowd, only a seedy photographer with his black hood and billy can developer. The picture lay in a shoe box in our cubicle back at The Balconies. With it, wrapped in tissue paper was something else I knew to be important if only for the stealthy manner I came by it.

When we were about to leave our Bellevue Hill house, while Carmel scolded Solly endlessly, Father took me to the front door. From under his coat he produced a screw driver and very carefully prized the little metal cylinder that was fixed to the top right hand of the door frame.

"I know it says in the books that you shouldn't take a Mezuzah down from the house, Jacob, but, but supposing

24

a Goy moved in eh? What would he know of it? Probably think it was an ornament or some Jew junk." He worked deftly until it came away, then he showed it to me. It had always been too high up for me to see and frankly I had been a bit frightened of it. Uncle Siddy was to blame for my fears. Smelling strongly of tobacco, he would grab me and lift me up to it, bellowing sarcastically, "Kiss the Mezuzah Jack, like a good little Jewish boy." And despite my struggles, on occasions my lips would be forced up against the little tube with its one opening like an eye through which I could see the Hebrew letter 'Shin' being the first letter of the unspeakable name of God. Father gave me the Mezuzah having first wrapped it reverently in the fine tissue paper he kept for gold. "For when you have your own home, Jacob." He stuffed it quickly into my pocket as Carmel's voice grew near.

As the ferry slid under the bridge I started in a half turn as though to go back to The Balconies for the shoe box. I stopped, gripping Solly's shoulder so hard his head came up, his eyes widening in an effort to orientate himself.

"Where are we Jack? Where are we going?" he asked softly.

"Stay here and I'll find out."

I surveyed the few passengers, trying to evaluate which face would give an answer and not be too inquisitive as to why two boys in thin clothing and wearing sand shoes would be crossing the harbour late at night. There was some sort of voluntary segregation, the way the women all sat inside the saloon, their skirts tucked primly under their legs defying the playful tug of the breeze. As I made my way forward to the outer deck, some of them pursed their lips in disapproval. Staring stonily ahead I went out on to the deck where pipes and cigarettes glowed.

The ferry rolled unexpectedly in the wash of a passing tug. Caught off balance, I grabbed for the stanchion, missed and fell heavily and untidily into a hard, dark serge shape that did not yield under me, not even when my flailing hands, seeking a grip, fastened onto cold, hard shiny buttons. A pipe clattered to the deck, its glowing dottle flared for a moment then disappeared over the side while its owner growled, "oh shit", threw me down and bent to retrieve the pipe. When he straightened up I saw the chrome numbers on his high stiff collar and the badge of the NSW Police on the cap beside him.

"You want to be a bit more careful, young fella-me-lad," and he tucked his big boots under him. In one smooth flowing action, he removed his cap from the seat and raised me up to sit beside him. "Going some where special ... Ikey?" The saloon door opened as a man woken from half sleep by the disturbance, went below. In the sudden shaft of light I looked up into the palest blue eyes and fair close cropped hair. Ikey? In the velvety darkness was I identifiably an Ikey? Did I appear to the whole world like the coarse comedian, 'Mo', who did the Jews no favour by 30 years on the stage perpetuating an archetypal Jew which, in pre-war Australia was the yardstick by which all Jews would be measured. I rubbed my hand over my smooth face; there was not the slightest trace of that charcoal that was Mo's trademark. I licked my lips too, afraid that without my noticing, they had grown thick and slobbery like his. But no, I was still Jacob, thirteen years of age, brown hair, brown eyes, a bit on the thin side and running away from the police.

The police! Here I was, as bold as brass, sitting right alongside one who was smart enough to be able to identify me instantly as a Jewish kid, here on a ferry in the middle of Sydney Harbour in the winter of 1939. What hope would Solly and I have of escaping to God knows where if every policeman could take one look at us and say to himself, "There go that pair of Yid kids we're supposed to be on the lookout for."

The ferry threaded its way up Middle Harbour and started to edge into a landing. Some passengers left our deck and headed for the gang plank; the policeman never moved, his solid body transmitting warmth to me. As the boat neared the wharf I could see the sign illuminated by the hazy blue light.

"I'm going to Gladesville to visit my aunty," I said and looked up into those clear blue eyes. It was not altogether a lie; Father had spoken in whispers about his aunt Bertha who shortly after her arrival in Sydney from London suffered a stroke and was admitted to the Gladesville Asylum, much to my amusement — I was actually quite pleased to have a barmy aunt and as he never took me or Solly to visit her, we could imagine what we liked about her. The policeman had re-lit his pipe. He demonstrated his great strength by lifting me down from the seat and giving me a gentle push. "Well you had better be going, young Ikey," he said. "Straight there, mind and don't talk to strangers." The ferry bumped the wharf and I was thrown off balance again but recovered quickly and shot down the stairs to find Solly where I had left him with his back to the warm flue pipe.

"We're getting off here, Solly," I shouted to him above the roar of the engines as they went into a shuddering reverse thrust. I had to lever him away from his flue pipe which he clung to like a bunny rug. The engineer had given him a packet of potato chips and he offered them to me. I brushed them aside and grabbed his hand, spilling the chips on the deck. Solly started to whinge about it but I lugged him down the gang plank and through the unmanned turnstile not knowing where I was going but suspecting that the young constable was hanging over the ferry's side watching us. The path rose steeply from the wharf; by the time we reached the road Solly and I were winded, the cold night air cutting into our lungs and robbing us of speech which was probably all to the good, neither of us having a clear thought in our heads.

Well, What Do You Say to My Boy?

Most of the women in our migrant community did not want their sons to follow their husbands' professions. This was the case even when a good living was being made and money wasn't short. The women wanted their sons to become educated men — doctors, lawyers, professors and the like. For why did they come to Australia if not to educate their children, to avail themselves of the schooling which was to be had here and not in their old home?

The men did not oppose their wives. Clearly the professions were better, more dignified, more secure than, say bottle-buying, hawking with drapery, labouring or even carpentering, which was said to be one of the best trades. Besides, the men too wanted their sons to be somebodies in the new land. Of course business men were the only ones with any chance of making fortunes, but learning came before money. Or so everybody said.

From this it mustn't be concluded that all the boys in our community became educated men. Many did, but in quite a few families the sons, when they turned fourteen, left school and joined their fathers at whatever they happened to be doing.

In our community no woman desired more ardently to educate her five sons than did Mrs Minnie Green. And no woman extolled more rhapsodically the virtues of learning than she did. And her husband seemed to be one with her in her aspirations, always keeping a serious face, always nodding his head whenever she spoke on the matter of education, which was frequently.

Mrs Green however had no success with her two oldest boys, Les and Izz. Neither of them liked school and as soon as each reached fourteen he had joined his father on his clattering, honking truck, buying bottles for three days a week in suburban streets and on the other three working days buying hides, skins and tallow and animal bones from farmers in country districts.

Mrs Green had not tried to stop Les and Izz from becoming

business men. She had accepted the position realistically, without much fuss. Concluding that her influence had not been strong enough to offset the forces against learning, to which they had succumbed, she set about making the home the all-conquering influence, a bastion of culture and learning, so that her other sons would not be lost.

Her third son Benny, who was then approaching fourteen and was a promising scholar, benefited from her policy. She surrounded him with objects which she believed would inspire him to higher things and cement his ties with learning and culture. She could not do anything else for him; she could not discuss his schoolwork with him nor could she help him with his homework. The truth was that Mrs Minnie Green could not read nor write in any language and she could not speak any language correctly, least of all English.

Thus it came about that she bought a piano on time payment. It might be asked why a piano when nobody in the house knew how to play the instrument and when not one of her five boys was receiving piano lessons? Partly it was because Mrs Green looked upon the piano as something inspiring and refining. And besides she was convinced that only the piano could counter the baneful influence of the guitar which her eldest, Les, was for-ever strumming inside the house. She sniffed at that stringed box as at an unclean thing.

Mrs Green spent much time with the piano, dusting it every day and lovingly polishing it at least twice a week. It stood out among the rest of the furniture in the dining-room, a formidable if silent ally of the mistress of the house. Silent it was for most of the time, but now and then the only musical member of the family, Les the guitar player, would run his grimy, thick fingers over the keyboard and produce a frivolous tone reminiscent of the guitar. It would grate on his mother's ears and make her wince.

'Why must you do that to the piano, Les?' she demanded. 'It is desecration, nothing but desecration,' she added, almost breaking her teeth over that stern word.

Les looked at her with feigned earnestness.

'The piano'll pine away Mum if it isn't touched sometimes,

caressed,' Les said. 'You know what I mean. It's like a human being,' he concluded, inclining his head respectfully, his lips set firm to prevent his face breaking into a smile.

She did not answer him. She looked at him with a puzzled frown as if trying to divine exactly what he meant. His earnest features set her at ease but she could not rid herself of her suspicions. Les had a most peculiar sense of humour. Vulgar it could almost be called. God knows where he got it from. He certainly did not get it from her and she was convinced he did not get it from her husband who, she was sure, was refined despite his uncouth occupation. Ah well! she sighed. The outside world, that rude world of money grubbing and vulgarity, had a habit of twisting people to its own image.

But for all this she was happy with her sons, particularly Benny the promising scholar, and happy with the piano which on the whole was performing its requisite cultural role.

The piano was not only the only object she brought to bear on the boy. There were the books, in great numbers, cluttering up the sideboards, tables and dressers, for there were no book-shelves as yet. To her great joy Benny devoured the books as if they were slabs of fresh honey cake. She watched him read with that look of pleasure and pride which young mothers ordinarily wear when their first born utters his first halting words. Benny was more than making up for her failure with Les and Izz.

Mrs Green bought most of the books from second-hand dealers, acquaintances of her husband. They sold them to her for next to a song. There were complete editions of Scott, Dickens, Thackeray, Kingsley, Marryat, Reade, Lever, Collins and other eminent nineteenth-century novelists and some leather-bound volumes of poetry. Now and again, a dealer, taking advantage of her inability to read, would palm off a cookery book or an abstruse, learned work like Locke's *Essay Concerning Human Understanding*. It did not make any difference to Mrs Minnie Green. She did not know one book from another but she blindly revered the printed word from which stemmed learning and thus happiness.

On almost all her shopping trips she dropped into the second-hand dealers first. Invariably she bought some books, which she placed at the bottom of her large shopping basket. But she could never resist carrying one or two under her arm like a student and she would succumb to the temptation of showing off, even boasting in the butcher's shop where there was always a goodly congregation of ladies, gossiping, treating the place as if it was a street or a backyard.

'My Benny only reads the best,' Mrs Green often boasted to the ladies. 'Penny dreadfuls never show their noses in my house,' she added with a faint blush for her words were not strictly accurate. Still they were nearly true.

Once, after she had made her familiar remark a lady who could read English looked at the book under Mrs Green's arm and asked: 'Does Benny enjoy Christian sermons too?'

For a moment Mrs Green did not know what had been said and she stared blankly at the lady who added with irony: 'Of course if you have to give him sermons it's as well that they should be by a Bishop of the English Church. After all what greater authority on Christianity can there be in an English country?'

Minnie Green realized she was carrying some kind of religious book; she had been had by that grubby, oily-mouthed second-hand dealer who often talked about Benny's reading, pretending to be interested. But suppressing her annoyance, with unexpected presence of mind and at the same time rising above her own beliefs and prejudices, she answered calmly: 'My Benny said, "Mum, please get me a book by an English bishop" and I hunted everywhere for it until I got it. My boy is very interested in religion and history and everything,' she added with a satisfied smile.

And before the other lady could open her mouth to cast doubts, Mrs Green, speaking rapidly, said that her Benny, in the pursuit of knowledge, would read everything, even the writings of Christians and heretics. He was like her late uncle of blessed memory, possessed of courage and curiosity. Her late uncle was not even afraid to dip into the pages of socialists and writers who said we stemmed from monkeys.

For all her words and her calm manner, the ladies in the butcher's shop did not believe Minnie Green. A sly second-hand

31

dealer had palmed the book of sermons onto her; how would she tell which was a book of sermons or which was a joke book if they were both placed in front of her? This was said after Mrs Green had left the shop with the parcel of meat on top of the basket, the sermons still under her arm.

Yet the community could not help admiring her. Granted, it was said, that she was a little green, a plain 'greener' as they termed starry-eyed, excessively optimistic newcomers. But there was no doubt that Minnie Green was naturally a refined, cultured woman, a kind of nature's lady with genuinely lofty ambitions for her sons. But how she had ever come to marry Sam Green, that coarse animal, that Samson of a man, was almost beyond their understanding. It was a great source of discussion in our community.

One of our most respected and best informed gossips, Mrs Fanny Snider, told a group of ladies at an engagement party that it was a fact that refined girls were often drawn to unrefined men. How could she say such a thing, everyone protested. Mrs Fanny Snider then repeated her statement, saying that it was as much a fact as that the sun rises in the morning. She gave instances: Minnie Green was one.

'The souls of refined girls are not parched raisins,' Mrs Snider summed up.

Whatever it was that had caused Minnie to wed Sam, it was undeniable that they were still fond of each other nearly twenty-two years after their marriage. And she looked up to her husband to such an extent that she could not understand why sometimes she heard him referred to as that 'Happy Bandit'. Maybe it was only a joke. But Minnie Green said: ask yourself what sort of a joke it is? She did not like it although she let it pass.

But when she overheard Sam described as a bushranger she spun around aggressively ready to do battle for her husband's honour and put an end once and for all to those unpleasant jokes which were not jokes at all. 'What was the meaning of it?,' she demanded.

'Now, now, Mrs Green, what is there to get excited about?' came the answer. 'Bushranger! Pah! Shame on you Mrs Green

32

for raising your voice. In this country bushrangers are the aristocrats, the leaders of society, honoured by everyone. You have something to boast about with a husband a bushranger.'

These exaggerated, swollen words placated her. Her Sam was certainly not a bushranger, a leader of society; but maybe he was a tiny bushranger. In a kind of way she was proud of her husband for his achievement. He was only a newcomer but he was a somebody already. So she accepted the explanation, relieved too that she did not have to quarrel for she was a peaceful woman and she cared for her dignity.

Yet she had many misgivings, deep inside. Whoever heard of bushrangers honoured! Honour was for learned men she had always believed. Evidently she did not know as much about her new land as she imagined. And that came from looking at the world with the eyes of a greener, the wise ones in the community said. But she could not help it. Everything about her told of a guileless nature, even her face which was broad and pink and unwrinkled with an expression which reminded one of a question mark, and her fair hair was done in a girlish Gretchen manner.

So it was not surprising that her husband, Sam, was not altogether as she saw him. He was regarded in the community as coarse and crafty and there was no doubt that he was worldly. It had not taken him long to know the new land, to become a real expert, a native in fact. And he had prospered as a bottle-o and a buyer of junk and animal bones which he sold to the fertilizer works. So well had he prospered that he had long discarded a horse and cart in favour of a motor truck; a poor spluttering thing it was but it suited Sam better than a healthy, handsome looking truck which only flaunted one's prosperity. In no time he had needed help, partners in fact. And what better partners than one's own sons when they were like Les and Izz?

Sam had taken the two boys from Minnie without her knowing it. Behind her back he always encouraged them to play truant and to come with him on his rounds, where he scoffed at school, extolling the self-made man as the best of men. What did they want education for? To make money all they had to know was how to read and add up and subtract in one's own

33

favour. They knew that already.

The boys had quickly fallen in with their father. They were very like him in many ways. The same humour, the same craftiness. And in their appearance the same heavy, powerful bodies, the same jet black hair. They made a fine team.

Thus, on their rounds, they were rarely out of each other's sight, Sam generally doing the buying and then helping the boys carry the bottles or the junk to the truck. They must pay for what they took; no thieving like other bottle-o's. Sam had laid down that rule at the very beginning of the partnership.

'You make more by honest commerce than by thieving,' he explained to his sons. 'Ever hear of a thief becoming a Sir or a Lord or even a Mayor? I bet you haven't. But plenty of business men have. There's that grocer, for instance, who is not only the mayor but he was knighted too. See what I mean boys. You've got to be legal to get on.'

They understood him quite well. You had to pay. That was the rule. There were no other rules.

When the boys had acquired plenty of experience and could take good care of themselves Sam allowed them to open up new territory, to go into backyards without him. When they returned to the truck they would relate all their experiences, tell their father everything.

Sam had an easy way with them so that they always treated him like a companion, a friend of their own age and not a parent.

One day, Les said to his father, pointing to an apartment house which provided a regular gold mine of bottles: 'The old girl in there fell for Izz as soon as she laid eyes on him. She told him he looked like a movie star. "Come round as often as you like," she said to him. "On your own," ' he added mimicking a woman's voice.

Sam looked admiringly at Izz who was the darkest, the best looking and biggest of the three.

'She thought you were an amorous drake,' Sam observed, 'and I don't suppose she's too far out.'

'What would I want with an old piece like that?' Izz said gruffly.

34

Sam shrugged his shoulders and smiled.

'She must have been forty if she wasn't a day,' Les said.

'So forty's old, eh?' Sam turned on his son. 'I suppose you think I'm a regular gaffer because I've had my forty-fifth birthday. I ought to be shuffled off the stage, eh? Is that what you think?'

Les spoke placatingly: 'A man's not old in his forties, a woman is though.'

'Too right,' Izz said. 'For me they're old when they turn twenty-one.'

Sam looked his sons up and down with contempt.

'A fat lot both of you know,' he said with a sneer. 'When you grow up you'll find out that old bones make very good soup.'

The boys winked, digging each other in the ribs with their elbows.

The argument ended in laughter. Most of their arguments did. The other bottle-o's and the men who worked the streets envied them, their happiness, their success.

When Benny was sixteen and in the leaving class at school his father was seeking an assistant for the dealer's yard he had just opened, one who could write letters, keep books and talk nice to important buyers, as he put it. And Sam Green thought of his son Benny, an educated boy if ever there was one. What a triumph it would be to snatch him from Minnie now that he was on the threshold of the university! The more Sam thought about it the more attractive the idea seemed and he was determined to capture his son.

But he could not inveigle Benny as he had Les and Izz. His third son was aloof and cool and rarely talked at the meal table, rationing his words as if they were really valuable. In a way he was a stranger to his father. How to get intimate with one like him was indeed a problem.

So it happened that Sam began to affect an interest in books and when it occurred to him that his son spent more time than was normal at his desk in writing, he asked Benny what he was doing, pretending that he was concerned, although the boy's scribblings were as much on his mind as yesterday's breakfast. Benny looked at his father shrewdly and answered non-

35

committally, giving him no information at all. Sam was rebuffed again and again.

'He won't talk, devil take it,' Sam muttered to himself. 'He looks like Minnie, the same fair hair, the same pink face but he hasn't got her innocent tongue nor her simple heart,' he told himself with self-righteous indignation.

Presently Sam lost patience and cast away all pretences. He approached his son directly and without any apparent guile.

'I want you to come in with me Benny,' he said. 'In a couple of years we'll have a great business. Green and Sons. Metals, scrap, import, export. We'll be rich. Millionaires.'

From the expression on Benny's face, Sam could see that he had sounded the wrong notes and he hastily began to sing a new tune.

'You'll have an easy life, son,' he said. 'I'll get you a motor car. You can do a lot with a motor car. You can take your girlfriend for rides all over the place,' he added, honestly believing that if the promise of money and an easy life couldn't do the trick a girlfriend in a motor car most certainly would.

To his astonishment however, Benny screwed up his face in an expression of utter repungnance.

'What makes you think that I would put a motor car and a partnership in Green and Sons as the height of my ambitions?' the boy asked haughtily. 'I know of a higher aim,' he added to his speechless father.

Sam was still furious when he spoke to Les and Izz a few hours later.

'What sort of a fellow's your brother?' he demanded.

'What do you mean?' Les asked.

'You ought to know,' Izz said glancing slyly at his father. 'You made him Dad.'

'I don't know him,' Sam snapped. 'He's a cold devil, that's what he is. No hot blood in him at all. He never laughs, he only sniggers, ever notice that?'

'He's all right,' Les said. 'He's got lots of brains, Benny has,' he added admiringly.

'Deep as the sea if you ask me,' Izz said.

'Deep, my old boots,' Sam snorted. 'Got plenty of airs though.'

For all his anger he was now more determined than ever to ensnare Benny into the dealer's yard. And Minnie, who did not know anything about her husband's intention, had no doubt whatsoever that Benny would go to the University the following year. In the butcher's shop, she boasted without pause. Although she did not know whether Benny wanted to do medicine she could not imagine that he would not want to become a doctor. So she announced that her son was going to study for medicine. It was a fine, noble profession. Doctors were respected and honoured everywhere and if they were not respected and honoured they were feared, and they always looked clean and very dignified which was more than could be said for most of the husbands of the ladies in the shop. And, as if making a concession to vulgar opinion, she said that doctors were never short of customers which could not be said of other professions from what she had heard.

Benny had other ideas but his mother did not learn what they were until Benny passed his leaving examination.

In honour of this signal occasion, Mrs Green had roasted a turkey stuffed with rice and garlic, laid the table with her best damask cloth and heavy silver cutlery, both wedding presents. And Benny was seated next to his secretly proud father, where he was fed the best pieces, fussed over by his admiring brothers and beamed upon by his mother who kept calling him 'Doctor Green'. The boy looked at her with a puzzled expression, repeating to himself the words, 'Doctor Green'. And all at once it dawned on him why his mother had bestowed that honourable title on him. He must put a stop to it. He would never be guilty of false pretences, he would never fly under false colours; he had long ago sworn an oath to himself to serve truth in all things.

'Mother,' he began in a solemn voice, 'if you think I am going in for medicine you are mistaken. In fact I am not even going to the university.'

Father and brothers suddenly stopped eating as if felled while Minnie Green kept repeating, 'no university', and going into a kind of daze, staring wide-eyed and blank across the table.

'That's right Mum,' Benny said, relentlessly faithful to the truth.

Sam cast a long, sideways glance at his son. He smiled to himself, pleased with the latest turn, his hopes rising, yet held in check for God alone knew what Benny had boiling in that head of his.

'What do you intend to do then??' he asked quietly in a matter-of-fact voice.

The boy glanced at his father with a determined, almost truculent expression on his face.

'I'm going to be a writer,' Benny said aggressively.

'A writer!' Sam exclaimed.

'Yes, a writer,' Benny repeated.

That brought Minnie to. She roused herself from her daze, fixed her eyes on her son and asked:

'What are you going to write Benny?'

'Stories of life, Mum,' he answered.

She did not understand him.

'Stories,' she repeated. 'Do you mean books, Benny?' she asked hopefully.

'Yes, books, Mum.'

'Books,' she cried. 'That's good. Did you hear Sam? Benny's going to write books.'

She was suddenly filled with an elation that drove away her former disappointment. What greater happiness could there be than to have a son a writer, the supreme kind of learned, educated man who wrote the books which others read and studied, even doctors.

Sam was hopeful. Now he did not think he would irrevocably lose his son who could become such an ornament to the firm, a letter writer and a talker of good English, necessary sometimes in business.

'Benny, how are you going to earn a living?' he asked.

Confidently the boy answered: 'By writing of course.'

Sam looked at him with pity.

'I'll tell you something you ought to know, Benny,' he said.

'On my rounds I've collected bottles off a poet, a big poet they say. You'd know of him if I could remember his name. Do you know his name?' He turned to Izz and Les. They didn't know his name either.

'Well,' Sam continued, 'that poet makes less out of poetry in a lifetime than a shopkeeper makes in a week.'

The boy exclaimed angrily: 'You're always bringing money into everything!'

Sam ignored his son's outburst.

'Look here Benny, if that poet I'm telling you about didn't work at something else besides his scribbling he'd starve like a homeless dog. In this country writers are on the lowest rung,' he added.

'We've got different ideas about the lowest rung,' the boy retorted angrily.

'I didn't say I believed it,' Sam said craftily winking at Les and Izz. 'Seriously Benny you ought to get into something that'll bring you in money and leave you time to write. Writing's only a hobby after all.'

The boy glared at his father.

'Sam, what are you saying to Benny?' Minnie exclaimed. 'I'm amazed at you. I thought you would show more understanding.'

'You misunderstood me Minnie,' he said and proceeded to tell her that he was thinking of nothing else but how he could help Benny with his writing career.

She was always ready to believe him. And he was relieved that once again she believed him. He did not want her to know the truth; he did not want her to suspect how he schemed against her. Till his dying day he wanted to keep up the pretence.

But more than anything else he wanted to get Benny into the business.

'I've been thinking Benny,' he said, 'that a writer needs to see everything. If you'd come down to the yard sometimes or go onto the truck with the boys you'd see such things that'd make you old in the head before your whiskers came up.'

It was tempting to Benny.

'I might accept your offer Dad,' he said.

'See, your Dad's not such a fool as you think,' Sam said with pleasure.

'Look, Dad, I've just remembered something,' Benny said, 'My old headmaster, Mr Fitsimmons would like to see you.'

'See me!' Sam exclaimed. 'What's he want to see me for? He doesn't drink does he? Or maybe he's been collecting brass door handles he wants to get rid of.'

'Sam!' Minnie cried in a shocked voice. 'What's come over you tonight.'

He instantly changed his tone.

'I can't see him tomorrow, Benny,' he said earnestly.

'Any day will do, Dad,' Benny said. 'He's spending his holidays at home.'

Several days later Sam Green was shown into the head-master's study. Mr Raynor Fitsimmons, a tall, imposing pedagogue with a silvery mane, extended his hand and declared in a deep, carefully measured voice: 'I've wanted to see you for weeks, Mr Green. I want to talk to you about your son.'

Under the magisterial gaze of the pedagogue, Sam Green felt he would agree to anything the headmaster proposed. As the saying he often repeated went, he was not a lion among lambs but a lamb among lions.

'I suspect your son might be a genius,' Mr Raynor Fitsimmons said. 'A genius!'

Bending over his desk he extracted a bulky handwritten manuscript from a drawer and thrust it under Sam's nose.

'Did my Benny write all that?' Sam asked.

'Unaided, Mr Green,' came the reply.

'Unaided,' Sam repeated.

'Only a very talented boy, a genius really, could have written this work,' Mr Fitsimmons declared. Putting the manuscript back in the drawer he fixed his steady gaze on the parent and spoke in his best manner: 'We must face the facts, Mr Green. Geniuses are rarely successes in the ordinary sense of the word. To put it another way, they never make money. In fact, they rarely make a living.'

'That's just what I've been saying,' Sam said.

'Benny will bring your home honour,' Mr Fitsimmons continued. 'But he needs freedom from all worries and petty concerns. I'm sure you'll be proud to see to that.'

'Of course, Mr Fitsimmons,' Sam said.

'I am glad to hear you say that,' Mr Fitsimmons said.

They talked for a few more minutes and then Mr Fitsimmons escorted Sam to the front door.

With a heavy heart Sam drove through the streets. Curse that pedagogue! Why was he so foolish as to call on him? Yet it was not that he would have to keep Benny for the rest of his days; it was that he hated to lose. Sam showed his unhappiness and his chagrin when he returned to the yard.

'You don't look too well, Dad,' Les said glancing at Izz.

'Some rotten cow take you down?' Izz asked sympathetically.

'We've got a genius in the family,' Sam said mournfully. 'And we have to keep him. That's what Fitsimmons asked me to do.'

'That's not so awful,' Izz said.

'Cheer up Dad,' Les said. 'It could have been much worse. Benny might have turned out to be a tea leaf and not a genius.'

'I don't know whether it's any better,' Sam replieid. 'A thief's got a chance but what chance has a writer, I ask you? You've seen that poet bloke. You know.'

'Benny won't take much keeping,' Izz said.

The boys were getting on their father's nerves without knowing it.

'Maybe it won't take much to keep him,' Sam replied irritably, 'but enough to cut you two out of a car. We'll have to economize.'

'Now Dad,' Les said.

'You're going too far,' Izz said.

'Perhaps I am,' Sam said wearily. 'We need letters written now.'

'I'll write 'em,' Les said.

'You, God help us,' Sam said.

Suddenly his mood changed as he recollected something.

'You know boys, the headmaster showed me what Benny did. A whole book of writing. I'll swear it was 10 by 8 by 3½. Remarkable,' Sam added proudly and returned to his work whistling. He wondered why he had worried; Benny would be his. He couldn't keep himself by writing any more than the poet did. Benny would soon be writing letters for him. The thought elated him.

And Minnie Green walked as if on air. Her Benny was a writer, a genius. In the butcher's shop she faced the ladies with great confidence.

'Well what do you say to my boy? A writer he's going to be. A writer of books. Truly our house has been blessed.'

Judah Waten

SEVENTY YEARS of YIDDISH THEATRE in MELBOURNE: 1909-1979

PART ONE

In 1892, there arrived in Sydney a very young man, a worker from Warsaw, named Chaim Reinholz. Having a fine voice and being familiar with the stage, he succeeded in becoming involved with the English-speaking theatre. He toured about the cities with a number of theatrical troupes, on one occasion, while in Hobart, vanishing from the troupe and surfacing at the Hobart Synagogue on Rosh Hashanah and Yom Kippur to conduct the prayers when the congregation had no-one to lead them. In 1905, Reinholz received Abraham Goldfaden's "Shulamis" which he had earlier not known. It excited him considerably and he decided to have it performed. Together with two ladies who knew a little Yiddish, he established a choir of thirty people, all of them non-Jews and rehearsed the piece with them. His own role he sang in Yiddish, as did, in parts, his two companions. Everyone else sang the text in English, the text having been specially translated for them. Reinholz, to his credit, did try to teach his non-Jewish singers the Yiddish text, but without success, for at the performance, they either forgot the Yiddish or so badly mutilated it that no-one in the audience knew what language they were using.

Thus, in 1905, in Sydney, was conducted the first Yiddish performance in Australia.

For Reinholz himself, it was the first and last attempt at staging Yiddish theatre, although he did give recitals of Yiddish songs for the benefit of Jewish communal institutions. He wrote songs of his own as well, mostly dealing with Jewish life in Australia, but in later years these

43

ceased to be sung, disappearing finally into oblivion.

On Monday 2nd November 1908, there arrived in Melbourne the actor Samuel Weisberg who came with the intention of founding a permanent Yiddish theatre in Australia. He had been born 46 years before on the 1st of May 1862 in Pyotrkov in Poland and by the time he arrived in Australia he had wandered throughout half the world with Yiddish theatre troupes. It had been on a friend's recommendation that he came to Australia to test his luck in creating a local Yiddish theatre. That may have been his ultimate dream but he soon came face to face with reality.

In an autobiographical sketch, [1] he writes as follows:

I arrived in Melbourne in November 1908 on the "Vulcania." As I disembarked, I was approached by a distinguished-looking Jew with a fine patriarchal beard, and he asked me, "Are you Mr. Weisberg?"

"Yes," I replied.

"My name is Malinski. I received a letter from London informing me of your arrival and requesting that I should meet you."

I was pleased indeed by the cordial greeting and by his warm welcome to the new land. I thanked him sincerely and Mr. Malinski took me home with him and introduced me to his wife

----

1. Samuel Weisberg: Reminiscences of Early Yiddish Theatrical Performances in Yiddish in Australia [published in the original Yiddish in the First Australian-Jewish Almanac---Melbourne 1937]

and six lovely daughters. The table was prepared for dinner and the atmosphere was a festive one, as though they were awaiting some important guest. . .

Mr. Malinski was an intelligent, easy-going, peaceful man. He was of the kind that one can only respect. Sitting at the table, we chatted naturally about different things. When we had finished, we went into his garden, which was blooming with flowers to catch a breath of fresh air.

It was a very hot day. As we sat on the garden bench, Mr. Malinski said to me: "Mr. Weisberg, according to the letter which I received about you from my brother, I know precisely why you came to Australia. I honestly regret to tell you that you have made a big mistake."

"You believe then, Mr. Malinski, that I shall not be able to organise a Yiddish theatre here?"

"Yes."

"Are there no Jews here?"

"There are, there are. But very few. In all of Melbourne there are only some 200 families. Most of these are English Jews or Jews who have been here more than fifty years and who do not understand--or do not wish to understand--Yiddish. Besides that, they are dispersed in all corners of the city. And where do they come together? In the synagogue; and that only twice a year, on Rosh Hashanah and Yom Kippur."

"Do you have no club? No cultural

institution?"

"Regrettably, no."

"Is there no working-class here? I mean, Jewish craftsmen?"

"There are some, but very few."

"And where do they meet?"

"There are two Jewish hotels--or, as we call them, boarding houses---and there they come to eat or to play cards---and to bet on the races."

"As I see it then, Mr. Malinski, I have been misled, fooled. I met an Australian Jew in London who told me that there are more than 10,000 Jewish families here and more than 8,000 Jewish families in Sydney, and that should I perform in Yiddish theatre in Australia I would make a fortune in a very short time. And as I have always been a pioneer throughout the world to open a way for Yiddish theatre, I did as he suggested. And now I seem to have fallen in quite badly. I have travelled 12,000 miles, lost so much money, so much time, left a wife at home. Think of my disgrace in the theatre world; I'll be the laughing-stock of them all that I should have made so bad a mistake."

I sat for a few minutes in bewilderment and said nothing.

"I am sorry, Mr. Weisberg, that I have caused you so much distress," said Mr. Malinski. "You asked me, and I had to tell you the truth."

"Oh, no Mr. Malinski. You have caused me no distress. I am a different sort of man than you think. I shall see for myself what I must do; I shall yet make Jews out of gentiles. I shall yet stage Yiddish theatre for them. And now, Mr. Malinski, you told me that there are two boarding-houses where young men, workmen, come together. Could you please show me where they are? I wish to visit them."

Following the directions of Mr. Malinski, who himself declines to accompany Weisberg because of the "bad repute" attached to the boarding-houses, Weisberg walked along Cardigan Street in Carlton where he met a man whom he "recognized immediately to be a child of Israel."

This fellow-Jew took him to the boarding-house where Weisberg introduced himself as a tobacconist from London. But the ploy failed. As he writes further:

In the dining- room stood a long table surrounded with chairs. At about six o'clock came the diners, all young men with different occupations---tailors, shoe-makers, carpenters, tobacconists. As the guest, I was placed at the head of the table. The landlord, Abraham Berman, introduced me to the others and told them I was a tobacconist. At the table the men spoke with enthusiasm mainly about the races, for the following day was to be the "hag ha'susim," the Melbourne Cup. The young man who sat on my right also came from London. His name was Reinholz. . .

As we spoke, several other Jews approached to play cards. One Jew entered whom I immediately recognized as Mr. Lubransky. I pretended not to notice him, but he asked, "And who is this young man?"

"A tobacconist from London," the others answered.

He moved nearer the table and studied me closely.

"No," he said finally. "This is no tobacconist. And I know I'm not mistaken. Hyman!" he then shouted into the adjoining room. "Hyman, come here! Look at him closely. Don't you recognize this bird?"

"On my life," cried Hyman, "it's Mr. Weisberg! Children, this is a Yiddish actor. I know him from the Princess Street Theatre, from Adler's Company."

The words "Yiddish actor" enthralled everyone. They all stood up and surrounded me and plied me with a hundred questions and the word spread like wildfire throughout Carlton, the Jewish area, that a Yiddish theatre troupe had come to Australia. In the next half-hour, the room became crowded with Jewish men and women trying to catch a glimpse of me...There also came people who knew me well. Foremost among them was Abraham Stone who had been my prompter in Capetown, and also a certain Tshan from the "Amateurs Club" in Johannesburg.

It suddenly became lively in the town. That same evening, a provisional committee was founded. We immediately sat down to important work and, as the next day, Tuesday the 3rd of November, was the sacred holiday "hag ha'susim," everyone had time to work out a plan. We sat together until two a.m.

The following day, the provisional committee called a

meeting of respected citizens. At that meeting, Weisberg proposed that, as he neither had a troupe with him nor was he familiar with the local Jewish public, a public reading should be arranged for the following Sunday evening and that news of this should be circulated among the Jews of Melbourne.

This was duly done. To his surprise, the hall was packed. He was received, as he writes, "with a hearty welcome and stormy applause."

"I took my place upon the stage," he writes, "and carefully studied the faces so that I should have an idea of what to read to them---a melodrama or a scene from life. I spoke to them briefly and decided upon "Gabriel" (better known as "Hinke-Pinke"). I tried my best not merely to read, but I performed the first act with all its different characters and sang the songs myself because I wanted to take the public by storm and win their support. After the first act, their enthusiasm was overwhelming."

Weisberg had intended to read two pieces but the chairman of the committee stopped him as he wanted to get down to more serious matters. That same evening, a club--the Lyric Club--was founded, which enrolled several hundred members, and 50 pounds was collected on the spot. To Weisberg's appeal that suitable ladies and gentlemen of talent present themselves before him for a future production of the complete play, "Gabriel," there immediately registered many young men and women.

"Within a few days," Weisberg continues, "I succeeded in assembling the necessary ensemble which prepared itself for the play, 'Gabriel.' Also a large choir of ten ladies and ten gentlemen did I gather together, all of them with fine voices and some musical ability. The trouble was that none of the ladies knew a single word of Yiddish, neither to speak, to read or to write. They had to write out their parts with English letters. I was more fortunate with the men. Nearly all of them could read and write Yiddish. However, I could not find a single primadonna in Melbourne and one had to be imported from Sydney, a certain Miss Dina Opitz. In the meantime, I organised a choir of 20 Jewish schoolgirls and taught them choruses from Goldfaden's 'Shulamis' and from 'Bar Kochba' as well as solo roles and Yiddish recitations. The opening night attracted an enormous crowd. Fathers, mothers were delighted to see their children singing Yiddish songs or reciting in Yiddish. The atmosphere was most homely and truly Jewish."

After several weeks of effort, Weisberg announced that on the 11th of January 1909, there would be staged in the Temperance Hall, the first historical Yiddish performance of the operetta, "Gabriel," by Joseph Lateiner.

"The operetta 'Gabriel,' Weisberg writes, "was performed with radiance and splendour. The event was highly successful and even today people are still talking about that first performance. After the first act, the public pleaded that the play be staged again and, indeed, four days later, this was done with even greater success, both moral and financial."

The "Jewish Herald" of January 22nd 1909 wrote of the performance as follows:

"Gabriel" is described as an operetta but is in reality of an unclassifiable nondescript character, partaking of tragedy, comedy, farce, vaudeville, and a number of other things too numerous to mention...Mr. Weisberg showed himself to be a comedian of no mean accomplishments and his sallies were greeted with roars of laughter and volleys of applause... Considering that Mr. Weisberg had only about six weeks in which to train his company, none of whom, with the exception of Miss Dina Opitz and Mr. Hyman Reynolds (? Chaim Reinholz anglicized--S.L.) had had any previous experience of the stage---many of them knowing little or no Yiddish---it speaks volumes for his industry and ability that he succeeded in giving what was on the whole a really interesting and entertaining performance."

What was not known to the audience or to the critic of the "Jewish Herald" was the little drama that, despite the success of the programme, was being played out behind the scenes.

As Weisberg writes in the climactic finale of his memoir: "The actors called a strike. They refused to go on stage until they were paid. The leader of the strike was Hyman Reynolds who played the lead role and demanded five pounds. He was paid the money before the performance. The others were finally placated with the promise by the committee that they would be paid at the Club on the following evening. This weighed heavily on my heart. I couldn't bear it. I instructed the committee to divide the earnings amongst all the amateurs and refused to take a single penny of that money for myself. I went home, packed my things and prepared myself for my journey back to England. I had had enough. Finished."

Thus--he concludes--ended the first attempt at Yiddish theatre in Australia.

In actual fact, Samuel Weisberg was incorrect on two counts. First, as already seen, his was not the first attempt at Yiddish theatre in Australia. Chaim Reinholz had preceded him by four years. More important still, however, was the fact that Weisberg remained in Melbourne and indeed took part both in the staging of several more plays and in bringing out other members of his family who were professional artists.

The success of this first Yiddish production in Melbourne made possible the creation of an amateur group under Weisberg's guidance. Not only that. It is worth noting that the first Yiddish cultural institution in Australia, the

"Kadimah," was founded in 1911 and one may well suggest that the Yiddish theatre may well have stimulated Yiddish cultural activity in Melbourne and possibly in all Australia. (Also worth noting is the total opposition of the local rabbis who issued a call--an unheeded call--for a boycott of the Yiddish theatre. If one may draw parallels with the American experience of the late 1890s, it would appear that their opposition stemmed from their attitude to theatre as a shameful trifling and also, being at that time of a more Anglicized nature, they may well have felt embarrassed before their gentile neighbours by the overt display of an essentially alien culture.)

The work around Yiddish theatre assumed concrete forms. The second production which Weisberg staged was Jacques Halevy's grand opera, "La Juive" ("The Jewess") also in 1909, which was performed three times. Considering the small Jewish population of Melbourne at that time, this was no mean achievement. Critical reviews of this production in the Australian press were warm. Even "Truth" newspaper, a widely-circulated paper, which was a mixture of cheap sensationalism, bawdy stories and anti-Semitism, praised the production, but did add the rider that the piece was performed in a "bastard" language. When Weisberg complained to the editor over this insult to Yiddish, the editor, far from retracting, replied that, to his way of thinking, English, too, was, no less than Yiddish, a bastard language.

PART TWO

It was after this second production that Weisberg brought to Australia his brother-in-law Reuben Finkelstein and his wife from Buenos Aires together with their children, three daughters and a son. In time, the whole Finkelstein family was to perform in Yiddish theatre. Their first play together was "Holy Sabbath" staged on the 26th of June 1911 and performed five or six times.

For some time, Weisberg worked together with the Finkelsteins but later they parted company over disagreement on the question of repertoire. Weisberg, an ardent follower of Jacob Gordin, held that above all they had to present Gordin's works before the public. Finkelstein was less particular.

Now, the question of repertoire was not merely an academic one. To appreciate this, one needs to digress briefly to the American Yiddish scene. There, until the 1890s, apart from the homely, folkloristic, tradition-bound works of Goldfaden, the Yiddish stage was dominated by what Irving Howe calls "shund" or trash. These were in the main hack pieces, usually naive mixtures of historical pageantry, topical references, family melodramas and musical comedies, pieces written in a matter of days, often mere sketches comprising a central situation and set speeches left to the actors on the stage to pad out with asides and free ad-libbing, plays that were either crude adaptations from Russian and German nineteenth-century drama sprinkled with incongruous homely Jewish touches or bombastic and wildly inaccurate renderings of Jewish history depicting the lives and heroics of such figures as Joseph, King Solomon, Judas Macabbeus and Bar Kochba. In these, there was a surfeit of burlesque, tomfoolery, clownishness and degeneracy, and the theatre was less a vehicle for the play than for personalities such as the legendary Jacob Adler and Boris Tomashefsky to display their charismatic talents. As one critic and playwright, Leon Kobrin, wrote: The theatre was a place where "clowns and comedians with glued-on beards and earlocks, sometimes in long coats but mainly in royal robes with tin swords and crowns of gold paper declaimed at the top of their lungs."

The quest for a better theatre in the 1890s produced Jacob Gordin who saw Yiddish theatre at that time as vulgar, false and immoral. He was the model of an enlightened Jewish intellectual imbued with Tolstoyan idealism, and intent upon lifting the masses out of superstition into culture. For almost two decades from 1891 with his first play "Siberia" until his death in 1909, he was a central presence in Yiddish theatre, a man trying to make Yiddish theatre like other theatres and grounding Yiddish drama in the soil of common life, translating and adapting the works of Hugo, Ibsen, Gogol and Shakespeare, bringing discipline to a stage too commonly marked by high jinks and chaos, insisting on strict adherence to scripts, limiting the use of ad-lib and attempting to create a system of painstaking rehearsals. Several of his plays, which bore the tag of "realism," became standard in the Yiddish repertoire; for example, "The Jewish King Lear," where an old and wealthy Jewish father makes the same mistake with his daughters that Shakespeare's Lear made long before, and "Mirele Efros," also called "The Jewish Queen Lear" again telling of the ingratitude of children towards their elders, and "God, Man and Devil," a reworking of the Faust story in which Hershele, a poor weaver, buys a lottery ticket from a salesman (the devil in disguise), becomes a manufacturer and a cruel sweater of labor and in the end, murmuring that "man is like a vapor that rises to the clouds and vanishes" hangs himself in remorse.

These, then, were the kind of plays over which Weisberg and Finkelstein parted company. In the years 1911 to 1914, Weisberg staged a series of Gordin's plays, these being "The Jewish King Lear," "Mirele Efros," "Chasye the Orphan," "Kreutzer Sonata" and "The Massacre," all of which were performed several times. Later productions of Weisberg were, among others, "Herzele Meuches," Joseph Lateiner's "Don Judah Abrabanel," "The Converted Priest," "The Golden Land," "Bar Kochba," "The Sacrifice of Isaac," and Goldfaden's "Shulamis." He finally gave up active theatre activities around 1915. In the seven years under his direction, the most active stars performing with him were Solomon Mendelssohn, Berensohn, Horowitz and Hoisy as well as the Finkelsteins. He was also aided in his attempt to assert the superior Gordin repertoire in Melbourne by a young actor named David Reitzin, who was billed as "the chief star of the leading American theatres." Reitzin was later to become Finkelstein's son-in-law. A large number of the plays which Weisberg staged and in which, even after his formal retirement, he performed were in support of the local Jewish schools and other cultural institutions.

Samuel Weisberg is rightly regarded as the grandfather of Yiddish theatre in Australia. His activities here were the stimulus to the development of other Jewish cultural institutions in the community, among which the "Kadimah" has already been mentioned. He was, by occupation, a hairdresser, situated at 110 Rathdowne St., Carlton, and died on the 27th November 1943 in his eighty-third year.

His brother-in-law Reuben Finkelstein had his own approach to theatre. Not too particular about repertoire, he also manipulated the actual plays according to his own sights. He gave them different names from the original, declared himself the author of a series of pieces which the public knew were not his, or performed familiar but ostensibly modified pieces in the name of utterly fictitious authors. As an actor, he permitted himself a series of liberties in order to draw public attention continually to himself. If all this be thought to be charlatanism or an idiosyncrasy, let it be known that he was merely imitating a long-standing tendency on the American Yiddish stage where actors and directors alike modified the written piece, mangled it sometimes beyond recognition, deleted scenes, added others and took liberties against which Finkelstein's efforts were pale mimicry. Finkelstein's wife, on the other hand, was a plain, modest woman, a talented actress in her own right who, nurturing a serious approach to theatre, continually demanded--fruitlessly, it would appear--from her vain husband, more integrity and responsibility both as an actor and as stage manager.

Between the years 1911 and 1915 the Finkelstein troupe performed a mixture of hack-works, though also of artistically sounder pieces. Alongside Goldfaden's "Shulamis" one sees Leteiner's pretentious "Alexander, Crown Prince of

Jerusalem"; also against Goldfaden's "Grandmother Yanke," one finds grand pieces such as "King Ahasuerus" and Leiner's "Uriel Acosta." Also staged were "Hannele the Convert" (or "Tate-Mame Tsores"), "The Sailor in Danger," "Yosele Miker," and Sharkanski's "Kol Nidrei." In 1912 the actor Mendelssohn in the capacity of impressario brought the Finkelstein troupe together with David Raitzin to Sydney where they performed Lateiner's "Alexander" and Goldfaden's "Shulamis" and "Grandmother Yanke." Each of these was staged twice; each proved to be a financial disaster; and Mendelssohn ceased his work as impressario. However, the troupe remained in Sydney for a while and played on its own account. Later, it travelled to Perth and, it is believed, to several smaller states....

In March 1927, there came to Melbourne the artist Jacob Ginter who had, behind him, many years of professional theatre-work in Poland. His first production in Melbourne with the Kadimah Dramatic Circle as it was then called was Sholom Aleichem's "Tevye the Milkman." In the same year, the Circle performed David Pinski's "Yankel the Blacksmith" in which the lure of the flesh is dramatised in all its intensity and Gordin's "The Stranger." In the years that followed, Yiddish theatre attained a still higher sophistication with the amalgamation of the Kadimah Circle and the Yiddishe Bineh and with the extension of the repertoire to include, among other plays, Hirshbein's "The Blacksmith's Daughter," Gordin's "God, Man and Devil," "Shlunke the Charlatan" and "Mirele Efros," Berkovitch's "From the Other World," David Pinski's "The Mother," Sholom Aleichem's "The Great Lottery Win," and "It's Hard to be a Jew," and Sholom Asch's "The Landsmen," "God of Vengeance" and "Uncle Moses" (dramatised by Pinchas Goldhar).

For many years the chairman of the "Yiddishe Bineh," Jacob Ginter initiated the trend to have all playbills printed in Yiddish and English and not, as had been done until then, all-English except for the title of the play which was printed in Yiddish. Only one English printer, an elderly man name Ford, a non-Jew, possessed some Yiddish lettering. After much error and confusion in the type-setting by the printer, Ginter virtually had to roll up his own sleeves and set out the playbill. Ford's was for many years the only place in Melbourne and probably in Australia where the printed Yiddish word could see the light of day. This was due, it was believed, to old Ford's weakness and affection for Yiddish; else he would not have troubled so much with the little Yiddish printing that he received. It was through him that the Yiddish word was enabled to be printed in Australia. It is also of note that it was largely as a result of the needs of Yiddish theatre that Yiddish was, at first, printed at all.

In 1936, Jacob Ginter's brother, Nathan, also a professional actor, arrived from Buenos Aires. Together with the Kadimah Dramatic Stage Union (note the new name), he acted in Sholom Asch's "Mottke the Thief" as well as in an artistic programme. Of Nathan Ginter, the Australian Jewish Herald of 31st March 1938 had this to say:

"He lives his part almost forgetting his real self. There is not a moment of stillness with him on the stage, silent or speaking, asleep or awake, according to the design of the part he always acts and acts artistically," while Sarah Ginter, his wife, the same critic Aaron Patkin wrote in another issue, is "an actress with feeling, who possesses a deep sense of stage craftsmanship."

In that year, 1936, Israel Rotman produced Gordin's "Kreutzer Sonata," Fraiman's "The Blind Painter" and Asch's "With the Stream," while in 1937 he also staged "The Jewish King Lear."

Nineteen thirty-seven, which saw the death of Reuben Finkelstein, also saw the arrival of Abraham Braizblatt, then a young folk-singer and recitalist from Warsaw. He performed in two concerts of song and recitations and at the invitation of

"The Kadimah Yiddish Theatre Corner," staged a revue "From Beyond the Sea," followed by B. Orlanski's social drama, "Blood," another revue, "Of All That is Good," Goldfaden's "The Mischief Maker," Leon Kobrin's "The Wild Boy," as well as several one-act plays in a series of cultural evenings held by the Kadimah.

The two momentous events in the development of Yiddish theatre took place in 1938 and 1939. Through the initiative of the "Friends of the Yiddish School Movement in Poland," Jacob Waislitz arrived on January 26, 1938. He had been one of the leading members of the Vilna Troupe, a cast responsible for many great contributions to the development of Yiddish theatre. In the year of his arrival, he performed in several artistic word-concerts as well as in several pieces with the "Yiddishe Bineh." Of his first appearance in public on the 5th of February 1938 at the Assembly Hall where he delivered recitations from Shakespeare's "Merchant of Venice," Rudyard Kipling's "Boots," and from Peretz, Asch, Bialik and Lutzky, Dr. Aaron Patkin wrote in the "Australian Jewish Herald":

"Jacob Waislitz, who is an exponent of the best and noblest tradition of the modern Jewish theatre, convinced us last Saturday that a real actor who was born into this troubled world with the dream of a poet, an artist blessed with a true love and devotion to his art, does not need any particular setting, painting, architecture, even music, to convey to the spectators the truth of his artistry.... Jacob Waislitz is a great artist--he brought here the Messianic message of the cultural rebirth of our suffering masses. His voice is the voice of true art and as such it must reach every ear which is not deaf to the sound of hope, freedom and culture."

It was at Waislitz's suggestion, on the first anniversary of the death of the famous Yiddish theatre director and Waislitz's mentor David Herman, that the "Yiddishe Bineh" became known as the "David Herman Theatre Group," the name under which it exists to this day. He took an active part in a series of cultural evenings until towards the end of 1938 when he sailed for Brazil. However, he was to return in 1940.

The second major event was the arrival to Melbourne on the 3rd of April 1939 of Rachel Holzer. In Poland, Rachel Holzer had played in works of Sholom Asch, Sholom Aleichem, H. Leivick, S. Ansky and David Bergelson as well as in those of Tolstoy, Strindberg, Gogol and Arnold Zweig, among others. Her sojourn in Melbourne was part of a wider tour. She delivered her first recital on the 15th of April 1939 which moved Aaron Patkin to write in the "Australian Jewish Herald" of 20th of April:

> (Rachel Holzer) "is one of the few chosen by God and nature to inspire those sparks of the poet's dreams with her own life, with her own spirit and soul....An actress by God's grace, a woman of engaging charm and simplicity, she conquered our hearts and told us in the holy words of artistic truth that our sources of creation are inexhaustible....(With her), nothing is left to mere chance, every movement of her body, every vibration of her magnificent voice is controlled by long schooling in stagecraft and indefatigable industry and perseverance.

In the first six months of her stay in Melbourne, she acted in Morozovitch-Shchepowski's "Three Women," which had been translated by her husband, Chaim Rozenstein, and in Verneuill'e "Frau Advokat" with Yasha Sher, as well as in many cultural evenings and concerts. After those six months, she prepared to leave and to continue her theatrical tour in the wider world. But the outbreak of World War 11 compelled her to remain in Melbourne.

With the return of Jacob Waislitz in 1940 and the pooling of talents of Abraham Braizblatt, the Ginters and others, the standard of Yiddish theatre was raised to an artistically high level....

Yiddish theatre was concerned not only with performing plays. It attempted to help materially a variety of communal activities and particularly the furtherance of Yiddish culture. Proceeds from the concerts were donated toward the establishment of Yiddish schools in the community, the creation of the first Yiddish newspaper in Australia and, among other things, the publication of a theatre lexicon, of Pinchas Goldhar's "Stories from Australia" (the first creative literary work in Yiddish in Australia) and Herz Bergner's "The New House."

To prepare a Yiddish play was a difficult enterprise. Each performance was preceded by months of rehearsals, the actors were in the main amateurs who worked in other occupations. With the progress of the war in the early forties, these difficulties were compounded. In 1941-42, Japan entered the war and brought the frontline to the shores of Australia. The country took fervently to the task of defending itself. Men up to their forties were drafted into the army, and of the Jews, those who were not yet citizens were drawn into special behind-the-front formations. There also reached Australia at that time the horrible news of the Nazi murders of Jews in Europe. Under such conditions, which struck at both the personnel and the morale, for the theatre group to pursue its work was a near-impossible task indeed. Performances were seldom held and, when they were, were conducted mainly in aid of Jewish and non-Jewish causes and appeals.

This state prevailed into the late forties. The new immigrant stream of refugees from Europe arriving at the turn of the fifth decade was, despite all the trauma leading up to it, a shot in the arm for local theatre. There arrived a number of gifted amateurs who, in time, became involved with the stage. The David Herman Theatre Group, now enlarged, resumed its activities. The audience, too, was naturally bigger.

In the years that followed, it became customary to stage at least three or four Yiddish full-length plays each year, among them old favourites like Sholom Alecheim's "The Big Lottery Win," Gordin's "Mirele Efros" and Goldfaden's "The Mischief-Maker," also social dramas like E. Morris's "The Wooden Bowl" and a variety of pieces not previously performed. New plays, sometimes experimental and avante-gard plays, such as Sigmund Turkow's "Sing My People," Bar-Yosef's "On the Walls of Jerusalem," Moshe Shamir's "Beth Hillel" and De Benedetti's "Red Roses." These titles represent only a small selection of the plays performed, but the range of the repertoire and the standard of the acting and the stagecraft made Yiddish theatre in Melbourne the equal to that of Yiddish theatre in Europe and America. As well as the above-mentioned plays, there were many evenings given over to one-act plays, revues, concerts, cultural gatherings, jubilee celebrations, Purim plays and other enterprises....

The actual quantitative involvement in acting of the David Herman Theatre has declined. Many of the regular members of the cast are involved in a variety of administrative functions, either within the Kadimah under whose auspices the Theatre has long been functioning or with, for example, Ethnic Radio 3EA, the chief among the latter being Yasha Sher. Also, there is the inevitable ravage of age. One-time artists have either migrated to Israel as have done Abraham Braizblatt and Abraham Zuckert, or have passed away, or have simply grown too tired to pursue the arduous round of rehearsals and performing that serious theatre requires. The public appears to be sufficiently content to be entertained by musical artists, comedians, raconteurs, and by imported films, particularly from Israel so that the demand imposed upon live Yiddish theatre has abated considerably. Although it is too early to expect very much from them, the arrival here of Russian Jews, many of them especially musically-talented

61

has not as yet made an impact on the theatre scene. There is a considerable number of young people in Melbourne who speak Yiddish and there is a Melbourne Yiddish Youth Theatre in existence. It has, in the past few years, staged Itzik Manger's "The Megillah," Arthur Miller's "The Price," Sholom Aleichem's "The Big Lottery Win," and the more recent Israeli play, "I'll Meet You In Two Weeks at The Kinnereth." Those who care for the future of Yiddish theatre place their hope upon the youth.

Serge Liberman

The Actor

By Herz Bergner

Translated from the Yiddish by Judah Waten

THE Jewish actor, Gedaliah Meister, paced through the house as he memorized a poem he was to give at his recital the following week. With every step of his big, soft body, the old weatherboard floor creaked as if answering him in its wooden language.

He was alone in the house. His wife was away at a neighbour's, his two eldest sons had gone to see a friend, and his youngest son, Abram, was playing cricket in the street with other boys.

It was a late autumn evening and the sun had just set. Inside the house, the glowing twilight spread over the small round table and the three well-worn armchairs that stood in different corners of the dining room. Each time Gedaliah Meister passed the mirror above the fireplace his pale, flabby face stood out very white in the darkening glass, as did his long, gesticulating hands like two white wings, and it seemed as if he was about to fly. He liked to learn his lines in the twilight when there was no one else in the house. As it grew darker, and the house filled with shadows, he still did not switch on the light. His rich bass voice echoed against the walls, rose to the ceiling as if it intended to lift it.

But Gedaliah Meister felt irritable and he could not calmly recite this Jewish poem, which he was certain possessed such dramatic fire, such moments of exultation, that it would capture his public. The more the words fired him, the more he became convinced that they would have the same effect on his audience. But he was impatient to get on to the stage and to enjoy the success. At the same time, he could not help wondering whether the poem he was memorizing was the right one. Until now he had obstinately given the public only those pieces which lay closest to his heart, and he liked to believe he would never have to lower his standards. Yet in truth he sometimes smuggled in a cheap piece, although he did not admit that to himself. This time the programme was a risky one. He had made a selection of the finest and most characteristic examples of Yiddish literature and he did not know how an audience living in such a non-Jewish world would receive them. He did not know whether he would be able to continue making a living as an actor, or whether he would have to accept the shrill, humiliating advice of his wife, a one-time Yiddish actress, and take up a business or a trade.

So GEDALIAH MEISTER could not recite calmly in the growing darkness and he switched on the light. Heavily he sat down in an armchair, but he could not sit for long. He stood up again and walked towards the mirror and stared at himself. In the last few years he had aged a great deal. All that now remained of his untidy long hair that he used to comb up high to disguise its thinness was a thin strand of hair, like a black leather thong stuck on to his shiny skull. Surrounded by little cushions of flesh, his big black, still manly eyes gleamed with fire from his flabby face. His jaw had lost its former stubborn strength and hung loosely in the creases of his jowls.

But he was far from accepting his fate and he did everything to maintain his looks. With dignity he held erect his big straight figure so that he would look even taller. Furtively he would dye the strand of hair that seemed stuck to his scalp. And when he came off the stage after a successful performance, surrounded by women with sparkling eyes who showered admiration on him, he felt brimming with youthful energy and enthusiasm. Then he was filled with hope and he recalled his past in Warsaw where he had walked the stages of the greatest theatres. It had been the same in the early days of his arrival in this strange, distant Australia. He had been filled with a great warmth and a belief in his work when he gave his first recital and produced his first play with amateurs who could hardly speak Yiddish. He remembered how many of the audience came up to him, pressed his hand and patted him on the back. He believed he had moved them with his acting and with the living breath he had brought from the old country.

"Marvellous," they had said. "Exactly as in life. A true picture. There wasn't a hair out of place. I saw my father, may his soul rest in peace. . . . There's no doubt he's a great actor."

But all this was in the past. It was not like that today. Even his own wife, who in their early days had acted with him, now constantly nagged him to put the stupid idea of acting out of his head and take to something that would make him equal with other people. She was always full of complaints; they were living in poverty in an old cottage while her friends had everything. . . . Swept by a sudden fear, Gedaliah Meister stopped reciting and began to walk from room to room as if searching for someone. From the street came the shouts of the boys playing cricket. He could distinctly hear his youngest son's voice. He liked Abram much more than he did his other two sons, who had turned away from him and did not understand him. He put great hopes on Abram.

As he heard the boy's voice, his heart was filled with joy. The boy's voice was beginning to break; it still possessed a shrill, child-like charm, although coming through was the half-formed male tenor. Sometimes the voice cracked, so that it sounded like a cry. It was just this that touched Gedaliah. It was only Abram who sided with him when he quarrelled with his wife; the other two boys sided with her. The eldest was something of a businessman who occasionally helped towards the upkeep of the house and gave his mother money for the "loud" clothes she liked to wear. His second son was studying, and he was always asking him for money for books; he, too, was full of complaints because his companions had everything and he had nothing. But Abram wanted nothing and never asked him to buy anything. The boy knew that, with his father's earnings as an actor, he could not afford to buy him much. Nevertheless, Gedaliah Meister bought Abram various presents, sometimes clothes, which he brought home secretly so that his wife and the other two sons would not see. At first the boy was thrilled with every present, but soon he began to give them back to his father.

"Take it back to the shop please," he begged, although he did not want to part with the present. "I don't need it. I can do without. I'm not a baby. You need the money for something else."

Gedaliah felt very lonely and yearned for Abram to come into the house, but the boy was too involved in his game and only his voice floated in. His wife was still at the neighbours; he imagined she was playing cards. His elder sons would not be home so early.

GEDALIAH MEISTER lay down on a bed in his clothes and turned off the light. Shadows began to play on the wall and ceiling, hanging crookedly, swinging like gibbeted figures in black cloaks on the gallows, then suddenly dropping into a dark tomb. Gedaliah watched the shadows without taking his eyes off them. He lay stretched out, his face staring upwards at the ceiling, motionless as if he was dead. He imagined that he himself was a shadow which had fallen down. He tried to remember some of his roles but he could not remember anything. Suddenly everything had flown out of his mind. Although it was not the first time this had happened, now he was frightened. Gedaliah could not make any sound, only his lips moved as if in silent prayer.

Out of sheer tiredness, his eyes closed, and half-thoughts and fragments of the roles he had played began to crowd in on him. He tried to shake himself free. Then abruptly he was carried far away, and once again he re-lived the strange lives he had played on the stage. He was lost in some faraway world which now had nothing to do with him. It tortured him that he could not remember his lines. It was a long time since he had played those roles; he had never had the opportunity in this alien Australia. But he had more than once recited whole passages to Abram before the boy went to bed. He told him stories of Jewish kings and Jewish heroes. Most of all, the boy liked to hear about David and Samson and Bar Kochba. Moved by these stories, Abram tried to imitate his father's bass voice and to act the parts of the heroes.

GEDALIAH MEISTER shook himself and woke up from a half-dream. The light had been switched on. His wife, Rosa, was coming towards the bed, pulling Abram behind her.

"Why the darkness? Why didn't you put the light on? Why did you lie down on the bed with your shoes on?"

Rosa burst forth with more complaints.

"Look at this boy of yours! Dirty and battered. He's been fighting with the boys again. He's a real devil. Always fighting. You brought him up like that."

Gedaliah wanted to look at his son, but he could not take his eyes off the loud and showy clothes which did not suit her age. Whom did she dress up for? Evidently it was for that Jewish fellow from England who had fallen in love with her, and to whom she sang those songs from comic operettas which young soubrettes used to sing.

IN WARSAW, Rosa had once been noted for her beauty. She had come to the stage from Staffke Street, one of the poorest streets in the city. Her success was due less to her singing than to her lovely face, her slender but full figure and the shapely long legs which she loved to display. Gedaliah fell in love with her when he met her at the Actor's Union. He tried to restrain her from flaunting her beauty on the stage and to teach her to behave with more modesty. But she said he was jealous and she did just as she wanted. In Warsaw she had never been given an important

65

part, but that did not prevent her in Australia from boasting that she had been a great actress. While she spoke about herself, she fell into a calf-like excitement and her boasting grew taller and taller. Although she had not appeared on the stage for many years and was no longer interested in acting, she could stand up in the middle of a game of cards and sing one of her songs and show off her still shapely legs just as she had done in Warsaw. People would laugh quietly at her hoarse, squeaky voice, her saucy glances, her bold, pretty yet sad green eyes. Still they enjoyed her songs. Her attire attracted their attention as well. She was forever dressing up. Everything she saw she wanted to put on herself: brooches, bracelets, earrings. Particularly she liked earrings; her drawers were full of them.

Rosa begrudged her husband his success although she had not been on the stage for many years. Since the London fellow, an elderly bachelor, had fallen in love with her in the autumn of her life, she did not know what world she was in and she kept rougeing and powdering herself, hardly knowing what to do next.

For many years Gedaliah had been indifferent to her and he could not endure her boasting. Now, when he saw her dressed up in her gaudy clothes, he smiled slightly to himself. His glance slipped off his wife and settled on his son who was covered with dirt, his clothes torn, his face scratched. Tears welled in the boy's eyes, but with all his strength he stopped himself from crying. As Gedaliah looked at Abram, whom he loved so much, his father's heart trembled. His son was attached to him and always did what he told him. He wondered what had suddenly happened to the boy. What change had come over him? Truth to tell, it was not the first time that the boy had come home looking so dishevelled. But the worst of it was that Abram never would tell what had happened to him.

Gedaliah decided that the time had come to get the truth from him. He gestured to Rosa to let the boy go. Then he put his hands on Abram's narrow shoulders to lead him into another room. But Abram with a sudden, strong movement pushed his father's hands off, looked angrily at him and moved away. For a few moments he stood apart from his parents and suddenly, as if he had remembered something, ran into his own room and banged the door behind him.

Gedaliah stood still, confused, and did not know what to do. Never before had the boy behaved like this. On the contrary, from childhood Abram had been an obedient son and his father had had a great influence on him. Tired and dejected, Gedaliah followed Abram. Carefully he opened the door of the bedroom, despite Rosa's angry beckonings not to do so.

Abram had undressed in the dark and had quickly got into bed, pulling the bedclothes over his head. In the green rays of the light thrown by the street lamp, Gedaliah Meister saw how the bed quivered. With quick, uneasy steps he walked over to the boy and placed a hand on the blanket on the boy's shoulder.

"What's the matter, Abram?" he asked quietly. "Who hurt you? Why do you play with boys who beat you?"

Abram did not reply. He held his breath and the movements of his body ceased. It was as if he was waiting for his father to take his hands away. But as Gedaliah did not take his hands away, and did not stop repeating the same question in his warm voice, the boy raised himself and angrily thrust his father off. Then

66

Gedaliah became angry, switched on the light and started to shout in a strange voice:

"You'll tell me what happened. At once! I'll knock the stubbornness out of you. I will . . ."

He raised his hand, but at that moment his wife opened the door and he caught her sad green eyes, gazing at him with such spite and malice.

"Why are you torturing the boy?"

She attacked him in her hoarse, high-pitched, grating voice, drawing out the words as if in a stage melody.

"Leave him alone. Look how he's picking on him! The old fool. . . . You spoilt him yourself!"

"Old fool." Those two words burnt into him. What had his wife against him? Why did she feel such a hatred towards him? Evidently the more she realized his defeat the more she disliked him. Perhaps she was hurt by his indifference towards her? Or maybe she was angry with him because he wasn't jealous of the old London bachelor and she really wanted her husband's love. Gedaliah knew one thing for sure; she was annoyed with him because he was still on the stage and she had withdrawn from it. No matter how she humiliated him to his face, behind his back she basked in his fame. Behind his back she praised him.

Now, filled with anger and contempt, she poured out the whole truth. It was not enough that the boy should have to put up with insults on account of his father, and have fights with the boys because of him, but he had to make complaints against the boy. Abram had stood up for him against the boys who had laughed at him because he went down the street, talking loudly to himself, gesturing comically with his hands and dressing outlandishly in such funny shirts and ties. He was a good son who was not ashamed of his father and stood up for him.

Rosa could not stop. As she poured out a torrent of words, fresh words kept coming into her mouth. But unexpectedly Abram jumped out of bed and put his hand over her mouth and silenced her.

"Don't believe her, Father. It isn't true!" he cried, and his protruding stubborn lip trembled. "Mother is telling lies."

Gedaliah said nothing and sat down on his son's bed. After a while he became aware of the boy getting back under the bedclothes.

ABRAM pretended to fall asleep, but Gedaliah felt that the boy had not closed his eyes. In the darkness their hearts grew nearer and they understood each other better. The boy could not fall asleep; all the time he saw the sharp, aggressive face of the friend who had hurled mocking words at him.

"Your father's cracked! He's mad. He talks to himself. He flaps his hands. Does he want to fly?"

Abram had kept it all to himself, never telling his father what was hurting him. As he lay awake until late into the night, tears welled in his eyes and his father heard his tremulous voice in the darkness.

"Father, I know you're a great actor—" His voice broke. "I won't have anyone insulting you. I like you very much. You like me, don't you? Mum wasn't telling the truth. It wasn't true what she said. Why did she have to say that?"

Gedaliah remained silent. Abram repeated his words.

"Don't believe what Mother said. I won't allow you to be insulted. You like me, don't you—"

"Go to sleep, Abram," Gedaliah said. "Of course, I like you. I think I'll lie down with you. Remember when you were small. I often had to lie down with you and tell you stories. You were a foolish boy. You were frightened to go to sleep on your own in the dark. Now you're a big lad. You understand a lot. You'll soon be barmitzvah."

GEDALIAH lay next to his son. The boy calmed down slowly and fell asleep. But Gedaliah couldn't go to sleep. He saw himself in Warsaw, and in the Polish provinces where he often went with a troupe or by himself to give recitals. He was young then, full of fire and great plans. The girls he had met in the townships stood before his eyes and they were so near to him that he could talk with them. There was Ruth, the slender tall girl with the dark face, and the dark narrow almond eyes, who threatened to commit suicide because of him. She sat down next to him and he felt her hand in his hair. She had a habit of stroking his hair with her slender fingers. She was the daughter of a rich man of the township and she wanted to leave and run away to Warsaw with Gedaliah. She was as beautiful as the world. She had long hair reaching down to the ground. He liked to see her hair falling loosely over her shoulders like a dark waterfall. From her hair came a cool fresh scent as from a well.

Gedaliah was now walking with Ruth and clearly he could hear her voice. It was a moonlit night and the fields near the township were covered with a silvery blue gloss. Nobody was to be seen. It seemed as if everything was covered in a thin mist and they were both floating in it. Ruth recited a poem and he gave his opinion of it and told her of his plans. It was nearly dawn and they still could not tear themselves away from each other. The next day they could hardly wait for the night. Gedaliah remained in the township. The troupe left without him. His wife, who was expecting, had created a scandal . . . and so had Ruth's father. Look whom she had chosen! A comedian!

When Gedaliah had to rejoin the troupe, Ruth had wept her eyes out. He kissed away the tears and promised to take her to Warsaw. But when she came to the city he was already back with his wife, who had given birth to a son. Ruth remained in Warsaw, and as if to spite him she married one of his friends. To hurt her, he went around with other women. She still could not forget him and she came to all his performances.

Through the window the dawn crept palely, and Gedaliah was still awake. His son lay near him sunk in sleep. His darkish fair hair fell into his eyes. Over his childish face flitted a calm, satisfied smile. Gedaliah did not want to wake his son and he did not move. But Abram, who even in his sleep was aware of his father's gaze, stirred and opened his eyes.

THE whole of the next day Gedaliah prepared himself for the recital and the boy did not leave his side. He would not go to school. For the twentieth time he opened the heavy album and looked at the photographs of his father in various roles. Gedaliah once again had to explain what all the roles were. Some remained deeply etched in the boy's mind.

68

When Gedaliah produced his plays, Abram had sat in the theatre, never taking his eyes off the stage. His father seemed so big, so mighty; his authoritative voice thundered, rose and fell. He was glad he had such a father and he was proud of him. In one play, there were many persons on the stage. The songs and music captivated Abram and carried him away into those other worlds where all the stage heroes floated. He sat in the dark hall and sometimes, becoming frightened, would move towards his neighbour. But he could never tear his eyes off the stage. When the lights went on, he woke as if from a dream and hardly knew where he was. Afterwards, Gedaliah had to explain everything he did not understand. Often, when there was no one in the house, Abram would look at his father's wigs and make-up paints. Although he was a little frightened of the wigs, he was strongly drawn to them. There were many kinds of wigs—black, fair, grey—and, as Abram tried each one on, he looked different every time; strange persons stared at him from the mirror. This gave him much pleasure.

RIGHT up till the recital, Gedaliah Meister had to recite to Abram all the pieces he was preparing. The boy gave his opinion about each and told him which he liked best. When there was no one else in the house, Gedaliah told him stories of Warsaw. He could not resist boasting of how popular he had been in Warsaw. He could not resist the temptation to tell how women ran after him; he told stories of Ruth who understood him so well.

"Ech, brother," he exclaimed, and sighed deeply. He straightened himself and became excited. "If you'd only seen me in those years! How I shone! I couldn't walk down the street . . . the loveliest women turned to look at me. It was a different world then. What would you know about it? They valued an actor. Warsaw was still Warsaw. It was a city full of Jews. Now everything's vanished . . . gone with the smoke. Gone, little brother."

Gedaliah suddenly stopped. He spread out his arms like wings and stood still, as if he had just finished a long monologue on the stage, as if carved from stone. Abram looked at his father with awe and in the boy's eyes he shone larger than ever.

BUT quite differently did Gedaliah look when he stood on the stage during his recital. The hall was half-empty and the empty chairs glittered coldly in the electric light.

Just after the destruction of Jewish life in Europe, people used to come in numbers to his performances and were moved by the sad poems he declaimed. But now the audience seemed indifferent.

As Abram looked at his father on the stage, his heart ached. With all his heart he wanted his father to capture the audience. But, as if to spite him, they would not give their attention to Gedaliah. He looked so sad. His almost bald head shone coldly in the electric light just like the empty chairs in the hall. His sparse hair, usually stuck down like black leather on his head, was now untidily disturbed. His big, still manly black eyes had lost their usual lustre. Abram could see that his father was calling up all his powers to please his audience, but without success.

Abram realized that all the time the people listened less and less. They began to whisper and talk. This roused Abram so that he wanted to run up to his father and embrace him protectively with his childish arms, and shout in his high voice to the people to keep quiet. Tears choked his throat.

WHEN the performance was over and everybody had left the theatre, Gedaliah and Abram remained behind, collecting the props. The boy packed the clothes, the beards and the make-up into a suitcase. The caretaker, who had been asleep in the corridor outside, suddenly woke up and put the lights out, plunging them into darkness.

It was late when they went out. It was a cold autumn night and the streets were dark and empty. Only outside a café and a dance hall was there any light, and couples hovered there like insects around a lamp. In a nearby side street, a red sports car pulled up outside a house. A young man and a girl got out. The young man wore a long coat and narrow trousers in the American style, and just as in the films he said to the girl: "See you tomorrow, Toots."

Gedaliah recognized him as he got back into the car. He was a Jewish chap whose mother sometimes came to the Jewish theatre.

Gedaliah and his son walked through the deserted streets, and now and then a drunk emerged from the shadows. Their steps echoed over the empty pavements. Gedaliah was wrapped in thought, not even seeing his son, who was walking beside him, trying to keep in step.

Abram's heart tightened, and suddenly he said to his father: "You acted very well, Father. I liked it. You've never acted as well as you did tonight. The people were a bit tired, that's all. You're listening to me, aren't you?"

"Of course, I'm listening," said Gedaliah, and a smile lit up his face.

————

Two Years in Exile

1

I wear out my first pair of pants on the fringe of swelling suburbia, where everything is mine. The sandy quarry belongs to me; and the scrub, the rocks, the potholes filled with mud, and the mounds of loam, crumbling and sinking beneath my feet as I watch the builders pushing back the borders. Home is where the feet run most freely, and I make my home anywhere, wherever there is dirt, wherever there is dust.

'What will your mother say?'

Mrs. Walters, spraying her delphiniums next door, shakes a pitying head.

Oh, to tug at the mole that sits on her chin. What bliss.

She stabs a forefinger upwards, probing for gaps in transparent void, and accuses me with her question, compelling, squeezing from me a display of shame and contrition and of whatever other humiliation she would have me feel. For she is a mother – though Colin's and not mine – and I am a son, and for each of us there are roles that we must play. So while Mother, my mother, is sequestered in Flinders Lane pumping stitches into the seams of blouses, this other mother shakes her head and probes at the void, cowing me into a shame I don't feel, my own fingers all the while itching, twitching to pluck at that prickly monster on her chin.

Colin, when he comes home from school, is a good boy. He

takes off his pants, folds them like royal linen, and replaces the holy gear with ragged blue jeans smeared and bespattered with paint and charcoal and grime. School is school; home is not its extension. Not in the Walters' rule-book anyway, where between school and home there is a demarcation, expressed most eloquently in a change of pants.

'What *will* your mother say?' This time more emphatic, crushing her words between teeth of steel, the harsher impact tempered by the swishing and lapping of spray on her delphiniums and gardenias.

'Mother's not home,' I manage, quite irrelevantly.

'Humph.' A puff of wind escapes from flaring nostrils in an upturned nose. Haughtily, mightily, with the airs that exalt her own virtue for being such a real, good, caring, stay-at-home, look-after-baby mother. Not like Mother, my mother . . .

But go betray Mother and tell this paragon of motherhood that I have only two pairs of pants. And that the other pair is in the cupboard, waiting for Sundays and visiting. Go tell this woman that, for folk who one year before came to this country with less, two pairs of pants are gifts of Providence. Go tell her . . . go tell her anything when she is a mother and I a son, and Mother, my mother, sits in a dingy dusty crowded workshop pumping away at a Singer, squeezing from its clatter and hum a pound of steak, a down-payment, a doctor's fee, a bus fare, a shirt. So I mime remorse as well as I can, hang my head, shrug a shoulder, bite a lip and toe into a clump of weeds on the nature strip.

Oh, to pinch that porcupine on the chin . . .

It is her own good lad, going against his will, I'm sure, who delivers me from the leaven of her scorn with a reminder clamoured from the window, 'Mum, the roast is burning!'

And Mum, with an 'Oh, my dear' and a 'Wouldn't you believe?' drops the hose as if it had teeth, and clatters up the stairs on hollow heels to rescue that wretched charred roast whose vapours drift out now, thick and sickly, to suffocate the bowed acquiescent flowers that the abandoned hose is still watering.

72

Colin's face behind the window is a smirk. There is little else to it, unless vegetable ears and freckles amount to anything. He is a good lad. He changes his pants on coming home, earns a few pennies selling Saturday's 'Globe' outside the Plaza, and shows his flair for music, of a sort, as he blasts his trumpet in a fanfare of violence.

His mother's prodding fingers on his hands, he points to the hose, still swishing and hissing into the roots of his mother's flowers.

'Will ya' be a sport, mate, and turn off the tap?'

'Do it yourself,' I would prefer to say, but I have tasted, felt, Colin's strenth before. So I make for the tap and watch, not him, but the rubber tubing shorten and convulse in a final protest and fall limp, like lead now, upon the grass.

'Ta, mate,' he says and ups his thumb. Transfixing a wad of void around his nail before disappearing into the deeper crypts of his red-roofed box that to him is home. Leaving me to wear out my pants on the fringes of swelling suburbia. Alone. Where Northcote ends. Waiting, in quarries, in potholes, on rafters and gums, for Mother's bus, or Father's, to bring them back from Flinders Lane where they pound out a life in this newer distant home.

2

Mother cannot forgive Melbourne, upon which, she says she has merely stumbled. Nor Europe, now left behind. And even while her feet tread the dry dusty earth of this firmer quieter shore, the ship of her existence floats, homelessly, on an ocean of regret and dejection, of reproach and tears.

We tread on our shadows, coming home. Behind us sinks the mutely drowning November sun, as we walk between two rows of red-brick cubes, set behind ordered squares of green, each fringed by delphinium and rosebush in a flush of conformity.

In which Mother is lost.

'Nice day,' says Mrs. Walters, smiling ever so nicely and resting on her broom to watch her husband and son thrash the shuttlecock through the air. The grass squelches under her husband's heavy bulk, while Colin, thin, lanky and nearly all bone skims over the surface as if to tread harder would mean to cause eggs to break.

'Good weather we're havin',' Mrs. Walters tries at conversation once more. Her mole invites. Only to betray. Like her smile.

'Yes,' says Mother, only now really noticing the weather at all. For factory interiors know no seasons.

''Ope it lasts,' hopes Mrs. Walters, resuming her sweeping in a last ritual before sunset.

'Good shot, Dad.' Colin leaps high to arrest the flight of the shuttle, but fails. Dad trills with the mirth of his success.

'Now serve it to me, son.'

The boy is dutiful. His left hand tosses up the feathered object, his right hand draws back, pauses, quivers and swipes at the white plumage. His straight orange hair, parted in the middle, rises and falls with each stroke, like flaps.

'Hit it up, Dad.' And Dad hits up, wildly, deliberately, giving to the shuttle the velocity of his own laughter.

The plumed cone wings and spins in reeling convulsions, hangs tremulously in mid-air, loses life, falls and thuds upon Mother's shadow at her feet. She recoils as though she herself has been struck. Her lips allow a murmur to escape, but Polish I don't understand and her curse remains her secret.

In one bound, two, three, Dad is over the fence, bending to pick up the battered shuttle and looking up at Mother through flushed amused eyes, his breath strong and rancid, a brew of stale tobacco from the lungs and beer from deeper wells.

'Sorry, dear lady,' he wheezes, his sorrow as true and deep as vacuum.

'You're a bit wide of the mark, Dad,' his son calls from behind him. 'Eh, Mum, did'ja see that shot?'

Dad stands up now, erect, as big and red as an ox. His right forefinger aims at an imaginary mark of Cain on my brow. 'Good boy you got there. Like to see a lad helpin' his mum.'

Mrs. Walters stands beside him. 'Yeh, 'e's a good lad.' She

74

tosses her head upwards, though really she is looking down.

'Yes,' says Mother again, more nervously, pushing me forward as though the Walters' were evil eyes falling upon me.

Behind her own door, within her own walls, her breath, smothered by apprehension, or disgust, escapes with relief.

Of all misfortunes available to the children of this earth, she bemoans, Melbourne was the one she had to choose. Melbourne, a tail torn from the rump of the world, where she is lost, amongst neighbours, generations, continents, galaxies apart from herself, a foreigner Jew in an Australian marsh. Like satin in tweed, perfume in tar, crystal in clay.

'A wilderness we have come to. What a wilderness this is.'

In the evening, our neighbour sings a song, or strangles it rather in his throat. Sings about a doggie in the window; sings a song he has caught like some contagion he would get rid of by passing it on. Sings, hoots, whoops, croups, then pauses, mercifully, for a semi-quaver rest, to raise the bottle to his trumpet, and then sings again, sucking in air sibilant with froth, throwing a toad's belch into his turbulent sonata for counterpoint. Daytime would swallow up his song, would digest it, absorb it, lose it without real loss in the symphony of clatter and roar of cars and motor-mowers and machines. But the evening is sated and regurgitates the serenade, and lets its breezes take it wherever they will to splash the sky and darkness with a cacophony of echoes. While in our own dim kitchen, Father reads the 'Jewish News', about Ben-Gurion and Peretz, about Jerusalem and Warsaw, singing, if he is moved to sing, in a muted hum, something private, something mellow, not giving his neighbours cause for even the slightest moment to remind themselves of him. While Mother would throttle every sound between iron and collar as she presses tomorrow's shirt, the moisture under the metal hissing, like herself:

'Why this wilderness, this curse, this Gehenna?'

And then the silence. Of midnight. And of Sundays. Of midnight and the wind rattling the window-frames and tree-tops brushing against the tiles or the muffled hum of a distant car bringing to Mother wisps of memory, memories of crowded courtyards and homely faces, of a Yiddish word and a rebbe's touch, in a cosier world now swept away. And then the silence of Sundays where not even grass stirs, lest its whispers be too loud in the unreality of cool, shimmering morning crystal. Sleeping city. Dumb city lying drunk, until the brittle crystal is broken by a milk-horse still limping from sleep and by the wheels grinding and the bottles rattling behind it. Then silence again, briefer and less durable, breached now by Father as he goes out with bucket and spade to scratch, scour and scrape up from the bitumen the horse's straw-coloured gift to feed his drooping tomatoes and struggling lemon-tree.

Mother hates both the noise and the silence, a silence that is yet not a true silence.

'A wilderness, a wasteland,' she mutters, fingering the curtains as she watches Father at his work of adjustment, and, daring to aim higher, casts her sight upon the empty lots beyond the crossing.

And the street, the cubes of red, the square gardens, the confines of her wasteland do not protest.

3

A wilderness. Five miles from the city's heart, Mother feels as if she were in a country town, a Siberian sovchoz or a displaced persons' camp again. Far away is High Street with its sprawl of shops, offices, arcades and picture-theatres. Further still, a light year away, there is – she knows – a Jewish face, a Jewish word, a Jewish melody. But at our end, her very existence is enshrouded in a pall of silence and of loneliness, while beyond, past the next crossing, along the dry, cracked and dusty unmade road stretches an empty nakedness that, for Mother, is worse even than the silence and the loneliness. And more threatening.

But the nakedness is being covered. This, Mother does not, cannot, will not see. Men in blue singlets and high gumboots blast the subterranean rocks, uproot wild shrubs, maul the earth and pound it into submission, cowing it to receive the edifices they are determined to erect upon it. The dry hard earth does not yield itself too readily. A thing of pristine virtue, it is too frigid,too severe to penetrate with tact. But muscle, machinery, dynamite and cursing overcome its resistance, and from the barren surface rise up wooden skeletons upon which brick and cement become flesh. Then are doors fitted, windows inserted, tiles slotted into place. Then, in a day, or two, or three, paths become cemented, bare surfaces covered with topsoil, seeds sprinkled, bulbs planted, and the house becomes a home as weak slender shoots become grass and reluctant buds blossom into full flamboyant colour.

So is a house built. So do the little coloured boxes of suburbia grow. House upon house coaxed to completion by the hum and roar of machines, by the vigour of men's curses, and by the laughter of a ten-year-old boy. My laughter. For as I swing by my arms from the horizontal beams and climb upon the rafters of each rising skeleton, in my imagination, which soars, I build it too, reaping as payment splintered knees, calloused palms and grit in the eyes. With my help, the perimeter where we live is pushed back and the city swells, enveloping us more rigidly within the carbon solidity of conformity.

Mother detests the perimeter. Father, with his tomatoes and lemon-tree, tries to adapt. But I, a bird on the rafters soaring high, thrive and flourish and grow within that wilderness. For the wilderness, the vacant lots, the wooden scaffolds, the quarry, the mounds of loam, even the ringwormed patches where puddles form belong to me. Its melody I have adopted, I know its silences, which are not truly silences, and treasure the emptiness. More than Mother could know. It has its own taste, a taste of that deeper more remote Australia that Mr. Cook teaches about. The Australia of open spaces, red deserts, towering gums, shearers, swagmen, jumbucks and wheat. Inspired by his mission to make me one of his Aussie kids, Mr. Cook brings me books, pictures, stories by Lawson, odes to

77

Clancy and to the man from Snowy River. My appetite he cannot satisfy. He tantalises my nostrils with the scent of eucalyptus and I swallow in mouthfuls whatever he feeds me. And – Mother should never know – I grow to love this country with the fervour of a proselyte, for the wilderness is mine. I become Mr. Cook's best pupil, his model child, his favourite. The questions he poses, he asks me to answer. The answers I give no-one else knows. Mr. Cook, who should know better, beams as he makes his way between the desks towards me, and laughs as he places his thin tendinous hand upon my shoulder, saying, too loudly, 'Well, son, you're a regular Aussie now.' Brian Simpson on my left sniggers, Russell McLean laughs, while Jim Reilly, Fisticuffs Jimmy to the boys, sharpens his knuckles which he will pound into me after school.

'Cissy! Teacher's pet! Sucker-upper!', he hisses behind raised fists. His blows hit whatever target he chooses. His mates urge him on. My left eye swells and darkens, I taste my own blood and tears.

'You're a regular Aussie now, eh?', he mimics from behind his fists. 'So show us boy, show us.'

Mr. Cook, who has stayed behind, now appears. The cheer squad flees and Fisticuffs Jimmy with it. This reed of a man again puts his mischievous hand upon my shoulder. It is dry, unfeeling leather, hairless and cool. It hints at barrenness and reminds me of the eucalyptus and gum, of open spaces and of the legend called Australia. I would like to love it still, but it has become remote, something not of my world at all but something that merely winked and taunted me with scented promises. Even the closer wilderness upon which I have helped to build with calluses and laughter mocks at having fooled me. And under Mr. Cook's withered solicitous hand now wiping my face of its blood and its tears, I weep, I weep, weep for the bruise that throbs around my eye and for the loss of a treasure that might have remained mine.

School ends. It is December. Month of warmth, excitement, festivity. Of respite from school and playground bullies. Of crystal skies and reluctant clouds; of crickets, sparrows, dandelions. Of Christmas, of Chanukah.

Colin stands upon the fence. I pray that it may tumble. His Highness stands upon his throne, casts a haughty eye, or a net, over Father's horticultural cripples, and asks, directing his inquiry to someone not at his feet but perched, monkey-like upon his shoulder,

'What are *you* gettin' for Christmas, mate?', himself itching, bursting to tell of promises made to him

Christmas? What is Christmas?, I ask myself, as I engrave a nail track into that too-sturdy fence. My ten years have not yet taught me. There *was* some fantasy performed at school, on the day before term's end. A Mary, a Joseph, three wise men with long black beards, bearing gifts, following a star, then craning their necks over a cradle which cradled a doll of plastic and straw. Ella Plotkin, the grocer's broad-nosed, fat and ugly daughter, played Mary – for acting at least she had a gift – and Peter Hughes, a blade of straw himself, so thin and so fragile, trembled through the rites of Joseph. While I, small, compact, chosen because unnoticeable, was made an angel in the company of twelve on a platform mercifully at the back.

'Well, mate, whatcha gettin'?'

What is Christmas?, I ask myself. But him I answer, because I must, 'Don't know yet.'

'Well, I'm gettin' a cricket set,' he says, finally bursting, so smug, almost drooling. The palings of the fence creak under the tremulous rolling of his mirth. The fence sways. Now for vengeance, I dare to hope, now for justice. But the fence stands firm. And if Colin has disappeared from his throne, it is because he has jumped off, not fallen nor crashed nor succumbed to my prayer.

'Colin is getting a cricket set for Christmas,' I tell mother. 'What are you buying for me?'

'My precious child,' Mother softens the blow to come. Her fingers, thin, a little crooked, the pulps flattened from pressing all day on seams, ruffle my hair.

'For us, there is no Christmas. Only Chanukah.'

Chanukah? What is Chanukah?, I ask myself, wanting but not venturing to escape from beneath her consoling palm. There is an illustration, I remember, in one of my books. A Temple of marble and cedar, soldiers prostrated before its altar, curtains, candles, lights marking miraculous days. That is Chanukah. And also a time – blessed season – a time for receiving gifts. So, Christmas, Chanukah, what's the difference? Gifts are gifts and know no distinctions.

And I get my gift. A table tennis set – bats, a net, a ball.

'For Chanukah,' Mother says, with love, as the gift becomes mine.

'For Christmas,' I say to Colin, he at my feet now and *I* upon the throne.

I wait for green envy to consume his face – teeth, freckles, pumpkin ears and all –, I wait for those mocking lips of his to set and his nostrils to bristle with the sap of unrewarded yearning. Oh, imminent moment of exultation.

But instead his eyes narrow into foxes' slits and his nose sharpens and his lips tighten, tighten taut into the tensed string of a bow, until drawn to the limit of their endurance, they yield and collapse, releasing shaft after shaft of hissing laughter that lashes and stings, that cuts and pierces. Our two yards combined cannot hold his scorn as it rolls, and tumbles, and trips, and sprawls on all sides, over wooden palings and creeping passion fruit into the Mertons' and the Sullivans', and the Mackenzies' and the Holts'.

'They're for babies!', he hisses, convulsing into giggles. The servant before the throne dares to be master.

I study my bats, see nothing to mock. Their borders are smooth, the edges well-filed; the handle is layered with ply, the palm cups it with professional ease; the sandpaper on their surfaces is clean, glistens as light plays upon the grains.

'Rubber!,' he shrills, 'rubber, rubber!'

And between shafts of his taunting, mocking, riveting laughter, in moments of sense between convulsions, his body, his hands, his teeth, his very screech describe the rubber bats that true champions use.

And against the real life-size cricket bat he now brings out from his own house and the red leather-cased ball that mirrors the sun's more muted laughter, my own precious treasure pales, pales from a gift of parental love to a heartless, cruel act of treachery.

5

The wound heals, while others fester.

December is the year's unwinding. Padlocks silence the schools. The hum and roar of bulldozer and drill die away. Dry dust settles upon the building lots, the wooden skeletons stand stunted and stark, and timber and brick lie in mounds in the midst of rubble and loam.

We kick the dust, Colin and I. And swing from the beams, nails barbing our sleeves, rafters scraping skin. We play. Not out of friendship. But merely because we have met in passing and the earth has not opened to swallow either of us. His shirt is a pepper-pot of holes, his jeans are split and grimy and torn at the cuffs. And his heels are worn down to wedges and the uppers frayed. He is a good lad, this Colin, wearing his out-of-school outfit to be torn, mangled, soiled. Out there, on civilisation's perimeter.

And in our dress, he would make of me his twin, as he kicks dust over me and throws wet sand down my neck, and probes and pokes and pulls and jostles, shoulder against shoulder, hip against hip, in a jest and ecstasy that is private.

Then, sated, or bored, he remembers something and has enough of play.

'Ta-ta, mate. See ya' at carols tomorrow night. Ya' must come. At twelve. Outside the Morgans'. Under the mistletoe.'

And he turns to go home. Leaving dust and sand to settle for

81

other opportunities.

Mother, at dinner, says her piece about my shirt. And wonders, aloud, who I think will buy my next pair of shoes. We have just finished eating the herrings and tomatoes. Mother is clearing the plates.

'I'll take him to the factory with me,' jokes Father. Whether to buy cheap shoes there or to work for them, I can't tell. But I laugh, to please him, and because I have something to say and need allies.

'I must go to carols tomorrow night.'

Mother is serving the soup. Chicken soup again, with noodles, for the third day in a row. While from next door, a roast tickles the nostrils. A myriad globules struggle afloat, a myriad bare lamps flicker and shimmer and glint upon the surface, reflecting themselves in these agitating oily orbs.

'Yes,' Mother says, 'I will wake you.' The ladle clatters confirmation against the pot.

Father looks at her. But her back is already turned as she steadies the pot upon the stove. And if Father has on his tongue a remark to loosen, he chooses instead to suck it down with the noodles. While I gulp mine with a helping of delight. For, surprise too great to countenance, I am going to carols tomorrow night. Outside the Morgans'. Under the mistletoe. At midnight.

And in the labyrinths of private fancies, I rejoice.

Until Mother, sated without having eaten, her hands knotted at the knuckles, starts to rock and heave in her seat, and sets sail upon an oft-sailed sea.

'We must move,' she says.

Father, having just licked and smacked his lips, winces under what may swell into an accusation.

'Out of this wilderness,' she adds.

The wind, this time, blows more gently. The sails flag. And Mother stops rocking, loosening the rudder she clasps between her palms. And, lapping me with eyes that could quieten storms, she draws breath, her bosom rises and lists, and she folds herself around me.

82

'My precious one, my little one.' Meaning, what is to become of you?

Thursday night, to be awake at the time of carols, I draw the blind early and sink into bed, even though the colour and smells and sounds of day still nudge at my window. Mrs. Walters waters her delphiniums and gardenias, her husband bays at a reluctant moon, while Colin, their good lad, violates and torments 'Come all ye faithful' on his trumpet. Mother darns my socks in the kitchen, Father reads about Warsaw and Tel Aviv and hums to himself. Fragile breezes break upon my window, crickets chirrup, a sparrow chatters on the sill, then flies away, flies away with my thoughts, my imagination, my dreams, holding them firmly, resolutely, until – until my eyes open, suddenly, to the glare of a blue and brilliant Christmas Day. Wheels, hooves and bottles clatter along the street outside. Then there is silence, fragile, transient silence, followed by the scrape-scrape-scraping of metal against asphalt as Father shovels up the horse's straw gift for his lemon-tree and tomatoes.

I could weep, and would, if tears and sunshine were meet companions under the same canopy of blue. But I don't, not until that evening when Colin, sensing blood, or amusement, creeps up from behind and seizes me with devils' claws.

'Don't ya' like our Christmas songs, mate?'

He is over me. As always. I lie spread-eagled on my back, the grass beneath cold and moist and unyielding, his knees pressing down, a vice on my outstretched arms, my own legs achieving nothing towards liberation. His face, freckles and all, scowls. His nostrils, black pits, flare. His mouth is a menacing crypt of fillings and carious teeth.

'We kill Jews, do ya' know?'

Words are his sole weapon, but the roots of my hair burn, as though he has set me on fire. The throb in my arms is as nothing against this fire.

'I am not a Jew.'

This, I thrust into every cavity in his teeth. And into the hollow of his throat.

Which makes him laugh.

I hate his laughter. If I could, I would seize it, throttle it, encase it, bind it to anchors of lead. If I could. But free, as malice is free, his laughter reaches all horizons.

'Colin, darling,' Mrs. Walters calls from her porch, intruding upon his mirth. 'It's time to come inside.'

He leaps up, pressing his knees for a last time into my arms and knuckling me in the ribs.

'Well, must go now. I won, mate.'

Leaving me crucified on grass still moist, my back cold and green, my arms aching, my ears throbbing with the laughter of his scorn. . . .

The wound festers, where others have healed.

I tell Mother everything. A weak shallow vessel, I can't contain it all.

Mother is a rock. Standing firm; absorbing my pain. Face set hard, chiselled marble, with cheeks suddenly high and cold. Touch, and freeze. I tell her everything, tell her more than everything. Adding things that might have happened, probabilities that Colin might have been capable of, had not his Mum, unknowingly, delivered me from his malevolence. I tell her everything. Hoping, praying to heat stone, to force a glow that might make her avenge all hurt and devour that freckled killer of Jews.

Father, too, has heard, but it is Mother who speaks.

'Did you hear your son?'

His silence torments like pain. He puts down his paper and rubs the bridge of his nose with forefinger and thumb.

'Your son is no longer a Jew.'

Ancestry and progeny have parted. The son has abandoned his past.

'What a country this is. There is no God here. See, now, what a shegetz is growing up under our roof.'

My arms ache. My ears throb. With Colin's cavernous laughter. And Mother's submission, and Father's cowed silence.

Just one word against that devil. Mother! Father! Don't beat him, don't even tell his father. But lay blame where blame is due, and curse him, him, and not me.

Mother salts and peppers tomorrow's soup with her accusations. Father – the hairs in his nostrils are too long and grow also from his ears – enshrouds me with the broad tallith of his hands and searches for contact deep within my eyes. Which burn. Which burst.

'Mother!' I plead. 'Father!'

Mother empties out the cup of her existence.

'We must move from here. See what this wilderness, this wasteland is doing to your son. Little brothers, blessed sisters. How have we sinned? Who is right in this world? And who is wise? And who is safe? Chaim to Siberia, Reuven to the gas-chambers, Sonia to America, Shimon to Israel. Leaves, feathers, scattered and dispersed, while we, silly, blind, pitiful yiddelech sink to the bottom of a barren trough, in exile, without a Yiddish book, a Yiddish word, a Yiddish geist.'

'Mother!', I try again, still seeking justice. Even though the plea sticks in the throat, trapped in a gurgle of incoherent meaningless sound.

And I discover a remarkable thing then. I discover that parents, too, can feel. Mother is weeping. A wind has blown against the rock. And it has crumbled. And disintegrated. With rivulets winding down the crevices and wrinkles beside her nose.

'My lost child, my precious one,' she says, burying my head in her breast, under a new tallith, a tallith woven of love and belonging, which I sense, or know, I shall wear forever. – As Mother wears the number on her arm.

Evening comes and passes. With sleep, for me, a century away, a universe away. Evening merges into night. Darkness overtakes the shapes of chimneys and trees which now disappear, dissolving into the void outside my window. Colin blasts upon his trumpet while his father takes to crowing. 'Silent Night' in the loudest of baritones, then 'Good King Wenceslas' amid the clinking of glasses and bottles and cutlery. Father sits in the kitchen, and Mother too, silently grieving over their shegetz. From behind a quilt of cloud, stars emerge. Solitary and nameless, meekly unassertive, as if to apologise for their very existence amidst the blare of Colin's trumpet and the scorn of his laughter and his father's raucous song. I watch them, am entranced by them, become as one with them. Until above the stars, Mother's face appears. Pale and drawn, wrinkled and in pain, quivering, throbbing, as each star becomes a tear. Shed for me.

6

Soon after, we move.

Goodbye, I shout to the neighbours. Goodbye Colin. And to you, Mrs. Walters, whose horny growth I shall now never pluck, goodbye. Sprinkle your gardenias with your devotion and shower your good lad with your love. And thrive on the dust of your wilderness!

Colin, swinging on the gate, smiles wryly, or squints, and raises a phlegmatic hand.

'Come and see us some time.'

'Yes,' I reply, 'I will.' The promise is genuine, from the heart, from the heart of a child with plenty to learn.

And before I can say goodbye again, he has turned his back, then takes one step, two, three up the stairs, and disappears. I see his smirk behind the glass of his window and his rash of freckles and that hollow mouth whose laughter has mocked so often. But it is only a memory that lingers there. Not Colin himself, not him. For he has already returned to his trumpet or his crystal set or to devising other mischief.

Goodbye, I shout again. This time to no-one in particular. But rather into the transparent air, idling mutely over green unruffled suburbia as Father places a box of kitchen utensils into my hands to take to the car.

We are on the way. Haii, I want to call out, we are moving! And to move is better than standing still!

Through the rear window, I see the wilderness recede, with each crossing, moving further out of reach. Enough of sand

and tadpoles, of quarries and mud. Enough of building boxes and pushing back borders. I have earned my share of calluses and grit in the eye. Goodbye, my wasteland. I loved you once. Before your people, with their special venom, ruined my love.

Father watches only the road ahead. Mother holds my hands. Her expression is solid. Impenetrable, the firm chiselled marble she must have worn when leaving Warsaw, Russia, Germany, France. Her chest barely moves with her breathing. Only the eyelids, blinking out of necessity alone, yield any hint of awareness.

So we move; come out from exile. Into a fruitshop set in the hub of chaos, in the greyer, rowdier, cruder centre of St. Kilda where Father rises early and Mother breaks her nails over potato and swede and succours the needs of her thirsty soul as she picks out from their boxes the mouldy lemon, the bruised apple, the withered grape. Grey is the colour of St. Kilda and foetid its every corner where I parcel out bits more of my childhood. Not grass, nor tree, nor flower dominate, but glass and brick and spouting and stone, all smudged, peeling, leaking, rusted, cracked. The street stifles under a pall of beer and rotting meat, it reeks of humus and dander, but here, here where the cats breed amongst potato sacks and the Herald boy shouts in adenoidal tones, and the drunkard staggers and reels, begging for a shillin' or a zak outside the Coat-of-Arms, here I thrive, I grow and thrive like some wild and reckless resilient shoot.

Mother complains still, but her cup is drained of its former bitterness. Three doors away is Glicksman's kosher butchery, opposite is Krampel's winestore, and within walking distance stand Rothberg's bakery, Kantor's bookstore and Glazer's delicatessen. Mrs. Tuchinski, fat and breathless, wails about her rheumatism, but recited in Yiddish, which is Mother's bread, the plaint is a melody plated with gold. The Kaplinskis buy from her and the Fleischmans and the Orbachs, each giving wings to memory reaching back into homelier times. And when I tell her of Harry Lewin who is in my class or of Benny Danziger or of Sophie Grundman who is the rabbi's daughter, an inner light pierces through the shroud of her weariness, to glow, to burn in a private fervour. And she touches my hair. Touches, smoothes, soothes, with hands coated with potato dust and love. Mother is gathering together again the splinters of her shattered self.

One evening, in the midst of reeking onions and wilted lettuces, Mother encourages.

'There is a boy in your class. Joseph Leibholz. His mother came in today. He sounds a fine boy.'

I seek him out, but cannot reach him, reach *into* him.

I try. 'Your mother knows my mother,' I say. And then ask, 'What games do you play?'

He stutters from shyness and looks away.

'None especially . . . Oh, . . . chess sometimes . . . And draughts . . .' Each phrase is a minor explosion of sound, each burst a revelation.

'Not cricket or ping pong or tennis?'

I see from his clean neat pants that he is an indoor boy, not one to roll in dust or chase after tadpoles or climb on the rafters of rising houses. When he shakes his head, it is not with regret, but with the contentment in knowing that what he does and what he is suffices.

'I . . . I also play the violin,' he says.

Slowly over the following weeks, I learn that he traverses regions that I have never yet encountered.

He is tall and slender and pale, and hugs the shadows, both around him and within. A fringe of strawlike hair sits over his forehead, his fingers are long and tapering candles of wax. And his eyes are drifting and dreamy, their colour that of distant oceans and as unfathomably deep. He doodles, he draws. He reads music as others read books and, in the shadows which are his alone, composes poems that Miss Quantrell praises in front of the class. I try to penetrate but he will not be penetrated.

'Will you play cricket with me?'

He shakes his head. 'I'm not good at it.'

'What about footy after school?'

'I don't want to.'

'But why not?'

'I don't like it.'

'It's easy.'

'No.'

His distance, his difference, inflames. He excludes every-one, but I can't bear to be excluded.

'All right, then,' I say, 'have it your way.' And in the days that follow, I set about him in different ways.

I kick dust into his face and splash ink over his sketches; I bruise him with my knuckles and poke hard fingers into his ribs. I call him 'Fiddler', 'Cissy', 'Sucker-upper', and mock at him with barbs honed with venom.

He does not whimper, this saint, nor resist, nor retaliate, though he is taller and could swallow me alive. His is the manner of martyrdom, denying the ultimate satisfaction to the victor of seeing pain.

Until one day, after I have tripped and spreadeagled him on the ground, he fixes his eyes, so blue and ocean-deep, upon me and stammers, as though rocks sat on his tongue,

'Why . . . do you try . . . so hard . . . to hurt?'

I have forgotten the original reason; the victim has always been so vulnerable and the opportunity ever-present. I have no ready response, so I laugh. I laugh, with the laugher of the victor, and fill the schoolyard with my mirth which spreads and tumbles and rolls into the street, its spiralling coils to be met there by another's laughter, by raucous hateful echoes that suddenly singe the memory and brand my own mockery with disgrace. For Colin has appeared. Colin. Not the real Colin, but his image, come to taunt the taunter and persecute the persecutor.

Later, Mother, wiping moist and grimy hands, takes me aside.

'Is it true that you've been hitting Joseph and fighting with him?'

I make sounds to deny, but the lie falters, strangles, still in the throat.

'His mother came in today. Is it true?'

I kick at the lettuce leaf trodden into the floor and squeeze a tomato until it splits. Silence is confession.

'What will become of you? Tell me. We have left the wilderness but the shegetz is still under our roof.'

The juice of the tomato drains into my hand. Its seeds slip through my fingers to spill on to the floor. They are your bones that I am crushing, Colin, and your blood that is being spilled.

'What *will* become of you?', Mother asks again, the rock of her fortitude beginning to crumble.

I cannot bear to look. I dread the appearance of those tortuous rivulets in the crevices of her cheeks. But she raises my chin with a hand become grubby and coarse, and sucks at my eyes with her own. Her brow is drawn, and smudged with dirt.

'We have left the wilderness,' she says. 'But have we really brought it with us?'

Jagged teeth of shame gnaw at the marrow of my being as, under Mother's gaze, I suddenly feel for Joseph and sense his pain. His sketches, his violin-playing, his poems – suddenly these return and, through the loom of memory, weave themselves into the warp of my earlier indifference, in turn, to dominate.

When, next day, I sit beside Joseph, I worship where, before, I had mocked. He sketches and I admire. He doodles and I imitate. He reads his music and I, cleaving, search among the dancing notes a pattern, a design, meaning. And when Miss Quantrell recites again a poem of his, I listen, and find it in myself to praise. To praise that which the wilderness, through default, had taught me to despise. The pallor of Joseph's face yields to a softer bashful glow. And gradually, the barriers fall as, caution his mentor, he admits me into the vast ocean of his dreamy drifting eyes where, chastened and converted, I find depths I have never known.

In that moment, I drown Colin. I seize that pagan laughter of his, throttle it, encase it, bind it to anchors of lead. With delirious fervour, I stifle his father's beer-sodden song and, with bliss too fabulous to contain, I pluck at his mother's bristled mole and trample upon those delphiniums and gardenias which she sprinkles with her very soul. Somewhere lies the perimeter I have helped to extend, the suburbia I have helped to cover. The quarries are filled, the puddles cemented. Little red boxes have taken their place. Somebody else scrapes up the milk-horse's precious gift. While here, far away, even in this grey drabness of my newer home, my joy swells; and rises; and soars. And transcends as, through Mother's and through Joseph's depths, I purge myself of the wilderness, of that wasteland, where a splinter of my childhood has, in our wandering, been lost.

Serge Liberman

Section 2

faces you can't find again

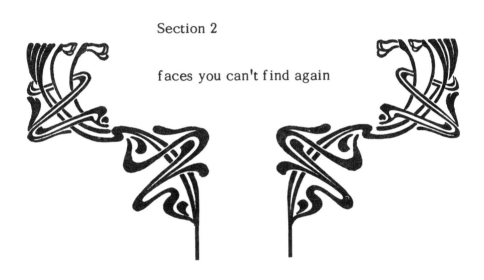

GARDEN ISLAND PEOPLE

FROM THE DARLING POINT balcony where I slept as a child, Garden Island was in middle view. At dawn I sat up in bed to watch the island float through mist and haze. The first sun brightened the top of a taller building while the much nearer western slope of land down to Rushcutters Bay, including the pale, mysterious facade of Kincoppal convent, was grainy still with night.

A childhood fear—that flame from gold and scarlet sunsets behind the island, would shrivel its buildings, lick across harbour water, scorch and consume us all. I was supposed to go to sleep at this flaring hour on summer evenings, but instead would call insistently, and very naughtily as "they" all agreed, for rescue and reassurance.

Some would scold. My thin, imaginative father would reason, but all the while I yelled and burned until first the sky, then water, turned lemon-pale and safe. Once my father fetched a white china basin to my bedside and into it dropped lighted match after match. Their fizzling was proof that water quenched fire. It was no proof to me who rightly perceived the blaze beyond Garden Island as fire of different order and quality.

WAR HAD REACHED the Pacific. I was just eighteen. Behind me were ten years at a famous city school where, despite myself, my loathing of school and my rebellion, I learned most of what I still know. During two years at a famous country school I discovered the value of what I had been taught elsewhere and for the first time in my life, to enjoy learning. One year I'd spent as an art student. My teachers at East Sydney Technical College believed I had talent but I knew that this ability was no more than sufficient for a hack career. Who, at eighteen, uncertain, shy and dreamy desires a hack career? Two months as a probationer nurse convinced me that my parents were perfectly correct in predicting that nursing held no future for their lazy, inept daughter whose notion of cleaning a room was to dab with a duster and stab with a mop.

So here I was. I, with exercise books full of the yearning, burning, hot and hating poetry of an unloved virgin, was unlovely in tortoiseshell spectacles, spotted with sporadic pimples, plagued with ungovernable hair and given to wearing art-student-sloppy clothes. I—a practising snob—professed the equality of man. I, miserable, exalted, black-moody, silver-lining optimist. I, above all suffering a dose of patriotism and war fervour as substitute, perhaps, for the adolescent "Religion with a capital R" which I never "got".

My defence against concerned, worldly cynical, loving adults who understood me only too clearly was to protest: "I am not understood".

Some six months since my family had moved from Darling Point to Pennant Hills. No buses served the area. After three quarters of an hour by electric train from the city, our cottage was reached on foot. Over the first half mile one tramped up a steep hill, then along a packed earth footpath to cross a cobbled back road whose stones were said to have been laid by convicts. After this there was an unmade, deep-rutted clay road lined with enormous wattle trees that met overhead. At weekends, on foot or hired horseback, I mooched about roads winding through little farms and orchards, or made scrambling explorations of steep gullies in the untouched bushland that stretched from the boundaries of my father's three retirement acres of orchard and vegetable garden, across to Dural in the west and down to Galston at the north. In the alone of my mind I listened to lines of poetry and thought of images from the bush around me—"the bark hangs from the trees in curls/like the hair of girls/and like their laughter/the lean bark . . ." And I rehearsed a future of valour, beauty (for I decided that at thirty I would mysteriously become beautiful), fame and unspecified (because I really could *not* guess, and had only once been kissed by a boy), eroticism.

Rumour—fairly accurate rumour—said that if one were not a student, and had no war job, one would willy-nilly be "manpowered" into any one of a short list of distasteful jobs—even, horrors, nursing. After a great deal of fearful thought, and determined not to take any of my family into my confidence, I one day voluntarily entered the manpower office in Martin Place where an amiable, tired and disillusioned gentleman listened patiently. No, not a factory. Not, and not again a hospital. He took my measure and reeled off a string of vacancies for unskilled clerks.

The second job he mentioned was on Garden Island. The Senior Service. Our Bastion. Sunrise. I heard nothing more. No doubt he mentioned the Accounts Branch and I, in honesty, should have explained that my dozen years of famous schools and their devoted, disappointed maths teachers, had left me incapable of reckoning the simplest sum.

Had I coped readily with simple sums I might have been appalled at the travelling instructions now given me. The ferry left the Quay at 8.30 a.m. The Ferry. The Ferry to Garden Island.

My family who had never been able to explain the changeling appearance of an arithmetical imbecile in their midst, soon set me straight:

"*Accounts* Branch? God help us all. 8.30 a.m.? Let's see, there's a train at 7.30 Arrives at Wynyard at 8.15. Time enough. Leave home at 7, so breakfast at half past six, say. How About The Winter?"

Misunderstood.

Early in 1942 Garden Island was still completely surrounded by water. To its north a hillock of rock, grass and trees rose from flat skirts of paved land near water level. The hillock dipped and was levelled for a few houses southwards, and then descended steeply to the large level southern area

95

covered with naval buildings. At the ferry wharf on the northern tip the man in police uniform who inspected my temporary pass told me to follow the narrow road along the eastern waterfront and I walked into smells of ropes and tar, past a marine stockade where a herd of little boats was mustered, towards an area of handsome buildings. Even the most utilitarian of Garden Island's late Victorian buildings are beautiful. Their dates, late 1880s and early 1890s, are carved above doors of rendered stone and decorative brick. On the south-west side, between the long, two-storeyed sail loft and a westward facing white building with a cool verandah, then used by yard police and hospital, stood a mean, peel-paint, fibro-walled-and-roofed structure which a wooden board identified as "Accounts".

Inside its door was a short lobby separated from a small office by a polished wood counter. Beyond was a big room flanked by glass cages—the Chief Accountant in a cage to the left and next to him a few typists in a long compartment against the eastern wall; the deputy accountant worked behind glass next to the lobby on the northern side. For the rest there were rows of deal desks, hordes of men in shirt-sleeves working at the desks, and rows of hats on pegs wherever there was wall space. Files were stacked high on tables, desks, floor, spare chairs, shelving. Each file was tied with red tape, which is pink. A couple of comptometers clattered somewhere in the middle of the room and two immense Burroughs adding machines clanked and rasped. On, over and through all a film of palpable grit perpetually showered from protesting harbour rock being blasted, a few hundred yards away, for the Captain Cook Dry Dock.

This cannot be me. This can't have happened to me. I am not here.

But, from the counter, a stooped old man with very white hair and very dull eyes led me to the accountant, Mr Keeling. Mr Keeling was stocky, middle aged, dark suited, not very terrible. He made some effort to set me at ease, noting the similarity in our names which, he trusted, would not lead to confusion. He also noted that I possessed not one single skill appropriate to an accounts office. I was frank in describing the qualifying Maths which just enabled me to acquire matriculation. He saw no present relevance in my famous schools, my spectacular Leaving Certificate passes in History and English or in my groundwork in Introductory Art.

The omnipotent unwisdom of Manpower cut both ways—Mr Keeling was landed with me, as surely as Miss Keesing with his office. Suddenly I was frightened. He cautioned about secrecy and I signed a form pledging that I would, for ever, keep my eyes and ears closed to what I should not see or hear, and my mouth shut about Everything.

Mr Keeling hoped I would learn fast and work well. He thought my arithmetical amentia would be least harmful in the Rating Section, so would I please follow him.

At the opposite end of the room, near the back window, stood a high, old fashioned desk surmounted by double shelves of pigeon holes. On top of these again were wire baskets bulging with files and sheaves of dockets, and at one corner an upright telephone. This barricade hid the occupant but did not dampen his voice which was loud, flat, ugly and addressed to a pale-skinned, black-haired, supercilious young man who stood beside his desk. He, having noticed Mr Keeling's approach, stopped listening to the voice and shrugged his shoulders in a languid way. Mr Keeling paid no attention.

". . . and if you can't tell the bloody difference between a wing bloody nut and a bloody countersunk screw you had bloody well better . . ."

" 'Morning Tim," said Keeling firmly and I too looked over the barricade to a Cruikshank gnome. He had a pointed brown bald head fringed with spiky brown-grey hair; blue and furious eyes under jutting eyebrows; full lips moist enough to keep a hand-rolled cigarette stump permanently stuck to the lower one through the most rapid conversation. Parallel steel pens, one behind each ear, were a frame for this head. The pale young man vanished and I was introduced to Tim Tapple. Mr Keeling then also vanished.

Tim Tapple stood up. He was shorter than I and bandy, with a very broad and powerful looking chest and shoulders. Probably I showed my dismay as plainly as he showed his. Something else sparked between us—dislike.

He indicated a yellow varnished desk directly in front of his own. That would be mine.

"Bruce," he growled, and the pale young man materialised and was introduced as Bruce Austin. He smoothed a swatch of hair across his forehead where a hint of coming baldness showed, and gave me a wry, superior smile.

"Where is that big girl?" snapped Mr Tapple.

"Miss Pulley," said Bruce, "will be back in a minute."

Mr Tapple grasped my elbow in his big hand and pushed me across to another row of desks. I was introduced to Bill Smithfield, a stout, florid man of about Tapple's own age—early fifties perhaps—who looked up from a thick leather-bound ledger into which he entered perfect copperplate figures. I realised that the Rating Section was defined by two walls and two aisles and that four or five of its desks were unoccupied.

A tall girl with spectacular bosom and hips and a tight skirt, her sturdy legs turned like pieces of furniture terminating in polished high-heeled shoes, swayed down an aisle.

"Here's my big girl" cried Tim Tapple joyfully. She beamed. Her dark brown hair, drawn back over a round head and pinned into a firm, plaited bun, was as polished as her shoes. She had round, bold brown eyes and a wide, bold, white-toothed smile, and looked about twenty. Taking her time she put a neatly folded towel, soap dish and handbag down on the desk beside mine. Then she swivelled, stately, to be introduced as Doris Pulley.

"You'll show Nance around," Tim told her, choosing the form of my name I most detested. Bruce Austin still lurked, but Doris looked over and through him at the same time, her searchlight smile all for me.

"And you can show Nance the cordage book," barked Tapple. On his way back to his own desk he snarled to Bruce Austin, "No work to do? Get on with it!"

97

Bruce sighed. He had won my sympathy.

Doris kindly lent me her towel and led me through the office, out the front entrance and down a side path to a small hut with two doors. An amateurishly lettered notice stuck to one door read: "Ladies now". Below was another scrawl: "Guard the tongue. Ladies sometimes present". Doris explained that these two lavatories were used by wharf labourers until last week when, for the first time, female typists and clerks were introduced to the Accounts Branch and it was realised that there was no provision for their exotic physical requirements. By next week it was hoped that both lavatories would be available for women, meanwhile a queue of wharf labourers came and went next door. There was a tap by the path for hand-washing.

"There'll be quite a few girls working here soon," said Doris. I envied her assurance amid these weird surroundings.

She was less awesome when she set out to explain the Rate Books which she only understood enough to perform the simplest routine procedures. She had no answers to my whys, and what fors? Doris arrived at the island a mere week ago after four years as a salesgirl in David Jones. She'd taken this job to "keep one jump ahead of the manpower" having no more liking for factory or nursing than I. This mature, confident girl was only six months my senior—far younger than I'd supposed. She lived with her widowed mother at Milsons Point and journeyed to and from the island by launch from Jefferies Street.

Doris had already garnered useful fact and rumour.

Fact: except for a few typists no women worked anywhere on the island till recently, but a number have been engaged for the Naval Stores office and many more are expected in Accounts.

Fact: Tim Tapple and Bill Smithfield have both worked here since the early 1930s. Bill can add four columns of cash simultaneously and *knows the timber ledger*. The timber ledger is terrible, but don't ask her why.

Rumour: Bruce Austin has been discharged from the Army because of ill health—so *he* says. Less creditable reasons are suspected. Tim and Bruce obviously can't stand each other—don't ask her why.

Fact: The men use awful language.

Rumour: Mr Keeling has given instructions that they must not swear when females are about.

Fact: The white-haired old man I met when I arrived this morning is Mr Perkins, the junior messenger. The senior messenger is that chap over there —the big one. "The one with the paunch?" Doris was pained by coarseness, but agreed. His name is Mr Hopkins and he is *awful*. Just—you—wait!! "But" I said, "I thought messengers were young kids. And tell me . . ."

"O.K. Big Girl," grates gravel in our ears. "Enough of the hen cackle. Now Nance—you ready to start? Doris has shown you what to do? Right. You can take over Naval Stores from Bruce. I've a lovely little job for him, ha ha."

Blank.

"Oh my gawd. Here Bruce, shove us a bundle. *I'll* show her."

The bundle was two inches thick: one day's transactions from the store called Naval Stores to distinguish it from all other Stores, Navy For The Use Of, which are called "Oil & Fuel" or "Boom Defence" or "Ropes & Cordage" or "Timber" or "Electrical". Tim repeats what Doris had already instructed—that I must "extend" the entries, and when I've finished with the white "notes" he'll tell me what to do with the "yellow vouchers" on the back of each bundle. He thrusts a heavy, black bound Rate Book before me.

"All the prices are here. The printed ones are Admiralty prices and the ones in red ink are local. Check your stock and rate by the local while it lasts and remember that though it says this costs two and a kick it stands to reason it couldn't because local prices aren't like that and . . ."

I Will Die. Or I Will Live And We Will Lose the War. The phone rings.

"O.K. Nance. Go ahead."

Into my misery Bruce slid. He will show me. His voice was a sly whisper. We two gentlefolk, he implied, must stick together against these hordes of inferiors.

At last it was five o'clock. Tim Tapple and Bill Smithfield were working back, but most of the office tidied desks, combed hair, put on its hat. All the men wore hats every time they left the office, even for a quick dash to the lavatory. Grey akubras mostly. Bruce's was a rakish brown pork-pie with a little feather in the band.

Bill Smithfield rescued me next morning. Whisky-stale of breath, hands trembling, he was methodical and patient.

"Take those white notes now. On that line there 'Sydney' is the name of the ship. Anyone from a ship authorised to collect goods from the stores, presents one of those to the storeman."

He explained how the storeman checked the signature of the officer ordering—there see, and initialled it with his own. For example this is for No. 4582, 8 oz 1" nails. The date is six months ago because the business of rating and costing is getting further and further behind the business of issuing. Before the war all the rating was done by Bill and Tim Tapple with time to spare for other work.

My job will be to find the price of those nails in the book, remembering that 4582 are different from 4581 and 4583 which are also 1" nails. (If it were as simple as that!) Actually, Smithfield explained, 4582 nails have been unprocurable for nearly two years and I will have to learn that when a destroyer asks for 4582, and thinks it receives 4582, it is in fact supplied with A011 the price of which will be found, not in the Rate Book, but in *this* hand-entered supplement. Eventually our 8 oz of 1" nails are found to cost 1/- per lb so we "extend" it, and over on the right hand side of the note, enter 6d. Simple?

We grind on. "Why?" I ask and "What for?" and "What does it look like?" Smithfield assured me that I would soon know "half the prices by heart". I did not believe him. He also said that each six months the prices would alter, according to an average of charges made by firms supplying material—"that's when it gets tricky," he said. "You have to adjust your memory."

Across the aisle Doris on "Ropes & Cordage" was racing through bundles at a tremendous rate. Bruce tackled "Electrical" with an expression of distaste. It was nearly possible to forget the terrible Tim. Then:

"Right Smithy" he rasped. "Enough of the love talk. Leave her to it. She'll never learn if you hold her hand all day." Smithy took his time, considerately looking everywhere but at my flaring face and neck.

"Give it a go on your own," he advised, "and I'll take a look-see at what you've done after tea-time." When he was half-way back to his own desk there was another roar, "Smithy!" but he carefully replaced his pens and ruler before turning back to Tapple. At the big desk they held a long, mostly muttered conversation. Every so often, Tapple's voice was skilfully projected to be heard all over our side of the office.

"Muttermuttermuttermutter . . . well she's bloody useless . . . muttermutter stuck-up private school bint . . ." and so on and on. Little of Smithfield's comment was audible until, still quietly:

"Oh, come orf it Tim. Y' can't expect them girls to do this job if they never even know what anything even looks like."

"Muttermuttermutter . . . maybe Doris, but not that bloody little —— —— snob. No —— fear!"

"Happy in the Service?" my father asked facetiously at dinner time. My replies were enthusiastic. I could not admit that I had made a mistake which might, this time, be even worse than the nursing debacle. Worse because so nearly impossible to alter. Even were I disposed to be truthful, words expressing my detestation of Tim Tapple could not be found.

MY GRANDMOTHER LIVED at Darling Point. After a late party I often spent the night at her house. I kept these arrangements secret, even from Doris, lest Mr Tapple should hear of them. To him the very name Darling Point, where the Navy had an establishment, "HMAS Rushcutter", was synonymous with privilege, hauteur, high-life and ultra snobbery.

Granny was over eighty and still pretty and animated. My failure to produce an instant supply of upstanding naval officers for her diversion was a great disappointment. I assured her, untruthfully, that I met scores of eligible naval types but they, and I, were far too busily conducting a war to allow time for frivolities. In fact we, in the Accounts Branch, had no occasion to pass the time of day with so much as a newly enlisted rating.

The best Granny could contrive, at this time, was a wild young man, son of a woman friend whom she had last seen in London thirty years before. This fellow, at twenty-three, had the distinction of being the youngest colonel in a certain colonial army. He was in Australia for a very hush-hush mission (to have his ears wiped, one might have supposed). He was the silliest and cheapest drunk in my admittedly limited experience, but this was not the kind of disclosure one made to Granny. She happily arranged for us to spend several evenings together. To be fair, it is possible that the young man drank so deeply to forget his trials for I was plainly not his type either, being an adequate but un-acrobatic dancer, bespectacled and unappreciative of horse-play. On his last night in Sydney Granny sent us off to Princes at her expense—I would return to sleep at her house.

We were late leaving the nightclub for Princes' doorman could not quickly find a taxi-driver anxious to transport a comatose colonel. That gallant recovered sufficiently to escort me down Granny's gravelled drive. With each trip and slip his footsteps exploded. His cap fell off, rolled under a shrub and was, with difficulty, found again in the darkness. As I at last turned the key in the lock he whispered shakily:

"You know Nan, when we go to bed together I'll be there too!" and lurched back to the impatient cab.

This was not a conversation to report to Granny who called me to her room when I got upstairs. For her I contrived a splendidly mendacious excuse for my early morning arrival. She, sympathetically and without warning me, told the maid who brought her tea tray that, "Miss Nancy is not to be disturbed early this morning". Consequently I missed the launch which plied between Rushcutters Bay and Garden Island. What to do?

Inspiration. Some of the glamour of the Colonel's parting declaration was still upon me. The new-fledged *femme fatale* found a public telephone and rang Bruce Austin. His sly laugh was unpleasant, but he *did* agree to wangle my passage on one of the naval duty boats which flitted to and fro across the harbour. So I met my first ratings, and was clandestinely set ashore beside the depot ship *Kuttabul,* a superannuated ferry moored close by our office. The breezy men aboard *Kuttabul,* busy with their usual morning chore of hanging strings of washing from deck railings, treated me, and my dapper escorts, to a frank commentary. Their cheerful voices followed as I scuttled for the cover of the Accounts Branch. Too late to punch the omnipotent bundy I had to seek horrible Mr Hopkins and sign a separate time book. And, he wished to know, by what unscheduled transport had I contrived to appear at this hour? His chins quivered with inquisitorial relish as I floundered—would I make trouble for anyone if I explained?

At this point Sir Galahad Austin sidled up to the Messengers' desk and quietly whispered in Hopkins' hair-sprouting ear. I was free.

No I was not. Austin lurked by my desk whenever he walked through the section, making plain my debt to him. He had something "on" Hopkins—and me. A bundle of vouchers from my "in" tray opened at a note in

101

Austin's curly handwriting: "What a dark horse *you* are", it said, "mysterious people intrigue me". No signature. And yet—it was not wholly unpleasant to have attracted his attention. When Tim Tapple, from behind his barricade, roared "Nance!" and for all the office to hear bawled his fury at an inaccurate total, Bruce drooped one eye in a wink and a few minutes later, managed to whisper condolence for "that oaf's uncouth behaviour".

•   •   •   ✦

FOR MANY MONTHS the women staff used the two outside lavatories and washed their hands at a standing tap beside the path. Even Miss Harland's complaints failed to gain more than promises of reform. But at last we were translated to a spartan but large room, appropriated from the sick bay, on the first storey of the handsome old building next door. It was directly above the ground floor office used by the Yard Police.

The window of our new washroom overlooked the Accounts Office in general, but in particular, its directest downwards view was straight into the window of the messengers' bolt hole. We were allowed new insights into the arrangements of Horrible Hopkins. Like Blessed Damozels Doris and I would lean over the bar; as soon as Hopkins realised our espionage he found another hiding place out of our line of vision for the bottle of whisky we spotted on a shelf under the counter. Another new amenity was a bank of large lockers against a wall. The top row was beyond the reach of any of the girls but there were enough lockers to share between every two or three of us. We had enjoyed our new comfort for a week or so when I lost my key ring. The locker was no problem because I shared it with Doris and could use her key, and it was easy to manage at home. My disastrous loss was an annual rail ticket, a metal tab which swung on the ring. It had some six months' currency, but according to the Pennant Hills booking clerk, was very difficult to replace. Hoping that the key ring would turn up, I bought a weekly ticket and reported my loss to Tim Tapple. I was sure I'd had the ring when I arrived on the Island the morning it vanished. Tim was less sarcastic than I'd feared and very helpful. He notified the Yard Police, pinned notices in every store office, the factories and at the ferry wharf. He and Smithy also peered under heavy furniture, persuaded Hopkins to move desks and a cupboard, shifted antique files, raised immemorial dust and located several items of great interest to themselves.

"Stone th' crows. Smithy! Here's that bloody file on *Sydney's* boilers."
"The one we had a search for in '39?"
"The very same."

"What 're y' going to do with it?"

"Lose it again, Smithy. Lose it again."

After a key-less week the Pennant Hills stationmaster said *perhaps* if I signed an affidavit, and attached a letter as proof of my place of employment, the Commissioner for Railways of the State of New South Wales might consider re-issuing my ticket. Tim, himself in perpetual warfare with railway authority because of a certain short-cut he favoured at his own station, said he'd make bloody sure the letter was a beauty and procured an impressive document on imposing letterhead from Mr Keeling.

No more than an hour later I was alone in the washroom and just about to go downstairs when, for some unexplained reason, my gaze fixed on a battered chair pushed into a corner. *Something* forced me to pull it over beside the lockers. Something made me climb it and grope in the dust between the top of the lockers and the ceiling. My keys were there.

How? When? I jumped down, replaced the chair, scrubbed my hands all before a couple of women came in. Had I, in some fit of aberration hidden the keys myself? And totally forgotten? I must have.

Years later when my university course included abnormal psychology I puzzled the affair again. Could months of Tim's nastiness, or subconscious worry about Bruce Austin and his half-threats, or shy misery about my boy-friendless state, or a combination of all these things have caused me to hide a heavy, clinking bunch of keys in an inaccessible place and wholly repress all memory. What else might I have done, and forgotten?

My immediate difficulty was how to tell Tim Tapple that all his solicitude had been unnecessary and that, thanks to my stupidity many other people had been inconvenienced. In some ways I thought I'd prefer to pay £12 for a new ticket—no inconsiderable amount from a weekly wage of £2.10.0. Certainly I could not swear on oath that my rail pass was lost when it lay in my pocket weighing a hundredweight. If I *did* confess to Tim, I thought, his new tolerance of my presence in his section would disappear and this time with good reason.

I dawdled down the stairs, perplexed and miserable with thoughts like these, and passed the open doorway of the police office. The elderly retired Inspector who had re-enlisted for special duties on the island during the war, leaned against the counter talking with his jolly middle-aged constable who inspected our passes at the wharf each morning. Mechanically I called "Hello" as I always did and Inspector Onions shouted: "Lovely day. Found your keys yet?" and I said: "Beautiful. No." without conviction and continued outside. Impulsively I turned back.

To Inspector Onions and the constable whose name—John—was all I ever knew of his title, I told my terrible tale. They enjoyed it very much. "Old Hopkins actually moved a cupboard," John chortled. "I don't believe it."

Inspector Onions said: "Leave the key-ring here. And stop looking as if you've lost a pound and found sixpence." After I'd said thank you, for what

103

I was not sure, he added: "Try and rub along with Tim, lass. Tim's the salt of the earth. You just leave it to us."

"Well what am I to do?"

"Nothing. Keep your face straight."

About an hour afterwards voices in the office stopped, heads turned, machines fell silent—always indications of something of interest somewhere in the accounts branch. At the entrance Inspector Onions, in full uniform, epauletted coat, braided cap, followed by an equally ceremonious Constable John, confronted Hopkins at the messengers' desk. Hopkins looked queasy. The Inspector's voice carried well.

"None of your business to know who we want or what we want. Please tell Mr Keeling we are here in reference to an article reported missing." Hopkins's face was a nasty shade of cream as he watched them march into Mr Keeling's sanctum. A sly little clerk in the costing section who was Hopkins's offsider in illegal peddling of race cards, grabbed his hat and scooted out the door, though where he expected to hide on Garden Island goodness knows. After some minutes the police strode the length of the office to Tim's desk.

"G'day Tim," Onions boomed. "A young lady in your section has lost some keys?"

"Yes. Nance there. Here, Nance."

The constable produced a damp envelope and from it took my key-ring, together with a very old, very water-logged leather purse. He held the exhibits towards me on the palm of his hand where they drew my eyes with the horrid fascination that snakes are said to have for silly hens.

"Would these be your keys, Miss?"

They would.

"And the purse?"

"No, that isn't mine." The purse was mystifying.

"I found them together, Miss. Under the ferry wharf. Just happened to look down a crack in the planking at low tide and I seen metal shining. So I rolled up me pants and took off me shoes and socks and in I went. Wonder who the purse belongs to? No name. Nothing in it."

" 'S a wonder you didn't cut your feet on the oyster shells," Tim said.

"Well I did." John smiled bravely. "I just got a bit 'f plaster and iodine from sick bay."

"I suppose you dropped the keys when you were showing John your pass one morning," the Inspector mused.

"I must have." Flustered I thanked them both several times until Tim intervened with gruesome stories of terrible poisonings arising from oyster cuts; the police assured him prompt medical aid would be sought if necessary. Horrible Hopkins, a better colour but still subdued, ushered them out of the office.

NO ONE FROM the Rating Section worked overtime on the last night of May 1942. I went home directly from work. My mother spent the night at Darling Point with my grandmother as she did once a week. This arrangement partly reconciled Granny to the removal of a third of her family to an area she regarded as halfway to the black stump.

At Pennant Hills, soon after dinner, we heard flights of planes overhead, and once, a sound which was unlike the accustomed vibrations from trains thundering north loaded with tanks, trucks, big guns and other heavy equipment. Next morning we learned of the raid by Japanese submarines on Sydney Harbour. All telephones seemed to be engaged but we decided, since the newspapers reported no damage to houses, that the household at Darling Point was untouched.

But there was tragedy on the island. At the end of the path leading from our office to the water's edge, the depot ferry *Kuttabul* was submerged nearly to the roof of her master's cabin, her funnel slewed, but high out of water, a line with a few pieces of laundry still pegged to it floated to and fro by the steps. All the men who lived aboard her were drowned.

All day stretcher parties trudged past our building carrying canvas-covered loads to the sail loft where space was cleared. After a time the divers could get no further. There was, then, no floating crane strong enough to pull the *Kuttabul* free of ooze and mud that sucked her deeper as months went by. Trapped men were left down there. We worked behind drawn blinds. The cheeky *Kuttabul* boys who teased and whistled girls as they passed the mooring to visit the canteen were gone, and death in all bombed cities, in Europe and to our own north was closer. Much closer. My friend Gertrude Scarlett gave me Kenneth Slessor's "Five Bells".

Where have you gone? The tide is over you
The turn of midnight water's over you,
As Time is over you, and mystery,
And memory, the flood that does not flow . . .

DeeDee did most to set our askew world straight again. On an early day in June she returned to work bearing a genuine medical certificate attesting her recovery from at least three ailments.

"It cost Bro. £5 from a medic. at the 'Cross'," she confided to Doris and me. She wore a diamond brooch, a heavy silver ring and a nondescript ornament called a "frat pin". Her hair was softer and a paler shade. To match a new brown linen dress she wore stilt-heeled kid shoes. ("Bro. has plenty of coupons") and wonderfully sheer silk stockings such as none of us had seen for three years ("Bro's sister mails them from the States").

Bro. was a Major. Alas he had been posted far away, but before leaving, introduced DeeDee to his friend Buzz, a colonel no less. Buzz expected to be in Sydney for some weeks and had taken over the lease of Bro's Potts Point flat.

.   .   .   .

AN OLD BUSH SONG called "My Religion" always brings a picture of Tim into my mind:

"To be upright and downright and act like a man,
That's the religion for me . . ."

it goes. I see his fierce face, his horizontal bush of eyebrow, the bristling pens behind either ear, the hand-rolled fag jerking on his lower lip, and hear his gravelly voice bellowing out the anti-clerical sentiments of:

"I will go to no Church and to no house of Prayer,
To see a white shirt on a preacher . . .
For parsons and preachers are all a mere joke
Their hands must be greased by a fee;
But with the poor toiler to share your last "toke",
That's the religion for me."

Tim described himself as a Calathumpian, but was probably Church of England. He maintained, with supporting evidence which was plainly true at least for Garden Island, that the public service was "given over to the micks", but did not hold this against Roman Catholics. He jeered indiscriminately at all formal religion, but formal religion was one of the few settled social phenomena that aroused no rancour in him. He thought that clergymen were completely out of touch with actual life, and relished an allegedly true story told by Blue because the tale reinforced those convictions.

Blue was told of an RAN chaplain who was assigned to minister to the fleet of small, fast Fairmiles soon after these craft were commissioned. He spent a few days aboard a Fairmile, and by the time he left, its formerly efficient and well-integrated crew were near mutiny. Zealous, wrathful and

106

satisfied with his reforms he reported in high places that he had remedied a disgraceful situation. A heavily braided personage listened, realised the havoc that had probably been wrought, and thundered:

"You have done as you thought best. This is an order. Never let me *hear* of homosexuality aboard one of our small ships again."

Smithy and Tim remembered when sectarian bitterness was acute in the Public Service and when, on Garden Island, the uniformed and civilian sides of the RAN were at loggerheads in conflicts whose bases were partly religious. One sometimes heard the last, diminishing sound waves of old disputes but these were petty and political rather than dogmatic or theological. About politics the Rating Section sensibly agreed to disagree. Smithy and Tim voted for opposed parties and we inherited the rule they had long ago made for themselves.

Actual religion was far less important than the borderline between honesty and expediency. Few people thought any the worse of a colleague who, occasionally, might "nick off" early for some good reason, having arranged with a friend to "punch the bundy" in his place. But a certain Mr Webley who "made a welter of it" was despised. Even so, no one would "dob him in" though, equally, no one "gave him the office" when detection threatened.

Marie first discovered Webley's ploy. She sat near his desk and noticed that he often went into the tea-room in the mid-afternoon. A minimum of sleuthing detected that he kept his attache case in a broken, unused cupboard just inside the tea-room door. Soon after three o'clock most days, Webley lowered the case from the window over the sink, and not long after, put on his hat and left the office as if for a wash. But he did not return. All he had to do was retrieve his case and walk ashore. As for punching the bundy, he and as it turned out, other men from elsewhere on the island, had made an arrangement with an unsavoury young clerk in the pay office. For several weeks before he was caught out, most of the Accounts Branch knew of Webley's deception and resented his dishonesty. But nothing happened until he got behind-hand in paying Hopkins for some losing bets. He blamed Hopkins for the fact that, soon after they had a bitter argument, a senior pay office clerk happened to walk by the back wall of the Accounts Branch just as Webley picked up his suitcase. He followed Webley for long enough to be sure he proposed an illegal exit, then "nabbed" him.

Small-scale pilfering was tolerated by most people. Tim used a kind of sliding scale of honesty. To take home a little glass jar of enamel, a handful of tacks, an electric light bulb, was allowable (though never in an attache case or gladstone bag which, in theory, might be searched at the police post). The art was to "stow the stuff" inconspicuously inside waistcoats and jackets. But the man who "fiddled" either large quantities of anything for himself, or anything at all to sell, was, by Tim's code, an outright thief. It followed that his opinion of the blackmarket was bedrock low. Someone who bought goods likely to have been smuggled or stolen was, he said, "as big a crook as the one that flogged it first". But Smithy had a stricter understanding of the laws of mine and thine. He would not even, said Tim with respect, "use a bit of toilet paper to wipe his nose on".

Alcohol was strictly forbidden on the island, but breaches of this rule were usually overlooked provided drinkers did not inconvenience other people. "Aw—shut up or I'll strike a match near your face!" Tim would threaten Hopkins in moments of rage. But a drinker who became so slipshod and unreliable that other people's job routines suffered, could expect little sympathy. The storemen were stricter. Henderson was known as a relentless "dobber in" of anyone who drank on the job in his store. He said: "Aleos are a danger to themselves and everyone else." Smithy and Blue were the heavy drinkers in the Rating Section but they only indulged ashore. Tim liked to "gargle a schooner" with his friends on the way home, and very occasionally "went on the hops" for an evening with a group of old mates. His hangover next day was always fierce.

Halfway between our office and the ferry wharf was a wooden boat harbour where small craft were moored. These were mostly fishing launches and family pleasure boats whose owners had relinquished them to the Navy for "the duration". *Saucy girl* and *Bubbles* transported workers, goods and messages between various harbour-side establishments and drew a petrol ration from the Oil Fuel store. One reason why oil fuel vouchers were so quickly rated was that week in, month out, the paper for these little boats and for *Peggy* and *We Two* and the rest of them, never altered.

The contrivances and frustrations of petrol rationing were one war-time inconvenience which did not touch my family at all. Neither my father nor anyone else had ever owned a car or wished to drive. I had no idea of what might be a reasonable number of miles per gallon for any kind of internal combustion engine, marine or otherwise. But I liked the little boats and was pleased that they were well kept and freshly painted, and hoped their owners would enjoy them again one day. They were glorified dinghies with awning-covered cabins, and one day as I walked past their harbour, I wondered to myself why *Betty Lou* should draw 10 gallons a week when *Happy Days* always had 60 and *Jason II* seemed to need 100.

"Tim," I asked, "how much petrol would one of the little launches use a week? Say, the one that takes the pay up to Darling Harbour?"

"Aw—if they was busy a coupla gallons a day p'haps. At the outside. Give or take a pint or two. About ten." I showed him that week's bundles.

"Stone th' crows! How long have these amounts applied?"

"I don't know for certain. Months. Years. I've never really looked at them."

" 'Course not. No one ever does. Oh my gawd!" He dashed into Mr Keeling's office with our Oil Fuel ledger. A great deal of coming and going followed all day. Gold braid flashed from the glass cage. Once Tim hurried back to the section and whispered:

"Shut your trap about this, girl. 'Nd if anyone asks you anything you're too bloody silly to understand. I want you kept right out of this blue."

108

No one asked me anthing but the news travelled somehow, for by next morning, the relevant store ledgers could not be found. Because our entries were more than six months behind the actual date, the disappearance of the store records made an immediate stocktaking impossible. For several days and nights Tim and Smithy rated oil fuel bundles until they were up-to-date. They were secretive about their findings. I cajoled Inspector Onions until he told me three men had been arrested.

"It's a damn disgrace," he said. "We've all blamed the Yanks for the petrol black market, but half Sydney's been getting its supplies right under our noses."

DORIS ARRIVED one morning so smiling, so rolling of eye and hips, that "Lay off it big girl!" Tim called, "you make me feel seasick." "She's the only girl I ever seen that smiles with her bum," he whispered, but not very low, to Smithy. Miss Harland said "Shush!" She also said archly: "My little bird tells me you'd better take your gloves off, Doris dear. You can't keep them on all day."

Her little bird had rightly discerned that the protruberance distorting Doris's left glove was an engagement ring—two splendid buttresses of yellow gold filigree supported a proud diamond.

Soon afterwards Marie received six letters, all delayed, "which was just as well—I got the happy ending first." Her Alan would return home soon. The bad beginning was a crash in a training plane that cost him his left arm. "Cheap at the price" he wrote. Alan would remain in Canada to be fitted with a new type of artificial arm and hand. "I could knit with the thing if I happened to want to," he told Marie.

Mrs Whiteley also displayed a marvel. She'd been given a pair of remarkable stockings called "nylons" and demonstrated their fineness by drawing one of them through her wedding ring. "They wear for *ever*," she said, "quite different from silk." "Of course," she said smugly, "it will be a long time before they're generally available—I just have a *very good* friend . . ." Hasten the day! I seldom wore the horrible war-time rayon stockings, but got up earlier each morning to apply tan-coloured leg paint with a sponge. It streaked through the day and rubbed off onto hems of petticiats and dresses, and after a late night it was a temptation to retire without first scrubbing one's legs and one's mother said the disgusting mess of leg paint on towels and bath was bad enough, but on sheets and pyjamas . . .

Peg, who read scientific literature, prophesied that after the war our lives would be changed by a substance called plastic. Many of the things we used every day, she said, would be cheap and disposable. We would eat off paper

109

plates and throw them away, and houses, moulded in shiny plastic would be cleaned by "a good sluice down". "God grant I die first," Peg concluded.

An editor accepted one of my poems. He was R. A. Broinowski of the ABC. He bought another. *The Bulletin* continued to return everything I sent them, but twice printed an encouraging line in the Answers to Correspondents column. Tim said *The Bulletin* was run by a set of lousy cows who couldn't tell a bit of good work if it was rubbed in their faces. I wrote poetry prolifically now, and much as I longed for publication was disconcerted by Tim's exuberant pride in a matter I thought private, almost secret. My ABC success had literally broadcast what I had carefully concealed before, and now Tim boasted of my radio success to all his friends and I let Inspector Onions down by not being able to supply a couple of lines he was trying to recall of "The Man from Snowy River".

Tim beckoned me to his desk and peered over the barricade to make sure no one was looking or listening. He lifted his heavy, brassbound leather gladstone bag up from beside his chair, opened it, pushed aside the morning paper and his lunch packet, and fished out a neat parcel tied with the white string (#32/15) which he preferred to any other. He opened the parcel himself. "Ever heard of *that*?" he asked. It was a brown, cloth-bound copy of *Jane Eyre*.

"Why yes!" He smiled. He patted my hand.

"Ah! But have you read it?"

"No Tim, I haven't."

"Would y' like to?"

"Yes I would; I read *Wuthering Heights* at school—it was a marvellous book."

"That's the *good* stuff" Tim said. "I'm no reader. Them books was Mrs Tapple's. I read 'em every year—never found another book I'd be bothered with."

I opened *Jane Eyre*. The pages were softened by much handling and dog-eared at the bottom corner of each page.

"Oh Tim. This is too precious to lend *anyone*. I'll get a copy from the library and read it. But if I lost this . . ."

"If you lose it I'll cut your throat and swing with pleasure. I want you to read *that copy*."

Several times I offered Tim other books I thought he might enjoy but he refused them. "Thanks Nance. I couldn't be bothered. I'm no reader except for them two I love and that's the strong of it. The paper'll do me."

Tim was leafing through some pay office records and found that my twenty-first birthday would be in a couple of months.

"You'll have to think about your future. What will you do when you leave here?" I told him, as I'd told Peg—no idea.

"Get cracking!" he snapped. "Find out. There must be lots of things. The Uni now?" I retorted that there seemed little point in enquiring about careers when I'd probably be a member of the Rating Section for years to come.

"It won't be bloody years. It's on the turn now. Them Russkis 've got the Germans running like a dose of cascara. Them Japs 'll soon find they've had it. This time next year it'll be just on over. You put up a reasonable proposition—I'll do the worrying about how it can be fiddled. Even with manpower there's ways."

My father always alleged that the man to distrust was the owner of marvellous references. "When I want to get rid of a clod I praise him to high heavens." So I laughed and told Tim his concern suggested a kick upstairs.

"Someone's got to bloody kick you *somewhere.*"

He nagged so much and so often that I made enquiries and heard of a Diploma course of training for professional Social Work at the University. It sounded interesting, required no mathematics at all, and took only two years to complete.

"You do it," Tim said.

"I can't—not just like that. I have to be interviewed for selection."

"Stone th' crows. If they knock you back *I'll* take 'em on."

The Director of the Board of Social Studies interviewed me. She was a perceptive Canadian woman who, I was sure, saw directly all my unworthy motives, and called every bluff in my hand. Nevertheless I was notified that, dependent upon a clearance from the Department of Labour and Industry, I might begin training as a Social Worker during the 1945 academic year. Tim and Mr Keeling set my application for exemption from a protected industry in train, but nothing about the proposition seemed feasible or even real to me. I did not wish to leave the island.

Only Tim, Peg and Blue seemed to find merit in my plans.

"How long is the course?" Doris asked.

"Two years."

"Two years!" Her eyes swivelled with shock. "Two years! Can you have a job too?"

"No. It's full time."

"You'll be broke."

"I've saved enough from this job for fees. And my family . . ."

"And you'll be *old!* All that *study!*"

We sat in Cahills' restaurant at the Cross waiting for our dinner—we were working overtime that night. Two hopeful GIs, who had walked behind us all the way up Macleay Street, whistling and admiring Doris's jaunty walk, had followed us inside. They now sat at an adjoining table trying hard to gain our attention. Doris picked up the menu and flashed her engagement ring with great spirit. The young men took the hint and left the restaurant.

"That's my future." Doris said, smiling at her ring. "Well—it takes all sorts."

TIM WAS CURIOUS about plans for my twenty-first birthday.

"Are you having a party?"

"Not really. I think just a few friends for dinner in town and perhaps a show afterwards."

"But you *will* be having a cake?"

"I'm not sure Tim."

"I'll *bet* your mother 's making a cake. How can you get your key and go through the door if you don't have a cake to cut?"

How indeed? How, without being offensive, could one explain my family's views about things like keys and doors, dolls on wedding cakes and Mother's Day.

"Oh Tim—I don't really think . . ."

"Listen, young lady. Tell your mother Tim Tapple says there's to be a whopping great key and a whopping great cake—and you can say he knows there's a war on but he likes marzipan."

Party plans. These days I had a group of friends who were quite unconnected with Garden Island. Four or five of us met every couple of weeks for a Chinese dinner at the Nanking in Campbell Street. For my birthday my parents had agreed to hire the Nanking's big private dining room for a dinner for our immediate family and these friends. But we planned only a small, informal celebration and had not thought of imposing a cake onto the exotic meal.

I explained to my mother that we'd have to contrive a cake large enough to yield a slice apiece for all my island friends. We laughed about the key. She said she supposed, if I really wanted one, we could polish up one of the mysterious old Yales that lurk in the depths of all Keesing sewing baskets. A cake was made and iced and the layer of almond paste was not forgotten.

Tim had arrived early at the office on my birthday to arrange a huge bunch of roses from his garden in a vase on my desk. When I thanked him he looked rather sly. As morning tea time approached he was restless.

"Where's Smithy? Where *is* Smithy? DeeDee, have you seen Smithy?"

"Not for a while."

"He had to go up to the stores office," Iris said.

"Well he should be back. Blast him!"

Smithy returned and then DeeDee disappeared.

"Where's that girl gone?"

"She'll be back in a sec." Doris said.

"Stone th' crows, it's worse 'n trying to start the bloody Melbourne Cup!"

But when Doris and Iris brought the tray of cups and a dish of elaborate biscuits, each of the section's desks was tenanted and Tim could stand in the centre aisle holding in his right hand, a giant key of heavy metal and in his left a small plywood model of a door. Reg Mulligan moulded and cast the key—on one side of its bulbous top are the figures "21" and on the other— Sept. 1944 / Nancy Keesing / from / Rating Section / Good Luck. The door was Tim's handiwork and before it was varnished everyone in the section, and other friends from all over the island, had signed it.

Tim's presentation speech was meant to be light and funny but I heard it differently. He spoke of Doris's arrival and how "hot on her heels Nance come, and I can't say we always seen eye to eye because . . ." "Hear Hear" from Smithy and "Oh dear" from Iris. Tim spoke of age and responsibility and "we been through a lot and we've all changed and . . ." I was cracking but Tim's voice did first; fortunately Blue interrupted with the opening bars of "Happy Birthday to you".

Not long before I left Garden Island two fishermen in a rowing boat over towards Athol Bight hooked, and with difficulty landed, a dead weight. Tied together with wire cord and weighted with a steel off-cut, the vanished store oil and fuel ledgers dripped on slimy bottom boards.

"It all turns up in time," Tim said.

And in time too a new giant crane called *Titan* moored alongside the *Kuttabul* steps and enormous grapples were fixed to sunken steel. The ferry's rusted hull was harder to raise than its salvagers expected and as it came free of mud at last it made a sucking sound pitched like a groaning sigh.

At the end my release came through more quickly than anyone expected or than I could quite believe. One day, for the last time, I sat on the mown headland with my friends and surveyed the harbour eastwards to the Bridge and westward out to the Heads where a boom defence vessel checked its installations. Behind us roofs and walls sheltered two and a half years which I expected to remember. But how well and often I would recall the place and those years I did not realise then.

With Tim, that afternoon, I visited stores and factories, workshops and offices and the police room, to say goodbye. We came last to the Naval Store and here was disappointment. For Mr Henderson and Frank were so ceremonious and stiff that the day's gathering sadness seemed hardly endurable. They fussed, alleging I looked tired, and as if for a stranger, dusted off a big packing case insisting that I must sit down while we spoke. That these three men, of all the people whose friendship I valued so much, should be so unnatural and . . .

Like a ball from a cannon I shot from case to ceiling, then rubbed my backside where it tingled from its sharp electric shock. Smithy appeared from behind a bay of shelving. Tim cackled like a maniac. We laughed until all we could do was fall against each other for support, and for the first and last time, I kissed them all.

"Stone th' crows," I gasped. "What a send-off!"

113

Regrets. That I cannot now tell Ken Slessor how I first came to read *Five Bells* in the beautiful little edition which he autographed for me years later. That I never saw Tim after I left Garden Island—we spoke by phone a few times and once I believe I glimpsed him on a crowded opposite footpath, but by the time I dashed across a busy road his bandy legs had been too quick for me. I used my invitation to the opening of the Captain Cook Graving Dock because I hoped Tim would be there but I saw few familiar faces in an immense crowd and his was not among them.

Marie asked me to her wedding and we kept in touch for a while but I have never heard of or seen Doris. DeeDee lives in a suburb near mine and we sometimes meet in our local supermarket, when we discuss prices, recipes and our children.

After I qualified as a social worker, the Board of Social Studies asked me if, for a month only and as a favour, I would assist an admirable elderly pioneer of the profession who was renowned and feared for her sporadic, ungovernable rages. We got on so well together that the month became four years. Once, in the remorseful calm that followed her storming, she marvelled that I could put up with her and was mystified when I explained that a Liverpudlian Calathumpian had broken me in.

A newspaper death notice told me years ago that the tide flows over Tim now. My reasons for remembering him are many—not least is that the voice of my conscience rasps and rattles: "Cut the cackle and get on with it. Stone th' crows. There's not all the bloody time in the world. OK Nance, get crackin'!"

Nancy Keesing

114

Africa Wall

Breakfast in Tangier for Isaac Shur was a short loaf of
bread, a tin of sardines or tuna, half a small watermelon,
sometimes too a bottle of Coke. No coffee. Isaac Shur had
no facilities for making coffee, his apartment had neither
electricity nor gas, and though he could easily have bought
a small primus stove, he preferred to leave his life the way
it was. Unencumbered. Uncluttered. Everything he owned
in Tangier fitted into two small canvas bags. He could
leave in a minute. He had a trunk of books and clothes
with a friend in London, and at odd moments he thought
it would be nice to have them here, to have all his things
together, but then he thought of porters and taxis and the
fuss at customs and the worry of thieves – everyone was a
thief in Tangier – and he decided, no. He didn't really
need all those books and clothes. He didn't need anything.
He was happy the way he was. Perfectly happy. Isaac
Shur had been in Tangier, now, for five months.

He bought his bread and his melon and his Coke and
his sardines or tuna always at the same place, the first
shop down the hill from where he lived. He was there

every morning at seven o'clock. He ordered by pointing, miming, smiling, shaking his head. Isaac Shur knew a few words of Spanish, Arabic and French – the lingua franca of this once international city – but he rarely used them. Speaking in a foreign language always made him feel that he was at a disadvantage. The first words he said, in a café, or restaurant, or shop, were, 'Do you speak English?' and when the answer was no, or a puzzled look, or a shake of the head, as it almost invariably was, then Isaac Shur would smile, *that* fact established, made clear, out of the way, good. Then he would launch into his performance of pointing and mime, happier with this, really, than speaking in English. In the shop at the bottom of the hill he was served each morning by the owner, a short, shuffling, always smiling Moroccan, shapeless in a dun-coloured jellaba, the Moroccan's cheeks, at that hour, frosted with grey bristles. The owner welcomed Isaac Shur each morning like a long-lost friend, throwing out his hands, calling out greetings, smiling hugely. Isaac Shur would smile back, then without further ado begin his business of pointing and mime. There were two black cats in the shop, lying about on sacks or on the floor just inside the door, warming themselves in the morning sun. The shop smelled of fruit and oil and Arabic coffee and bread and dust, and there was another smell too, surrounding all these others. This smell was not just in the shop. It was everywhere in Tangier. Isaac Shur had sniffed it in Spain too, and in Greece, but in Tangier it was sharper, more pervasive, impossible to ignore. Its exact cause or component was to Isaac Shur a mystery, but he had a name for it. He called it, to himself, the smell of poverty. He planned one day to write about it. Isaac Shur was a poet and a playwright. His first play had been bought by the BBC. Three of his poems had been published in magazines, one in the *New Statesman*. He was twenty-six years old, an Australian.

Isaac Shur sliced his watermelon with the Swiss army knife he had bought in Copenhagen. He was sitting at the table where in half an hour he would begin work, his typewriter and papers pushed to one side, the door open, the windows open, the shutters folded back, his view of bushes and trees, his garden. Sun fell onto the tiled floor. A breeze passed through the trees onto his face. Isaac Shur looked at his watch. Ten minutes past seven. Good. He felt alert and alive, as he did every morning. This was the best time of the day. From now till ten. Three hours. After that it would be too hot, too hot to think, too hot to work. Three hours. Two and a half. Well, that was enough. That was plenty. He would work till ten, maybe even till ten-thirty, and then walk into town, have his morning coffee, buy a newspaper, a magazine, sit, stroll. Then lunch. Then . . . well, he would see.

Isaac Shur wiped the blade of his Swiss army knife on his jeans. He used this same blade for watermelon, bread, forking out sardines, sharpening his pencils. He finished his bread, washed it down with Coke. His apartment was really just one room, but large, and odd-shaped: where he slept was up two steps and around a corner. Sitting at the table, finishing his breakfast, he could see only the foot of his bed. His two canvas bags beside it. A spare shirt. The kitchen was a narrow space behind him, a sink and a tap. The toilet, behind it, had to be flushed with a bucket. There was an oil lamp beside the bed, another one here on the table. Isaac Shur's was the garden apartment in a block of three floors. Isaac Shur brushed the breadcrumbs from his table and from his lap, lit a cigarette, and stepped outside.

It was a walled garden, the wall made of grey concrete blocks, and along the top of it a glittering necklace of broken bottles and shards of sharp glass set in cement: the terrible teeth of all walls in Tangier. Isaac Shur ignored

117

this. He had learnt not to see it. The garden was wild and unkempt, shaded and private, Tangier locked out. Except in one place, where Isaac Shur stood now, where the ground rose, affording a view beyond the wall, as though the wall were not even there. A view that sailed clear of the hill, past the rubbish dump just beyond the wall – a dusty, smelly mound of earth and iron and feathers and bones and newspapers and broken bricks and God only knew what else. Sailing past all this, quickly, barely touching it, away, and then along a green valley, a soft green cleft that ran as far as he could see, into the fuzziness of distance, into the vague shape of hills.

Isaac Shur stood with his cigarette. The valley was why he had taken this apartment. He had looked along it, that first time, and the doubts he had had about living in a place that had no electricity, no gas, that was half an hour's walk from the centre of town, a walk he would have to do at least twice a day, probably four times. But more than that, the place was so isolated, no one he knew lived anywhere nearby, and the rubbish dump just outside ... but then he had looked along the valley, that first time, and all his doubts fell away. Yes, he had said to himself at once, the decision made. I will work well here. I will be happy. This is what I want. Yes. The valley was green at all times of the day, no matter how hard the sun blazed down, and always that same green, soft and hazy, an English green, the green of Hampshire and Sussex and the other counties Isaac Shur had travelled through. And though, at that particular time, he had felt no especial rapport with the English countryside – regarding it merely as pleasant scenery, as he had seen the countryside in France or Denmark or Germany – now, seeing it in Tangier, it struck a chord, it awoke something inside him, some memory, some need. He never tired of it, he could stand for hours looking along its greenness, his eyes endlessly travelling its hazy length. Halfway along the valley there was a village, and then a second, and then a third. Three clusters of white buildings patterned onto the green, but the second, Isaac Shur knew, was not a village but a cemetary, the tricks of perspective and light housing the dead as it did the living.

Isaac Shur threw away his cigarette. He turned his back reluctantly on the view. Time to work.

Isaac Shur had begun, a week ago, a poem on his mother's hands. His mother had died when Isaac Shur was twenty-two, and then his father had died, a year later, a year to the day. Isaac Shur's method of work was to write down, in grammatically perfect sentences, everything he could remember. His mother's hands slicing bread. Putting on lipstick. Dialling on the telephone. Flying to her heart when she laughed. Her fingers. Her wedding ring. Her nails. Her palms. His mother's hands covered, so far, twenty-odd pages. Isaac Shur felt he had hardly begun. There would be twice that number of pages again, at least. And when that was done, when he had recalled everything, he would put the pages away, unread, never look at them again, and then he would write his poem. He wrote quickly but carefully, his letters large and well-formed, and when he heard the clamour at the gate, his mouth fell open, as though he had just been woken from a deep sleep. For a moment he didn't know where he was. And then he did, and he knew what was happening. It was the same thing that happened every morning. Isaac Shur rushed out into his garden, waving his hands, shouting.

There they were, as they were every morning, clambering over the gate. Two of them were already inside the garden.

'Go away!' Isaac Shur shouted. 'Beat it! Scram!'

The two in the garden stood there, smiling idiotically.

119

Isaac Shur ran at them. They ducked behind a bush. A third dropped down from the gate.

'Get out of here!' Isaac Shur shouted, wheeling around. 'Leave me alone!' Now the other two were in too, not just smiling but laughing, dancing on thin legs, waving their arms. Isaac Shur ran at them, but they were too fast, they were always too fast, ducking effortlessly out of reach, and then standing still, taunting him with their idiotic smiles. He ran again, his hands grabbing empty air, and then he remembered, instantly panicking, that his door was wide open, the windows, the shutters. Two of them were already inside, the little one, the one he called The Hot Shot Kid, and the tall one, the one with the shaved head. When they saw him, they ducked behind the table, over-turning his chair. Isaac Shur saw that The Hot Shot Kid had his Swiss army knife. And what else? What else had they taken? His papers lay in turmoil all over the floor.

Isaac Shur, in true anger now, slammed the door. Right! Rushing for The Hot Shot Kid, he stumbled over the chair. The tall one laughed, and then was gone, fast as water, out of the window. Then he appeared at another window, smiling like a loon. Isaac Shur ignored him. He advanced on The Hot Shot Kid.

'The knife!' he shouted. 'Put down that knife! Put it down!'

The Hot Shot Kid, for the first time, looked afraid. He was a small boy, about five or six years old. He looked over his shoulder, at the slammed door. The game had become serious. Isaac Shur lunged and grabbed him. He grabbed the knife. The Hot Shot Kid broke free and ran for a window. Isaac Shur let him go. He was shaking. He was wet with sweat.

The shutters, the windows. He locked everything. He shot the bolt on the door. They were laughing outside

120

now, calling out. Isaac Shur picked up his papers. The Swiss army knife was in his pocket. What else had they taken? His pencils, his pen? No. Nothing. It was all there. He picked up the fallen chair, sat down. They were throwing dirt now, at the shutters, at the door. In another minute it would be stones. Isaac Shur saw, when he lit a cigarette, that his fingers were trembling.

It was his fault, of course. He had encouraged them. The Hot Shot Kid lived in the apartment above. Two of the others lived in the block too. The rest were from somewhere around, local kids, playing most of the time on the rubbish dump. Isaac Shur had noticed them there, vaguely, on that first afternoon, when he had moved in. On his first morning in his new apartment, Isaac Shur, walking around his garden, had seen them standing at the gate, looking in. He had waved to them, and smiled, and then, having bought a too-large piece of watermelon that morning, he had offered them each a slice, and some Coke too. He had unlocked the gate. They came into the garden. Isaac Shur had felt sorry for them, for their thin legs, their thin arms, their ragged clothes. He had given them some bread too, bread and sardines. They were polite that first day, standing in the garden, looking in his open door but not going inside, and Isaac Shur had invited them in, showed them his typewriter, his pencils, his papers, his Swiss army knife, explaining to them, pointing and miming and smiling and shaking his head, his work, his reason for being here, his life. That was the first day. On the second morning they had appeared in his garden. The gate had been locked, they had climbed over. They were still polite, still well behaved, but smiling more now, laughing, friends. Isaac Shur shared his watermelon with them again. From there to how it was now had happened in a rush. And getting worse every day. Worse and worse.

Stones banged against his closed door. Isaac Shur sat

121

furious at his table, puffing on his cigarette. Ignore them, he told himself. Don't make a sound. They'll go away. He reached for his papers. With the door closed, with the shutters closed, it was almost too dark to see. Isaac Shur lit the oil lamp on the table. He picked up a pencil. Her hands when she sewed on a button. The way she held the needle. The little finger of her left hand. The needle dipping. Her hand pulling the thread tight. The oil lamp pushed out heat in solid waves. Isaac Shur unbuttoned his shirt, and then took it completely off. He flung it away savagely on the floor. And then his jeans too, his shoes and socks. He was enormously hot. He could hardly breathe. The smell of his crushed-out cigarette was foul in the room. He lit another. Now they were kicking his door, shouting wildly, banging the shutters with sticks.

Isaac Shur had written his play in London in a large cold room in Maida Vale, the upstairs front room in a cracked grey house of bedsitters, on the slum fringe. His view, when he looked, was of identical cracked houses both ways down the street, as far as he could see. His only heating was a tiny gas fire set in the wall. The windows rattled with wind. A draught blew under the door. The linoleumed floor was ice to his feet. Isaac Shur was cold when he went to bed at night, cold when he awoke each morning. He had written his play in ten days, then ten days more for a second and final draft, typing as fast as he could, cold all the time. His fingers were white with cold. Coming back from his literary agent, he had seen, at Oxford Circus, a large colour photograph, a poster, an advertisement, for South Africa. The photograph showed three girls in skimpy bikinis laughing and jumping into the sea, and Isaac Shur had felt his muscles tighten with pain, looking at those bare bodies. He had shivered violently. He had felt sick with cold. His literary agent phoned him that night, ecstatic with praise, and a week later the play

122

had been bought by the BBC. Beginner's luck? Isaac Shur knew no other writers, he had no experience of rejection or waiting, and though he was, of course, delighted, delighted and thrilled, the full measure of his success was unknown to him. This is the way it happens, he thought. Good. He had been in London, then, for a month and three days. Before that, for a year, he had travelled, never staying anywhere longer than two or three weeks. A week in Vienna. Ten days in Prague. Three weeks in Copenhagen, two in Stockholm and Oslo. This was his first time in Europe. He wanted to see it all.

Two days after his play had been accepted, Isaac Shur was at the flat of a friend, a fellow Australian who had been in London for two years. This friend, Graham Tinsdale, was a film editor. They sat before a small fan heater. Wind rushed unimpeded through the bare branches of the trees in the square outside, the windows of the flat uncurtained, cold black rectangles of night. Isaac Shur told Graham Tinsdale the details of his sale to the BBC. Graham Tinsdale looked amazed. 'That's terrific,' he said. 'Are you going to do another one?' Isaac Shur looked at the black windows. 'I don't know how anyone can live in England,' he said. 'It's so cold.' 'Go to Greece,' Graham Tinsdale said. 'Greece is good in winter.' 'I've been to Greece,' Isaac Shur said. 'I think I'll go to Tangier.' Isaac Shur had no idea why he had said this. Tangier. He knew nothing about the place, he had no real desire to see it, it was just something that had come into his head. Tangier. He heard the wind rushing outside. He shivered. 'When?' Graham Tinsdale said. 'I don't know,' Isaac Shur said. 'Tomorrow. The day after. Listen, is it all right if I leave a few things here? They're all in a small trunk. Won't take up much room.' Two nights later Isaac Shur was in Paris, waiting to board the midnight train to Madrid. He stayed in Madrid for four days, and from there hitchhiked down, and the closer he got to Tangier the more he recognized that he was afraid.

Why am I doing this? Isaac Shur asked himself. Because I had said to a friend in London that I would? That was nothing. I could have stayed in Madrid. Madrid was warm. Blue skies every day. The Prado. Good wine. Isaac Shur hitchhiked down, through Valencia, and then along the coast, Malaga, Estapona, travelling not very far each day, staying in hotels, rooms, and each night the fear growing. Why? Why?

All new cities are fearful places, but Tangier remained fearful to Isaac Shur longer than anywhere else he had ever been. And not only at night but during the day too. He was frightened of the shopkeepers, the touts, the beggars, the endless boys forever plucking at his sleeves, always with the same litany: 'How are you, my friend?' What frightened him more than anything else was that he knew his fear was visible to all. He radiated, he knew, not only discomfort but vulnerability. It was in his eyes, in the way he sat at a café, in the way he walked down a street, in everything he did. He wondered should he go somewhere else, but he didn't know where. He could think only of London, but that was too cold. No, he told himself, I don't want to travel. Not yet. I've had enough travelling for a while. Hotels, rooms. I want to be in one place. I want to do some work. Then Isaac Shur began to meet people, Americans, mostly, people his age, other writers, painters, college dropouts, kids having a good time. He moved from the hotel where he was staying to a cheaper one, he established habits and routines, he settled into good work. He developed a manner of walking down a street, of sitting at a café, of not seeing those things that he didn't want to see, of ignoring the hands forever plucking at his sleeves, the litany of pestering voices. He erected around himself the necessary shell or disguise that every-

124

one developed, he told himself, to exist in this city. He learnt to keep his right hand always in his pocket, tight over his wallet and passport and traveller's cheques. Very quickly, he did this without thinking; it became second nature to him.

A large stone slammed against Isaac Shur's door. The door shuddered, daylight, for an awful instant, showing all around. Isaac Shur leapt up from his table, a shout in his throat.

What was the use? What was the point? Isaac Shur knew that even if he chased them away, which was probably impossible, even if he sat them out, did nothing, waited, didn't utter a sound, it would make no difference. The best hours of the day were gone. His brain was in turmoil now. The morning was ruined. He looked at the last words he had written. They lay on the page. They meant nothing.

In the kitchen Isaac Shur splashed himself with cold water, combed his hair. He dressed again in his jeans and shirt. Passport, money. There was a wild scramble in the garden when Isaac Shur stepped outside. Isaac Shur didn't look up. He locked his door, unlocked the garden gate and locked it again, then pushed the keys deep in his pocket under his passport and wallet. Still not looking up, paying no attention whatsoever to the children waving and shouting and advancing and dancing back on their thin legs on the edge of his vision, he started down the hill. Just before the shop where he went every morning he saw a woman sitting on the ground, a baby on her lap. The palm of the woman's held-out hand was as crinkled as a dead leaf. Isaac Shur kept his hand tight in his pocket over his wallet and passport and traveller's cheques. The only acknowledgement he allowed himself to make of her presence was a curt shaking of his head. Give to one and you give to them all, he had learnt long ago. They were endless. Any-

125

how, he told himself, I don't have any small change.

It was not yet ten o'clock, but the day was already hot. Dust swirled in the road. That smell that Isaac Shur called the smell of poverty filled his nose. July. August, Isaac Shur had been told, was the worst month. Everyone went away in August. August in Tangier was unbearable. Even the nights were hot. Isaac Shur thought for a moment of going to Portugal, a month somewhere on the Atlantic coast, but the idea of travelling again, just now, of finding a place to stay, of having to establish his habits and routines all over again, was annoying, too complicated, and he pushed it away. He would think about that later, another time. Instead, quickly, he thought about where he would go for his morning coffee.

Isaac Shur had no one particular place. He left it, each morning, for his mood to decide. Some mornings he enjoyed the Café de Paris, on the corner of the Avenue Louis Pasteur, diagonally across from the French Consulate. This is where he had sat that morning when the *New Statesman* with his poem in it had arrived, the magazine open nonchalantly at his page – or so he had hoped it looked – sipping his coffee, smoking cigarette after cigarette, his eyes casually moving over the elegant lamps and the mirrors and the burgundy-coloured leather seats and the waiters in their clean aprons and stiff white shirts and black bow ties, and the parade of people moving past in the street, and the French Consulate with its classical facade and the tall palm trees in the garden, the tall iron gates, the black official cars. Isaac Shur's eyes drifting over all this and then back, again and again, to his poem on the marble table. The Café de Paris was expensive, but Isaac Shur didn't mind that. On the mornings that he went there he usually bought *The Times*, and took his time with it, sitting there for an hour at least, reading every word, even the obituaries and Court Circular. At the Café de

126

Paris Isaac Shur was always alone, and he liked that too. He enjoyed the quiet hour, his newspaper, his cigarettes, the coffee.

Or he would go to Claridges, which was further along the street, on the other side, and sit inside, on a stool at the bar, and have a croissant with his coffee, sometimes two, looking up from time to time to see himself reflected in the mirror behind the bar, his face serious and dimly lit amongst the bottles of whisky and brandy and liqueurs and gin. At Claridges Isaac Shur felt international, a seasoned traveller, mature and self-contained, someone who knew the ropes.

No, Isaac Shur wasn't in the mood for the Café de Paris this morning. Nor for Claridges. He continued down the street that led down to the Socco Grande, past the Minzah Hotel, where, Isaac Shur had been told, Ian Fleming had always stayed whenever he had been in Tangier. Isaac Shur had had his morning coffee there several times, in the garden, sitting under a vast umbrella by the blue pool. The doorman, a turbanned and costumed tall black African, stepped out of the way on the narrow pavement as Isaac Shur went past.

In the Socco Grande Isaac Shur saw the usual crowds milling around the usual dilapidated buses, the usual vendors with their portable stalls – the man who sold scissors, the cakes man, the man with the scarves and belts – and the usual beggars, the usual touts, the endless wheeling boys. Hands reached out for his arms, his shirt. Faces appeared, serious, smiling. 'How are you, my friend?' Issac Shur walked not quickly but not dawdling either, crossing the large dusty square, his right hand firmly in his pocket, his eyes enjoying the scene, but his face fixed straight ahead. The cafés. The shops. The different sudden smells, of charcoal and meat, of noodle soup, of gasoline, of bread, of chickens, of dung.

127

Halfway across the square Isaac Shur saw, standing together, in their usual place, the fatimas. Isaac Shur had employed a fatima only once. An old Fleet Street journalist, a man who had stepped ashore at Tangier on his way to somewhere else in 1939 and never left, had told Isaac Shur about the fatimas. 'Go down there, Isaac,' he had said, 'and for three dirhams you'll get your clothes washed and your floors scrubbed and your bed made – they'll even cook your lunch. But don't pay them more than three dirhams, understand? Not a penny more.' Isaac Shur had gone down to the Socco Grande at eight o'clock in the morning, pointed to the nearest woman, and then taken her back with him to his apartment on the bus, a thin woman with lined hennaed hands. Isaac Shur had sat in his garden in his shorts while the woman washed his clothes and his sheets and his towel, washed them in cold water, pounding and pounding them, and then spread them out on bushes to dry. After she had scrubbed his floors, she had come out to where Isaac Shur sat in the garden and mimed eating, her thin hands flying to her mouth, and then pointing at Isaac Shur, raising her eyebrows. At first Isaac Shur had thought that she wanted to make him lunch. He shook his head, no, he didn't want lunch, he wasn't hungry, he would eat later. Then he realized that she was telling him that she was hungry, that he had to feed her. 'Oh,' Isaac Shur had said, blushing red, and had run down to the shop where he bought his breakfast every morning and he bought what he always bought, a tin of sardines, bread, a melon. The fatima had eaten these in the kitchen, crouched in the furthest corner, her back turned on the open windows, the trees and bushes, the view. When she had finished Isaac Shur gave her three dirhams and she had fallen to her knees on the floor and blessed him, and at the gate had told Isaac Shur, pointing and miming and smiling, that she wanted to come again,

128

that she would always come, that she would be his fatima. Isaac Shur had wanted to give her another dirham, for the bus, but his hand stayed in his pocket.

Isaac Shur entered the street that led down to the Socco Chico, the arched entrance to the market on one side, with its wet smell of flowers, a tight, steeply downhill street crammed with tourist shops. He walked faster here, both hands in his pockets, the left one touching his Swiss army knife, feeling its smooth, familiar shape. A sudden gust of boys – three? four? Isaac Shur didn't look – appeared around him, touching, laughing, crying out, and then they were gone, and Isaac Shur was in the Socco Chico.

Saint-Saëns had written his *Carnival of Animals* here, in the front first-floor room of the hotel to Isaac Shur's right. Tennessee Williams, Isaac Shur had been told, had sat here too, often, at one of these cafés, and watching the endless parade had conceived *Camino Real*. And William Burroughs had sat here. And Paul Bowles. And a young Truman Capote. The whole world passed through the Socco Chico, if you sat here long enough. This, anyhow, was the constant refrain of the Americans, the painters and writers and college dropouts whom Isaac Shur had met and befriended, in particular, George Matthews, a black-bearded New Yorker who was Isaac Shur's closest Tangier friend. George Matthews was a great sitter. Four or five hours at a stretch was nothing to him. That was his norm. George Matthews would sit, sometimes, the whole day through, and then, after dinner, come back, around ten or eleven, and sit another three or four hours, ordering, from time to time, a cup of coffee or hot chocolate, smoking a cigarette or two, but mostly doing nothing, just sitting. George Matthews always had a book with him, Spinoza's *Ethics*, or something by Hegel or Toynbee or Kant, once it was Marx's *Das Kapital*, but Isaac Shur had never seen him reading. A book was just something that George

129

Matthews always had with him, a justification for sitting, a prop. He had graduated from Columbia University, but not in Philosophy, as Isaac Shur had supposed. His thesis had been on how to win at Monopoly.

Isaac Shur saw George Matthews sitting at his usual table at the Café Central, his left hand resting lightly on a small green book. 'George,' Isaac Shur said.

George Matthews looked up. His black-bearded face, which always looked gruff, broke instantly into a naive, innocent smile. 'Hi,' he said, seeing Isaac Shur. 'Hey, sit down, whatcha doin'? How's things?'

Isaac Shur pulled out a chair. There were three other people sitting at the table, two painters named Vincent and Berkeley, and a girl everyone called Bunny. Isaac Shur said hello to them, and then turned back to George Matthews.

'Those kids,' Isaac Shur said. 'Those kids are driving me crazy. I couldn't do any work this morning. Again.'

'Naah,' George Matthews said. 'Kids is nothin'. Don't let 'em hassle ya. Kids is kids.'

'Not these kids,' Isaac Shur said. 'These kids are vultures. They won't leave me alone. You know what happened this morning? One of them grabbed my knife. The little one, The Hot Shot Kid. I went crazy.'

'Yeah?' George Matthews said. 'The Hot Shot Kid, eh?' He smiled. 'He's some kid. So clip him one in the ear, he won't hassle you no more.'

Isaac Shur lit a cigarette. 'A clip in the ear,' he said. 'If you can catch him.'

'Listen, don't let 'em hassle ya,' George Matthews said. 'You want hassle, go to New York. Man, that's the capital of hasslin'. Here, you just relax. Take it easy.'

'Yes,' Isaac Shur said.

The usual waiter appeared, the one everyone called Dopey because of his drooping lids and bald head and

130

slow, faraway manner. '*Con leche?*' he said to Isaac Shur, not quite looking at him. Isaac Shur nodded. The waiter poured out the coffee and milk simultaneously from the two silver pots he always carried, hardly looking at the cup, but getting it, as always, exactly right.

'How ya doin' there, Dopey?' George Matthews said. The waiter smiled the faintest smile and shuffled away. 'Isn't he terrific?' George Matthews said. 'The most terrific coffee pourer on the whole damn continent of Africa. In the middle of an earthquake, I bet he still wouldn't spill a single drop.' He laughed, and then turned back to face the square, his eyes darting, taking in everything, vastly alive, endlessly amused, under his black brows. Isaac Shur sipped his coffee and smoked his cigarette.

Ten minutes passed, fifteen. There was some talk at the table, the sort of talk there always was, small talk, light gossip, never about work. Work was never mentioned. Work, if you did it – or didn't – was your own business, a private thing. When Isaac Shur's poem had come out in the *New Statesman*, he had shown it to George Matthews, here, at the Café Central, at this table, and to the other people who had been here too that day, one of whom, a thin, crew-cutted Canadian named Steven, was a writer, working on a novel. Isaac Shur, excited, had not only let everyone read his poem but then launched into an exposition of his method of work, how he filled page after page with sentences in prose, and then put them away, unread, in a drawer, and wrote his poem. When he had finished telling everyone about this – it was the first time he had ever explained his work to anyone in his whole life – Isaac Shur had expected that there would be some talk about it, that Steven, anyway, would talk about how he wrote, but there wasn't. No one said anything. The talk, when it began again, moved where it always did, into small things, light gossip, and Isaac Shur wondered if this was Tangier

131

or whether all creative people everywhere kept themselves buttoned up. Whatever, Isaac Shur had never talked about his work again.

Another ten minutes, another fifteen. Isaac Shur had finished his coffee. He didn't feel like another. He didn't want another cigarette. A Moroccan youth appeared at the table, a regular at the square. Isaac Shur instinctively put his hand over his cigarettes on the table.

'Hi there, Muhammad,' George Matthews greeted the Moroccan. 'How's it going?' The Moroccan shook George Matthews' hand, and then slapped him on the back. He shook the painters' hands too, and smiled at Bunny, nodding his head seriously. Isaac Shur ignored the outstretched hand when it came his way, countering it with a short smile, a quick nod, then busying himself with a cigarette. George Matthews invited the Moroccan to sit with them. The Moroccan sat, smiling. After three or four minutes he stood up, shook hands with George Matthews again, with the two painters, nodded and smiled at Bunny and Isaac Shur, and left. Isaac Shur stood up too.

'Hey, where ya goin'?' George Matthews said. 'What's the rush?'

'Well, I thought ...' Isaac Shur began, counting out the money for his coffee. 'I've got some things to do.' He nodded at Bunny and the two painters. 'See you,' he said.

'Wait a minute, wait a minute,' George Matthews said. 'Listen. Why doncha come round for dinner tonight? I'll fry up a chicken.'

'OK,' Isaac Shur said. 'What time?'

'I don't know,' George Matthews said. 'Nine?'

'Fine,' Isaac Shur said. 'Nine o'clock.' Isaac Shur signalled to the waiter, pointing to his money on the table.

'Ya feel like Monopoly?' George Matthews said. 'I'm in the mood.'

'You're always in the mood,' Isaac Shur said, moving

132

away from the table. 'See you. Nine o'clock.' And then, remembering, 'I'll bring the wine.'

It was half past eleven. Isaac Shur, both hands in his pockets, ignoring the bustling bodies all around, walked down the street that led from the Socco Chico to the sea. He would walk along the beach, he decided. He would sit somewhere quiet for a while and think. He would have lunch. He passed, on his left, the mosque, and saw, through the open door, the tiled mosaic walls, the fountain at the entrance, barefoot Moroccans ritually washing, and, further inside, others sitting cross-legged, silent in prayer. Isaac Shur decided that tomorrow he would go to Gibraltar.

Isaac Shur went to Gibraltar about once a fortnight, going on the ferry at nine o'clock in the morning, coming back around six, a two-hour trip each way. Once, suddenly impatient, excited, the prospect of that two-hour trip too much for him, too predictable, too slow, he had taken a cab to the airport, and flown over, and then, at five, flown back, the trip, this way, costing him five times what the ferry did, plus the cabs. It had been worth it though, to see Gibraltar from the air, the thrill of landing on that impossible airstrip, that tiny neck of connecting land, the sea on both sides, the plane coming down on almost no space at all; and then, coming back, for the first time he had seen Tangier the way he had been told by old residents it used to be, in the twenties and thirties, before it had been 'discovered', a magical city floating pale blue on its hills above the Strait.

In Gibraltar, Isaac Shur changed his traveller's cheques – the rate was better than what you got in Tangier, though lately it had been falling – bought a pile of the latest English magazines and newspapers, sometimes too a couple of books, then he had lunch in a Chinese restaurant, and then, in the afternoon, sat in his favourite place, the small park and sailors' cemetery at the end of the main street, and quietly read. In Gibraltar he also bought a bottle of duty-free whisky – Johnnie Walker Black Label or Haig and Haig Pinch – two cartons of Camel cigarettes, and a box of Havana cigars. Ramon Allones, usually. Sometimes Punch. Isaac Shur was no great cigar smoker, but he liked the image of himself smoking a fine cigar in the afternoons whilst sitting in his garden looking across at the green valley and its three white villagers. Every afternoon, around six o'clock, the day's heat dying, this is what he did. Unless the children came again. But usually in the afternoons they left him alone.

Yes, Isaac Shur said to himself, tomorrow I'll go to Gibraltar.

The street he was walking down suddenly widened, and Isaac Shur, looking up, saw the sea. Palm trees. Sea-gulls. The road was torn up here, pipes were being laid. There was the usual commotion of tractors and trucks. Isaac Shur, turning left, made for the beach.

He walked for about half a kilometre, and then sat down, on a bench under a tree. He lit a cigarette. Between the beach proper and where he sat there was a row of beach clubs, places where, for a small fee, you could use the changing rooms, hire a locker, shower, buy a drink at the bar, but the real business of the beach clubs was sitting. The beach at Tangier is wide, a long trek across the hot sand to the sea, and Isaac Shur had discovered, on the two or three occasions when he had been to one of these beach clubs, that hardly anyone ever actually swam. Swimming was too much trouble. It wasn't worth it. It was too far. It was a sweat. Instead, everyone just sat, sprawled in deck chairs, smoking, talking, sipping Cokes, for half the day, and longer. Isaac Shur, even when with his friends, or with people he knew, had quickly felt restless, awkward, and each time had left after less than an hour.

134

Isaac Shur walked the length of the road that paralleled the sea as far as it went, and then back, and lunched, alone, at a noisy café on the harbour. Calimari. A glass of white wine. Coffee and a cigarette. A television set on a shelf above the counter was showing an old film starring Montgomery Clift. The film, dubbed into Spanish, was probably being transmitted from Spain. Isaac Shur didn't know what the film was, he couldn't follow the story at all, but he watched it intently as he ate, not at all bothered by not being able to understand what anyone was saying, enjoying the shots of buildings and cars, the interiors, the details – the telephones, cigarette lighters, elevator doors opening and closing, the clothes. He debated having a second cup of coffee and sitting until the film was over, but the café was too noisy, people coming in and going out all the time, money changers, touts, prostitutes, beggars, and though he would have liked to stay, Isaac Shur knew that he would be pestered if he sat here alone too long.

Isaac Shur walked back through Tangier a different way, up through the French quarter, the New Town. In the windows of the shops he saw cameras and watches and tape recorders and handsomely packaged bottles of after-shave, and Isaac Shur felt growing inside him an acquisitive urge, a desire to own – what? He looked at playing cards, battery-operated record players, transistor radios, silk ties, pondering each item, considering. A Dupont cigarette lighter? A pair of French sunglasses? No, this is ridiculous, Isaac Shur told himself, as he did every day, I am not going to pay these prices. I can get all this stuff cheaper in Gibraltar.

No children rushed at him when Isaac Shur unlocked his garden gate. Nor were they on the rubbish dump. The day was hot with silence. Inside his apartment, Isaac Shur opened the windows but left the shutters as they were. He saw the pages lying on the table as he had left them, his typewriter, his pencils, his pen, and for a moment he thought of sitting down, continuing his work, but no, he was too hot, he was too tired, he shouldn't have had that glass of wine at lunch. He sat down on the end of his bed and took off his shoes and socks. It wasn't the wine. Not just the wine. He unbuttoned and took off his shirt. He thought, if I lived in town, if I didn't have to do that walk every day. He put his passport and wallet and traveller's cheques under his pillow. He was almost too tired to take off his jeans. There was no wind outside, not a breeze, not the faintest stir of air, but Isaac Shur smelt, for an unaccountable instant, that smell of poverty. It filled his nose, his head, and then was gone, replaced by nothing.

What woke Isaac Shur at five o'clock was the garden gate rattling. At first he thought it was the children, and felt himself stiffen. Then he remembered. Today was the day he paid his rent. 'Coming, coming,' Isaac Shur called, dressing quickly, but not bothering with his shoes and socks.

She stood at the iron gate, haughty and enormous, wearing the spotless dove-coloured jellaba of the finest wool she always wore on these visits, golden slippers peeping out. Isaac Shur unlocked the gate, smiling apologetically. She swept past him, down the three steps that led to the garden, into the apartment. Isaac Shur, relocking the gate, saw at the kerb the battered black Vauxhall in which she always arrived, her son – one of her sons – sitting at the wheel, staring dumbly through the windscreen straight ahead. Isaac Shur hurried inside.

This woman had once owned, Isaac Shur had been told, the most expensive brothel in all Tangier. Certainly she was rich. She owned, beside this apartment, two buildings in the town, one of them a shop, the other offices and apartments; her mouth flashed with gold; on her left wrist sat a large Swiss watch, there were diamond and gold rings on most of her fingers, and the Vauxhall was hers. Yet, when Isaac Shur had gone to see her, to negotiate the leasing of this apartment, gone with the English painter who was relinquishing the apartment and returning home, he had found her living in what looked like abject poverty, in three cramped and crowded rooms in the heart of the Medina. In the first room Isaac Shur had seen an old man asleep in a chair, two young girls sitting on a battered sofa, a baby lying on a scrap of blanket on the floor. Flies crawled everywhere. The only hint of affluence was a television set in a corner. The other two rooms were filled with beds. The smell was appalling. Isaac Shur had had to go outside, to conduct his negotiations in the street. The English painter had done all the talking, in Spanish mostly, but with a few words of Arabic and French. Isaac Shur didn't know the woman's name. He called her Fatima.

'Fatima,' Isaac Shur said, coming into the apartment.

She was walking around the apartment, looking at everything, the typewriter, the two canvas bags, the shirt on the bed, her head high, aloof, completely disregarding Isaac Shur. Isaac Shur remembered that his wallet and passport were still under the pillow, took them out quickly, and began to count out the money for the week's rent.

'Fatima,' he said, holding it out in his hand.

Still she ignored him, looking around the apartment. Isaac Shur placed the money where he always put it, on a corner of the table. He watched the woman's eyes taking in his newspapers and magazines, his bottle of Johnnie Walker Black Label whisky, the Ramon Allones cigars, his cartons of Camel cigarettes. Finally, she sat down in Isaac Shur's chair.

'Whisky,' she said.

137

Isaac Shur fetched from the kitchen a glass and poured it half full. He handed it to the woman.

'Cigarette,' she said.

He offered his pack of Camels, lit one for her with a match. The woman's face said nothing. She raised the glass to her lips. Then she heard something, they both heard it, a sound outside, a step. The woman dropped the glass of whisky to the floor. The cigarette fell from her other hand. She sat, silent, stone, her eyes on a corner of the ceiling.

Isaac Shur went to the door and looked outside. It was nothing. There was no one there. The sound must have come from the apartment above.

'Nothing,' he said, holding up his hands, smiling.

The glass was not broken. Isaac Shur poured the woman another drink, lit for her another cigarette. Once more he offered the week's rent. Again she ignored him, sitting straight in his chair, puffing on the forbidden cigarette, but not inhaling, blowing the smoke away. Isaac Shur watched the glass go three times to the woman's lips, but each time it seemed to him the level remained the same. Then there was another sound, and once more she let fall the cigarette and glass.

She stayed for half an hour, never once looking directly at Isaac Shur, but the money disappearing, as it always did, into her jellaba, and when he unlocked and opened the garden gate for her, she swept past him as though she had never seen him before.

Now Isaac Shur stripped again, and standing in the kitchen washed himself all over, shaved with cold water, regretted for an instant not buying one of those handsomely packaged bottles of after-shave, then dressed again, this time putting on his spare shirt, fresh underwear and socks. He rinsed out the glass the woman had used, poured himself a good measure· of whisky, selected and trimmed a Ramon Allones, and stepped out into the garden.

138

Isaac Shur stood with his drink and cigar and gazed along the valley. He felt awake and alert, refreshed by his sleep, his wash and shave, but not as he felt in the mornings. This was a different kind of wakefulness. Or was it wakefulness at all? Isaac Shur thought of the poem he was writing, and at once his brain felt tired, sluggish, annoyed to be forced to think of that. Then of what? Isaac Shur saw, on the rubbish dump, The Hot Shot Kid, the one with the shaved head, another one of them too. He took a step back, quickly, not to be seen. There was a concrete bench under a tree. Isaac Shur sat down.

George Matthews had said that what Isaac Shur needed was a Spanish girl. Spanish girls, he had said, were the best. No complications. No involvement. They knew what was what. He had even picked one out for him, a small frizzy-haired girl with large dark eyes who worked in one of the tourist shops on the Avenue Louis Pasteur. 'Don't be silly,' Isaac Shur had said. 'What are you talking about, "don't be silly"?' George Matthews had said. 'There's nothin' to it. You just go in, give her somethin', I don't know, a bottle of perfume, somethin' like that, then, well, you ask her to come for a walk. Tell her you've got your own apartment, that'll do it.' 'I couldn't do that,' Isaac Shur had said. 'Anyhow, I don't know enough Spanish.' George Matthews had laughed. 'Listen, you don't have to *talk*, for God's sake,' he had said. 'Look, you just rub these fingers together – like this.' George Matthews rubbed his index fingers, two naked bodies, side by side. 'Says the whole thing.'

Isaac Shur wrote once a fortnight to a girl in Australia. They had gone out together for nearly two years, a blonde girl named Ann, an interior decorator, and Isaac Shur knew that all he had to say was 'Come' and she would be in Tangier in a week. He had sent her, from London, a pair of Victorian jet pendant earrings, and she had had herself photographed with them on, three small photographs, pasted on a card, a triptych, two in earnest profile, smiling in the one in the middle. Isaac Shur kept this in his wallet, and each fortnight, before writing to her, he would look at it, at the three faces. Isaac Shur told her, in his letters, what he was doing, what he was seeing, what he was writing, he said how much he missed her, he signed his letters 'love', and as he wrote, what he felt was certainly true, but afterwards, reading his letters over before posting them, he saw how careful they were. They were not his voice; not the voice he employed in his speech or his poems.

Isaac Shur watched his garden filling gently with night. When he stood to refresh his drink, he saw that the valley had almost disappeared. Faint lights in the villages were the only sign of its existence. His apartment, when he went inside, echoed with emptiness, the sound of his shoes enormous on the hard, tiled floor. Isaac Shur poured himself another drink. He threw away his cigar and immediately lit a cigarette. He stood in the centre of the room and looked at the unmade bed, his two small canvas bags, his things on the table, the empty chair. It was still early, not yet seven o'clock. George Matthews didn't expect him till nine. He debated an hour at the Café de Paris with *The Times*, or maybe a stroll down to the Socco Chico, see who was there, a cup of coffee, a cigarette. He remembered he would have to get a bottle of wine. He would get that at the shop down the hill. Gibraltar tomorrow, he remembered. A breeze stirred the trees outside in the garden. Isaac Shur crushed out his cigarette. He felt, suddenly, impatient. He put down his glass of whisky, crossed quickly to the windows and closed them, stepped outside and locked the door. He would buy that bottle of after-shave, he decided, as he unlocked his garden gate, in that shop on the Avenue Louis Pasteur, the shop where the Spanish girl with the frizzy hair and the large dark eyes worked. Yes. He would do that now.

Isaac Shur walked home from his evening with George Matthews. It was after one o'clock, the sky blown full with moon. On the Avenue Louis Pasteur he passed the shop where the Spanish girl worked, where he hadn't gone in, but his thoughts were not on that. Two Moroccans walked hand in hand on the other side of the street. A woman stepped out of a doorway just ahead of him. Isaac Shur, walking past, saw for an instant her eyes above her black veil, the white flash of a naked ankle. Then he was past, walking quickly but not outwardly hurrying, the street empty ahead.

They had played Monopoly, as they always did, five fast games, the board set up and ready when Isaac Shur knocked on the door. They had played during dinner, and then afterwards, game after game, sitting in that curious windowless room in the centre of George Matthews' apartment, a large photograph of Humphrey Bogart hung crookedly on one wall, Beethoven's Fifth booming on George Matthews' record player. He had brought the record player with him from New York. He was never going back there again. He was through, he said, with all that hassling.

George Matthews, as always, had won every game. After the fifth game he had suggested they switch to Scrabble, or chess, but Isaac Shur had said no, he was tired, he wanted to get up early, he had to work in the morning. 'Anyhow, you're tired too,' Isaac Shur had said. 'You're nearly asleep.'

George Matthews had been smoking kif all evening. His eyelids drooped. The smell of his many pipes was sweet in

141

the air. Isaac Shur had never smoked kif, and whenever George Matthews asked him why, as he had again this evening, Isaac Shur laughed, smiled, sipped his wine. 'I haven't got anything against it,' he had said again tonight. 'I just don't need it, that's all. I'm relaxed enough. Come on, it's your go.' There was something childish about George Matthews, Isaac Shur had always felt, something lacking, some essential quality, but exactly what it was Isaac Shur couldn't pin down. But did it matter? Isaac Shur accepted him as he was, accepted the endless games of Monopoly, the endless sitting. He liked him. He was glad that George Matthews was here in Tangier.

A café was still open on the corner where Isaac Shur turned up to ascend the hill to his apartment. Isaac Shur saw Moroccans in drab brown jellabas slumped at the tables, felt them looking at him as he approached, his footsteps ringing loud in the night, and his impulse was to cross the road, but he didn't. Instead, he inspected them coldly as he walked past, his eyes moving from one face to the next, pleased to see each one looking down, looking away, turning from his hard gaze. No one spoke. Isaac Shur began the walk up the hill.

He passed the shop where he bought his breakfast every morning, the shop closed now, but a wan light dimly visible inside, oily and feeble through the dirty window. Isaac Shur felt in his pocket for his keys. He was almost upon her before he saw she was there, the same woman he had seen this morning, sitting exactly as she had sat then, as though she hadn't moved all day, and the baby too, sitting against a wall shadowed by the moon like a pile of dirty clothing thrown there on the broken pavement. Isaac Shur made to step around her, automatically, that reflex action he had done in this city so many times, but she moved, her hand reached out, and when Isaac Shur took another step, quickly, away from her, out onto the road, she came after him, he felt her fingers on the fabric of his jeans. Isaac Shur jumped as though he had been struck. 'Oh, go away,' he said, 'go away!' The sound of his own voice startled him. He hadn't meant to speak, to cry out. He heard his voice as though it had come from someone else, heard the sound of it, the tone. Isaac Shur panicked. He began to run, the key to his iron garden gate already out, gripped hard in his tight hand.

At two in the morning Isaac Shur awoke to hear a sound in his garden, a sound of scraping and chipping, a sound of masonry. He lay dead quiet, too terrified to move, his hands frozen by his sides, his heart thundering high in his throat. He listened, but he didn't have to listen. Isaac Shur knew at once what the sound was, without a second's doubt. Someone was taking away his wall.

Isaac Shur didn't move. He heard the grey concrete blocks being lifted away, one by one. He couldn't move. His fear was enormous. He lay, his heart hammering, naked in the dark. He thought of the oil lamp by the side of the bed, but he knew that to light it was for him, now, impossible. He couldn't move his fingers. He couldn't raise his hands. The room was as black with his eyes open as it was with them closed. Another block, and another. He listened, terrified, to the mortar being chipped away. And then he felt something else, inside him, beside the fear, a first prickle, and then stronger. He began to breathe hard through his mouth, his anger growing, his outrage, growing and growing, pushing aside the fear. He sat up. He stood up. When he opened his door the moon felt inside at his feet like a page of paper.

An old Arab sat cross-legged on the rubbish dump beyond the wall, scraping broken bricks with a knife and putting them into a burlap bag. Curled beside him lay a thin yellow dog, the colour of bad cream in the light of the moon. Isaac Shur stared at the Arab's thin hands, but the Arab's face, bent over his bricks, was to Isaac Shur in shadow, a blackness, a void.

Isaac Shur caught the four o'clock plane to Gibraltar the next afternoon, the connecting flight to London at half past eight.

MORRIS LURIE

144

the house
on lafayette street

michele nayman

I had bought a cowboy hat – a real Stetson – in Cheyenne, Wyoming, and on the bus to Denver I was able to cover my face with it and sleep.

After arriving at the Greyhound Depot on Nineteenth Street, and after collecting my suitcase, I straightened my hat and grinned. Denver! Denver, Colorado: tracing the footsteps of Jack Kerouac and Neal Cassady – larrikin angels of the Fifties, automobile fanatics in an automobile city (parking lots where landmarks should be), symbols of irresponsibility and irrepressibility. Denver! I emerged from the depot, bus-trip tired, bus-trip happy.

The guidebook suggested the Y.M.C.A. (women accepted in addition to men), so the Y.M.C.A. it was. I found a taxi, the driver of which told me it would be quicker on foot. He gave me directions and I walked along the flat, wide streets, passing anonymous office blocks in various stages of construction, aware of a preponderance of cowboy hats and boots and belts. Later I discovered that I had stumbled into town just in time for the annual National Western Stock Show. I was delighted, and thought that perhaps I might be able to pass off my Australian accent as some regional variation from an obscure part of Texas. No-one believed it for a minute.

The Y.M.C.A. did not look promising. It was already dark, and several men of undefined age and various racial backgrounds were standing or sitting on the steps in the front. I walked up the steps, trying to achieve the optimum combination of aloofness and friendliness: I wanted no trouble. One of the men whistled at me; the others seemed bored.

The price of a room – payable in advance – was one dollar fifty more than the price listed in the guidebook. "Take it or leave it," said the middle-aged man with the thick glasses who sat behind the desk. His hands were stained with nicotine, and I noticed that he had trouble writing my name even though I had slowly spelt it out for him. He gave me the key to a room on the sixth floor ("you should be safe there") and said that check-out time was 11 a.m.

There was a drunk in the corner of the lift, asleep. I pressed the button marked 6. A man got in at the second floor and ignored both me and the drunk. When I got out of the lift, I found myself facing a large expanse of window through which could be seen an uninterrupted panorama of buildings and streets. An elderly woman in a pink cardigan sat at a card-table in front of the window by the left wall. She was painstakingly piecing together a jigsaw puzzle, and the light provided by the window created an almost halolike effect around her white hair. 'But no,' I said to myself, 'that is how Kerouac would have seen it. You are not Kerouac and it is not the mid-Fifties. It is 1979, and you are Eileen Scott, and you are here to see Denver with your own eyes.'

There was a long corridor to the left which smelled of urine, vomit, and disinfectant (vomit, I thought – are there junkies here?). In the doorway of the room next to the one allotted me stood a tall man – a Puerto Rican I think – who stared at me but without interest. I wondered if maybe I should try to find a hotel. But my room was furnished and more or less clean, and I turned the lampshade around so that its faint bloodstain faced the wall.

After having a shower, I put on a delicate patterned shirt, hid the pieces of camera equipment in different places around the room (in a pillowslip, under the bed, in the bottom drawer), locked up, noticed uneasily that the Puerto Rican was still standing in his doorway, retraced my steps down the corridor,

146

found that the drunk was no longer in the lift, and entered the evening.

Josephina's is a restaurant in Larimer Square, a rehabilitated nineteenth century collection of shops. The restaurant was full, and the man at the front told me that a table would involve a ten-minute wait. I took a seat at the bar and ordered a glass of milk.

Ten minutes later my name was called ("Miss Eileen," the man said; I hadn't given my surname), and I gathered hat and handbag and was about to follow the waiter when I heard a deep voice behind me ask for a table. Partly out of kindness (because I knew there would be a wait for a table), and partly out of curiosity, I turned around and said "Are you dining alone?" The man with the denim shirt, denim jeans, and thick greying hair nodded. To which I replied "I am too; you are welcome to share my table."

We followed the waiter and sat down.

"Graeme Tyler," announced my dinner companion. "Actor extraordinaire – theatre, television, film, radio, drama, comedy, documentary, farce. I'm thirty-nine and I've lived here for ten years."

"Eileen Scott," I reciprocated. "My friends call me 'The Eel'. They say I'm slippery."

Graeme looked at me as if he expected me to say more. "Well?" he demanded when I didn't continue.

"Well what?"

"Is that all?"

"I've just completed a degree in Literature," I said. What was I meant to say – I'm not sure what I'm supposed to do now? I'm not too clear on who I am? I've come to Denver to follow Kerouac's ghost?

"What are you doing in Denver?"

"Trying to order a meal."

Graeme smiled and we ordered *paella* for two, which turned out to be an excellent choice.

There was a band playing – a four-woman band called *Sunday Ladies.* They alternated between gutsy rock and gentle folk, and the lead singer – a full-bodied woman with thick black

147

curls – sang with a strong, round voice. Graeme immersed himself in it.

"I've been to see her every night this week," he said. "Her name's Marie. I think I'm in love with her." He got up from his chair. "Excuse me," he said, and walked over to the bar. A minute or so later he returned to his seat, and the barman placed a bloody mary on the loudspeaker next to Marie. Graeme got up from his seat again. "If we move the table," he said, "we'll be able to see better." And move the table we did.

At eleven-thirty the band announced its last song, and Graeme, from the middle of the restaurant, sang along in a deep baritone, applauding vigorously when the *Sunday Ladies* had finished. The band started packing up. Graeme walked over to the platform and said to the lead singer, "I think you're terrific, can I see you sometime?"

"No," said Marie, and that was that.

Somewhat crestfallen, Graeme asked if I was interested in accompanying him back to his house to read some children's books. I said that I was.

After seating me on some cushions in his living room, Graeme took three children's books from the old mahogany bookshelf, and began to read one to me. It was a fable about a caterpillar. Graeme chuckled as he read aloud, and made me examine the illustrations – "No, look more *closely*" – so as not to miss all the funny little objects and visual surprises that ordinarily I would have missed. "A child's world is so magical," Graeme said; "actually, I'm still a child myself."

I was offered the couch for the night – "Don't worry," he said, "there are no strings attached. A few loose threads, but no strings" – but I was concerned about my camera equipment at the Y and so I asked Graeme to take me back. He did, and I didn't move into the wide-verandahed house on Lafayette Street until three days later, by which time I had become so ill I could hardly breathe.

Graeme insisted I move in so that he could "look after me." When his doctor said over the telephone that he was not prepared to take on new patients, Graeme became furious and announced that henceforth he was looking for a new doctor. He hung up and paced around the kitchen, his forehead furrowed and his eyes bulging slightly. "I've been going to that bastard for six years," he said. "I first went to see him when he was just starting up and had no patients at all. And now he won't see my *friend.*" It takes Graeme quite a while to wind down when he's angry. I was to discover this several times over the following few days.

But we did find a doctor, who gave me penicillin for a strep throat, and various other prescriptions for an ear infection and swollen glands. Having a temperature of $101°$ made me feel as though there was an invisible wall surrounding my head. Everyone and everything appeared not quite real. I started laughing a lot. Graeme gave me a pair of his pyjamas that had shrunk ("I'm not too good on laundry," he explained), and plumped me up with pillows, a hot water bottle, a portable colour T.V., a radio, and a selection of children's books.

The bedroom was an attic with a sloping ceiling and a large window facing the street. The window was part of a small alcove with ceiling levels different from the rest of the room. In the alcove was an antique drawing board ("I bought that from a sale of government furniture in El Paso twenty years ago") and a chair with a broken leg ("I don't like objects which aren't defective in some way." "People too?" I had asked). It was a fairytale room.

I stayed in bed for two days. Graeme woke me every four hours to remind me to take my assortment of pills. If he wasn't home, he would telephone from wherever he was. At night he got into bed and watched that night's ice-hockey game on T.V. He wore headphones, so I was spared the sound. I could, however, hear Graeme's odd whoops of encouragement or disapprobation at unevenly spaced intervals. After the game, Graeme read for a while then turned off the light and wrapped his arms around me after placing a chaste kiss on my forehead.

When I got over the worst of the virus, I came to realize that there were two other people living in the house. One morning I heard Graeme espousing his views on the tyranny of government interference, a topic I had heard him broach several times. There was a low murmur in reply, though I couldn't make out the words. Graeme left to tape the voice-over for a documentary film. A couple of hours later, I went downstairs to make a cup of tea, and found a cuddly bear-like man wearing a cream sweater and heavy black-rimmed glasses. He was drinking coffee and reading a newspaper.

"Hello," I said.

"Hello."

"I'm Eileen."

"Yes," said the cream sweater.

"Who are you?" I asked hesitantly.

"Tate Tyler," he replied, and resumed reading.

When Graeme got home that evening I asked him about Tate. "Is he related to you?"

"No," said Graeme. "Tyler wasn't his original name. It is now, though. He changed it by deed poll."

"Why?"

Graeme didn't answer my question directly. "Tate has been living with me for seven years. After I had been in Denver a while, I wrote Tate and said that if he wanted to leave Texas he would always have a home here."

"What does Tate do?" I asked.

"He reads a lot," Graeme said. "He introduces people to one another."

"Yes, but what does he do for money?"

"He doesn't really need much money. He lives frugally. I don't charge him any rent."

The other person in the house was Caroline Tyler, who called Graeme 'daddy'.

"Her original name wasn't Tyler either," Graeme explained, "and actually she wasn't really my daughter. But she is now."

"Did you adopt her?" I asked, wondering by this time why the questions I asked – which seemed perfectly reasonable to me before I asked them – always came out sounding silly.

"Actually, no," Graeme said, then started talking about something else.

I started feeling well enough to go out. Donning cowboy hat, I went a second time to the exhibition of livestock and agricultural machinery at the Coliseum, which probably was where I had picked up the virus. Thin teenage boys sauntered self-consciously, munching hamburgers, and wearing T-shirts printed with slogans like "If you ain't a cowboy, you ain't shit".

150

The rodeo was checked shirts, frenzied broncos, hats thrown on sawdust; and muscled cowgirls on stockhorses, manoevering obstacles and cracking whips. I clapped and whooped with everyone else and managed to push aside that tight chest-lump of anxiety that had been following me around ever since I had left Australia.

After the rodeo I started feeling healthier and more positive. I still didn't know what I'd be doing when I got home, but not knowing began to worry me less.

It was time to leave. I had stayed in Denver far longer than I had intended. But each time I said I was thinking of heading off, Graeme would say that I wasn't ready yet. And so, each day I would venture out and discover a little more – the parks, the mountains, Bill Cody's grave, the Red Rocks Amphitheatre, the town of Boulder – and come back again to the house on Lafayette Street.

One day I returned to find a large blonde woman sitting with Graeme in the kitchen.

"Hello," she said pleasantly, "you must be Eileen. I'm Janice Tyler. Thought I'd drop in to say hello."

"Are you Graeme's wife?" I asked.

"No," she said, surprised.

"His sister?" I asked, determined to get to the bottom of this.

"No."

"A cousin?" I asked faintly.

"Why no," said Janice, her face expanding into a grin.

And then something clicked. I grinned back.

The next day I packed my things and took a taxi to the Bus Depot. I bought a ticket to Albuquerque and looked forward to another two months on the road, after which there would be the trip home. Graeme and I had hugged when the taxi came and I had promised one day to return.

I felt light-hearted, and this feeling must have been obvious on my face, because a man of about twenty-seven came up to me and said "You look happy. Our bus won't be here for nearly an hour, so I thought I'd come up and introduce myself. I'm Jim Davis."

"Pleased to meet you, Jim," I replied. "My name's Eileen Tyler."

JEWS and MAORIS

Samuel Marsden (1765-1863) was a Yorkshireman and promoter of the first missionary endeavors to New Zealand. He explored New Zealand and recorded much of his conclusions. Perhaps he was cynical about social conditions in England. He migrated to Australia in 1793 and functioned both as farmer, magistrate and officiating minister of the Church of England. Marsden visited New Zealand and on Christmas Day, 1814 held the first Christian service in New Zealand. He purchased land for New Zealand's first missionary settlement. Prior to visiting New Zealand, Marsden had met certain Maoris visiting New South Wales and had been very impressed. He reached the conclusion before arriving in New Zealand that the Maori "are a noble race---vastly superior in understanding to anything you can imagine in a savage nation."

Marsden made a second visit to New Zealand in 1819 and by now concluded that the Maori had descended from one of the lost tribes of Israel. He believed that the Maori had sprung from dispersed Jews at some period and that this view could be proven from a study of Maori religious superstitions and customs. He believed that the Maori had somehow reached New Zealand via Asia. . . .

Marsden, however, was a superficial observer who only recorded what suited his theories. He declared all else was a manifestation of satanism and must not be documented, and was better lost for all time. Fortunately, many intelligent laymen, among them a Jew by the name of Pollack, took a different view. There were two main Maori streams of thought. One of these, the cult of Io, was esoteric and for very few. Most had never heard of Io. Io was a formless, shapeless, eternal deity. As Io matua, the parent, he begat all things yet he begat no being. He had no parents. No eye may behold him. The soul of life emanates from him. His name could not be pronounced lightly. No image could be made of him. He could only be worshipped outdoors and never between sunset and dawn. Early lay observers believed the Hebrew Jahweh or Jehova had contracted to Iahou or Io. Oriental scholars believed then that Ea or Ia or Aa was identified with the Hebrew Ya or Jah. The Maori pronounced Io as I-aw, Jehova as I-awa, there being no letter "V" in Maori. These pronunciations facilitated the identifications of Io and Jehova. . . .

In the 1860s an attempt was made by a nationalistic movement to set up a new state called New Canaan. The highest title of honour in that society was to be the Maori word "Tiu" meaning Jew.

The attraction to Jewish concepts probably lay in the fact that the Maori in suffering and revolt prayed to the Missionary deity and found his prayers unanswered. As a rule during the last century the Maori saw himself as the Jew, deprived of his land. This belief based on hope developed the concept that the Almighty would again return that land to him. The militancy of the Old Testament was inspirational. The archangel Gabriel appeared to Te Ua Haumene and the outcome was a substantial nationalistic revolt that ultimately failed. Other Maori intellectuals developed the thesis in the 1860s that the Maori had once followed the total law of Io, had forsaken this with pollution and corruption of Maoritanga or Maori life, with resultant tragedy and disaster.

Te Kooti Rikirangi, a great warrior, developed a new

153

theology and church in which, like Te Ua Haumene, he explained the decline of Maoridom as being the result of false beliefs which had been introduced. The Ringatu church which resulted from his ideas advocates subjection to and obedience to the will of God. Te Ua Haumene called his followers Israelites and forbade all intercourse with Gentiles. Together with Te Kooti Rikirangi he identified with Moses. Te Kooti had been exiled abroad and escaped. He saw his escape as his exodus from Egypt; his capture of a ship and his return to New Zealand as the beginning of the return to Canaan. He promised a return to Canaan to all. Te Kooti introduced his variant of Passover on July the twelfth. He laid emphasis on the Old Testament. Every Ringatu tohunga, or priest, must be able to recite by rote substantial passages of the Old Testament. The Sabbath is Saturday.

The living Ringatu faith today, like Judaism, awaits the Messiah. The last such prophet Rua Kenana (Canaan) died in 1937. He was the son of Kenana or Canaan Tumoana, who was killed while fighting for Te Kooti.

In the present century and currently, Jewish tradition and history have little direct influence in Maori involvement in Anglican (Episcopalian) Catholic and traditional non-conformist branches of Christianity. However, Ratana who founded a new religion in the 1920s, a modification of Methodism, still saw the Maori as a child of Israel, the Chosen of God. The fastest growing and most active proselytising religion among Maoris today is the Mormon Church. This church sees the Maori as the descendant of the Jew and teaches that Jared left Israel for North America about 2300 B.C., and that the Maoris descends from those American immigrants who migrated into the Pacific.

The Maoris had their own battalion in the Second World War and it was not rare for Maoris---who considered themselves as Jewish descended---to taunt Nazi prisoners who had

154

required blood transfusions, that they had been transfused with and owed their lives to Jewish blood. . . .

The Maori rapidly adopted the European system of names. Many given names were of Biblical origin. Surnames were more difficult. Sometimes a Maori would adapt the name of somebody he admired. Miscegination between Jewish visitors and Maori was not unknown. Many Maoris boast of their Jewish ancestry today. It is difficult to know how often this is a wish fulfillment, how often it is factual. Names such as Solomon, Isaacs, Nathan are common in Maoridom. There are still essentially Maori settlements called Jerusalem and Judea. There are in New Zealand in an Anglican Church in Rotorua and also in a Catholic Church at Waahi stained glass windows portraying Christ as a Maori. Pictures and Christmas cards of Christ as a Maori are not rare.

Papahurihia had a serpent Nakahi who only appeared by night and who gave messages. There is no word for snake in Maori and nakahi almost certainly derives from the Hebrew word, Nakas. All Maori nouns must end in a vowel.

Many early missionaries had a profound knowledge of Hebrew and compiled lists of semitic words with Polynesian equivalents. As the Polynesian migration was through the Malayan peninsular, it is easy to understand how many semitic words could be incorporated into Oceanic languages. This, however, is a study for the specialist.

The early missionary and educated layman and scholar were often of the opinion that the Maori had descended from one of the lost tribes of Israel or had had substantial contact with Judaism at some time in the remote past. Many aspects of Maori behavior were accepted as vestigial forms of Jewish

155

belief or behaviour. These attitudes had a profound influence on the 19th century Maori, especially in periods of nationalistic revival and rebellion. Te Ua Haumene, Te Kooti Rikirangi and others preached to their follower that the Maori were the chosen people of God, the children of Israel. This view is still encountered. However, although there are analagous practices in Judaism and Maoridom, it does not follow that these have a common origin. Marsden had preconceived ideas, as had many of his contemporaries, and they sought and found in New Zealand proof for these ideas.

*   *   *   *

MEDICAL HISTORY OF NEW ZEALAND PRIOR TO 1860

The question arises, what is a Maori? For the purpose of this paper a Maori is anyone of any degree of Maori descent who regards himself as Maori. Skin colour is of little importance. Many individuals, extremely Maori in their orientation may have so much European blood as to appear European or Pakeha, yet despite skin colour, often these people remain Maori in their orientation and are acccepted as such by other Maoris. The view of a Maori university graudate is quoted: "I believe that Maori is a language and a nationality and an orientation and a fact. We are not browned skinned Pakehas who have vague longings towards something called Maori. We are Maoris." Another advanced the view: "A Maori is first and foremost a Maori and only secondarily a human being, the laws of western psychology do not apply to the Maori."

Yet another Maori told me he had once heard a speaker at a Maori meeting declare that Maoris were the chosen of God and Maori was the language of God. The audience shuffled and looked somewhat embarrassed but nobody dared contradict the statement.

Many Maoris today take the view that the Pakeha has his world and they have theirs. All Maoris, individually and collectively have need of their own private world. They feel they have lost much of their culture, what they have left is minimal but it will remain their own. This of course, leads to the view that none but the Maori can understand the Maori. This is a view embraced by Maoris of all levels of education and social status. These attitudes, all expressed in recent years relate to the problems and feelings that go with being members of a racial minority.

There can be no doubt that Maori is merely a multi-dimensional concept with concrete and abstract facets of which language, mythology, nationality, skin colour and culture are merely definable parts. The abstract concepts are indefinable. Maori is essentially an attitude and an orientation to life. The Maori may take pride that there are certain illnesses and certain conditions basically specific to himself. He takes pride in his family loyalties, his tribal traditions and hospitalities. He takes pride in his prowess in war. He takes pride in the fact there are certain foods relished by the Maori that appear repulsive to the average Pakeha. He takes pride in many aspects of his social life which would not be acceptable to the Pakeha and he is very proud of what is known as Maori Aroha or love in the widest sense of toleration and acceptance.

Putting it another way, the Maori believes he is in some way specifically and indefinably different from the Pakeha. The Maori believes he has subtle differences which cannot be understood nor communicated to any non-Maori.

Such views are of importance in so far as they tend to lead the Maori to believe the European doctor will not be able to understand him or his problems or those diseases specific to the Maori. These views tend to perpetuate Maori cultural and mythological beliefs even though these may become modified with civilising influences.

The ancient Maori recognised death as being due to three causes:

1. Death by war or mate taua.
2. Death by decay and old age, mate tara whare or mate aitu.
3. Death due to supernatural influences known as mate atua.
The word "atua" meant a spirit, "mate" meant sickness or death.

Mate atua was of two types:
1. That in which there was no intervention by any human agency or mate atua proper.
2. That in which illness or death occurred by supernatural concepts invoked through the medium of human agency. This was known as makutu. Makutu is the personification of an ancient deity who lived in the depths of the underworld with the lizard and reptile gods.

There are many synonyms and variants of these conditions which are not germane to this paper.

Among other things, the European brought many new diseases to New Zealand. These diseases, often with high morbidity and mortality were described collectively as mate Pakeha or the diseases of the white people. As these diseases came from the European their cause was non-Maori. All Maori illness became known as mate Maori to differentiate it from mate Pakeha. Mate atua became known as mate Maori. The meaning of Maori is not clear. Some believe it to mean indigenous or native. Makutu retained its original meaning.

Today mate Maori may be used either in its true sense or as a term for all forms of witchcraft. The same applies to makutu. Today makutu is generally used as a term for all black magic and this will be the general meaning of the word makutu used in this paper unless otherwise specified. The word wheiwheia is often used. This word means enemy and may commonly be used by individuals afraid to use the term Makutu or Mate Maori. Many believe it dangerous to even speak these terms. A full classification of the many varieties and clinical types of Makutu is a function of ethnopsychiatry rather than of medical history.

Makutu and Mate Maori were the explanation of both pathological and functional illness and indeed often still are. There is no purpose in delimiting physical or psychiatric disorders; neither of these can be discussed individually. What applies to the one applies to the other. To the Maori the aetiology of both was identical.

The origin of the Maori is unknown. He probably came from Hawaiki, South East Asia, arriving in New Zealand via Melanesia or Micronesia or both. He is thought to have arrived in New

Zealand between 1200 and 1400 A.D. Maori legend has it he arrived in a number of great canoes of which the most important were Aotea, Arawa, Tainui, Takitimu, Horouta, Matatua. The canoes are important in so far as many tribes and many individuals trace their ancestry back to them and there may be both rivalry and hostility based on ancestry.

Cook, who re-discovered New Zealand, estimated the Maori population in 1769 as 100,000. Observers in the twentieth century have felt a truer estimate is between 200,000 and 400,000.

Trade with Australia commenced about 1788. Sealing and whaling commenced about 1792.

By 1850 the Maori population had fallen to something like 60,000. This was because of the numerous epidemic illnesses, venereal disease and alcoholism brought to New Zealand by the Pakeha. The Maori rationalised this racial decline was due to his gods withdrawing their protection as the Maoris abandoned their traditional way of life. By 1854 there were 32,000 white settlers in New Zealand.

As in so many other societies, the Maori had both exoteric and esoteric beliefs. When the European discovered New Zealand, the Maori had not yet left the Stone Age. Although he had not discovered the use of metals or the manufacture of pottery or bricks had not discovered the wheel, had no rational system of medicine, he had evolved a metaphysical system with a cosmogony, theogony and anthropogony on a level comparable with and in some ways as advanced as those of monotheistic religions. Most of this culture has been debased or degraded or modified through the influences of civilisation and other religions. As the Maori had no written speech, his beliefs could only be passed on by word of mouth. They could only be passed on to those considered worthy of receiving them. Missionaries mostly took the view that these Maori beliefs were manifestations of satanism and as such were best forgotten and did not record them. Maoris converted to Christianity adopted a similar view. On the other hand, those Maoris who remained staunch to their traditions and beliefs—and there were not many—naturally refused to impart their views or their beliefs to those who had left their faith.

The esotericism of the Maori was known to few. For completeness it is worth mentioning. It is believed that originally there was nothing but a vast expanse of space inhabited by Io. Io was timeless, formless, unchanging. He was the origin of all things that begat no being. Nobody could look upon him, nobody could

159

behold him. The cult of Io was essentially benevolent. He was served by a priesthood of the highest order and this priesthood had no connection whatsoever with the doing of evil or the practising of black magic.

The esoteric belief of the Maori is virtually lost. It was only ever known to the few, its metaphysical concepts being beyond the comprehension of the many. Esoteric belief was based on a supreme deity Io. This name probably has the same origin as the word Iho, umbilical cord. Io was a highly abstract concept. As he was never born he is sometimes called Io the parentless or Io— Matua—Kore. As he was also formless, no image could be made of him; he had no incarnation, nor could sacrifice be made to him.

Houses of learning, almost universities were conducted by the Priest of Io for the very select few. Such an institution was often known as Whare Wanganga. The Maori divided all knowledge into three divisions.

1. Kete aronui; all knowledge that is applicable to the public good, including human welfare and human sympathy.

2. Kete tuatea, all knowledge that is detrimental to the public good, such as black magic, death and destruction by supernatural means.

3. Kete tuauri; knowledge of ritual, tapus.

Details of the cult of Io were not recorded until the 1850s. The data was provided by Te Matorohanga.

The cult of Io was a cult of white or sympathetic magic. It had a ritual relating to birth, sickness or death. But of its associated practices nothing is known. The name Io was so sacred it could only be mentioned in the open air and never in a dwelling place by the initiates.

Io was served by a priesthood composed of individuals of the highest ancestry, intellect and ability. These were known as the Tohunga ahurewa. It is inconceivable they had no system of medical knowledge. It is debatable, however, whether this medical knowledge was available to the many.

There is much superficially, in common between the cult of Io and the Old Testament Jehovah. Both are timeless, eternal shapeless and formless. Both created yet neither beget life. The Maori made in early days little active endeavour to oppose the activities or teachings of Christian missionaries. It is likely the influence of the Priest of Io was a factor in this acceptance. The Priest of Io, of necessity was a Maori intellectual and was probably quick to see the altruistic and idealistic concepts of the newer religion.

The printed word and the newer techniques of education facilitated the spread of the newer knowledge. Most priests of Io were submerged beneath and absorbed into various branches of Christianity and perhaps believing their beliefs of yesterday were satanically inspired did not record them. The missionary held similar concepts of Maori beliefs and likewise failed to record them.

From the exoteric view point, the primal gods were Rangi the Sky Father, and Papa the Earth Mother. These embraced, lived in close contact and had some seventy children all of whom were male. The parents were in such close contact no light could penetrate between them so their children all lived in darkness, coldness and misery. Soon talk of a revolt arose amongst the children and one of them, Tane, who ultimately became god of fructification, proposed to separate the parents, to force Rangi up and let Papa lie suspended in space. The children would then have enough room to live in comfort and light between the parents. This revolt occurred and sky and earth was separated as a result. Tane came to be worshipped as a god in his own right.

That there is some connection between the cults of Io and Tane is likely. Tane, in the form of the sun gave the signal for the opening of the Whare Wananga. Tane obtained for man from Io the three baskets of knowledge previously referred to. Tane also created the first woman of clay and put into her the breath of life, then mated with her begetting the human race. The cult of Tane includes many concepts of the cult of Io but many of these concepts instead of being abstract are now concrete and personified. Basically Tane symbolises benevolence for mankind, or white or sympathetic magic.

Not all the children, however, wished to revolt and live in light. The opposition to the revolt against the cleavage of the parents was led by Whiro. Whiro has become the god personifying darkness, evil, malevolence, illness and misfortune.

There are many myths relating to the common story met in many cultures of the fight between the powers of light and darkness, good and evil. In this case one brother, Tane, personified light, one brother, Whiro, personified darkness.

After a long and difficult struggle, Tane defeated Whiro and Whiro was compelled to stay for ever in the underworld or darkness or Te Po. As Whiro Te Tipua he is responsible for all forms of human evil and disaster. He has as emissaries the Maiki Nui. These personify disease and sickness and wage a constant war

161

against all mankind. They inhabit the tai whetuki or house of death. All evil then emanates from Whiro and his servants. In the common language he was known as Whiro the thief. He lay in wait planning to steal the life 'and soul of man both individually and collectively. Whiro then was considered the origin of all evil on this earth. In the house of death in the spirit world black magic originated. As will later be seen, Whiro had his own priesthood, the Tohunga Makutu, the adept of black magic.

It has been mentioned that the seventy children of the primal gods were all males. These constructed out of earth the first woman, Hine-ahu-one. She was endowed with life, kindness, courage, industry and benevolence by Whiro's brothers. Whiro could not agree with this and he endowed Hine-ahu-one and all her issue with the sum total of mankind's evil propensities; thus the common conflict seen in many cultures between good and evil or morality and sin entered the first mortal. In this world Whiro was symbolised by the lizard, sometimes in a highly stylised form. To the Maori the lizard symbolised Whiro and death and indeed in clinical medicine it is often found a lizard still symbolises death. Should the gods decide to destroy a man or withdraw their protection, the lizard would be introduced into his body to cause illness or death. The lizard would gnaw away at the vital organs and illness or death resulted.

The lizard gods lived in the depths of the underworld. Even today morbid fear of the lizard in real life is frequently encountered and the sight of certain types of lizard is taken as an omen of impending disaster.

The seventy children of Rangi and Papa became known as second-class gods or gods in charge of individual departments such as war, agriculture, earthquakes, edible ferns and many others.

A third system of tribal gods existed. These were essentially personifications of natural phenomena interpreted on a supernatural level such as the god of rainbows Uenuku, or the god of comets Upokoroa.

Many of these gods of personification were believed to predict or to punish or to inflict disease. These gods were interpreted by a priesthood or by a human medium.

A fourth type of god also existed who was essentially a spirit or ghost of an ancestor or stranger and as such had to be respected. This type of spirit god might inhabit an individual or influence an object for better or for worse.

The third and fourth classes of gods were the powers which

162

rendered the black arts effective. The third and fourth classes of gods were those known to the bulk of the populace.

Each type of god had its own priest known as a Tohunga. A Tohunga really means an expert, a teacher, an adept, a master much the same as the term magister in other occult arts. The widespread superstition and ignorance of the Maori rendered him a ready victim to the Tohunga who wished to practice as a wizard or a shaman.

The practice of magic to be successful must be productive of results. The existence of such results must be accepted by the populace. In other words, in any community in which individuals can exercise the power of magic there must be a system of laws or rules or regulations or a defined standard of conduct and behaviour. Deviations from these standards calls forth the wrath of supernatural forces, sometimes directly, i.e. Mate Maori; sometimes indirectly through a human medium, i.e. Makutu; both resulting in unhappiness, illness or death. The powers or forces responsible for this magic or Makutu are known as mana and the exercise of mana depends upon what is known as a breach of tapu. Monographs could be written on these concepts alone.

The following statements are generally true but like all general statements they are over simplified. The gods created tapu and lacking the gods, tapu could not exist. Tapu is best and most simply considered as a series of things that are forbidden, a series of things which must not be done, a series of positive prohibitions, thou shalt nots. As these laws of tapu were imposed by the gods, any breach of these laws led to punishment by the gods. Such punishment was negative in so far as the gods purely and simply withdrew their protecting powers over the individual concerned. To the Maori this was both serious, dangerous and anxiety producing. He believed that in the world there were ever active evil forces marshalled by Whiro and these forces sought to destroy both his body and his soul and only other benevolent gods were protecting him against these. The withdrawal of the god's protective powers when tapu was broken left the Maori powerless, without any spiritual, physical or emotional defence against the ever active evil principles controlled by Whiro. This simple philosophy meant of course that offences against the gods were punished, not in the next world but in this world. Tapus pervaded the whole of Maori society, the whole of Maori culture from birth to death. Individuals, objects, material possessions, geographic areas, foods, the subjects of discussion, social and sexual customs, all had

163

tapus. Their number runs into hundreds. For instance, to eat the food or use the utensils or a blanket of a tapu person could lead to sickness and death. The shadow of a tapu chief falling on a house would ensure its destruction. Burial grounds in particular are tapu. Tapu is involved in the handling of the dead and their possessions. Substantial numbers of tapus are still observed in clinical medicine among the Maori.

Goldie(1) a nineteenth century physician wrote: "The violation of tapu includes any interference of tapu objects, persons or places and the disease inflicted by the gods for committing these breaches of tapu are always considered very serious, by some they are believed to be incurable. The patient must die."

In theory, Christianity should have dispelled the concept that a breach of tapu leaves the individual spiritually blind against the powers of evil. Clinical practice often shows this is by no means the case.

There is a common saying, "if you cannot defeat a movement, incorporate it". Certain missionaries did this and they assimilated certain Maori words into their church services and one such word was tapu. Today it means sacred or holy in the christian sense. Altars in Maori churches may be inscribed with the word "tapu". This has helped to keep the word currently both in use and in misuse. Many modern Maoris place a different meaning on the word from that inscribed on the altar.

Many pseudo-tapus have arisen and these are often accepted with the force of an old time tapu. These are based on European influences. They may include desecrating the sabbath, taking food into a churchyard or a graveyard, not emptying the pockets of money or tobacco before going into a cemetery, being irreverent in a holy place, marrying outside a particular sect of christianity against theological advice, having the Bible at a meal table or discussing Christian concepts over a meal or even permitting operative surgery.

The priests of Io were trained in a special establishment known as a Whare Wananga facing the rising sun. The priests of Whiro studied in a special establishment known as the Whare Maire facing the setting sun. The priest of Io was taught in the day time, the priest of Whiro at night time. One was the priesthood of light and life, the other the priesthood of dark and death.

Today's Tohungas receive no formal training. Most are self taught, a few are taught by other Tohungas. Many claim their powers by inheritance from the mana of their ancestors. Some believe a Tohunga can transmit mana to his successor before or at death either verbally or by special ritual.

The name Whare Wananga has been taken by at least one modern theological institution and many a Maori has said to me somewhat cynically but with deep meaning words to the effect that, "even a new religion must flourish within the framework of the old Maori order".

Without the gods there could be no tapu, without tapu there could be no mana, without mana there could be no makutu. There is no precise nor adequate English translation for the term mana. It is something abstract, not concrete and it can not be clearly defined. Mana may be attached to gods, rangatiras or chiefs, Tohungas or adepts or other celebrated individuals. Mana may apply to possessions such as a mere or a club, it may apply to possessions such as food being consumed. It may apply to substantial or communal possessions such as land or houses or canoes. It may apply as has been mentioned to the shadow of a chief, to the footsteps of a chief, to the site where a chief has been sitting, to the fire of a chief or even a shadow of a tapu hill. It may apply to excreta and dejecta. It is often put to me this way—mana is like god but not the Christian God. It is something that no power can stop. Mana goes on for ever and ever. It can either kill or cure according to circumstances.

Words or a glance too have mana, hence the efficacy of the curse or a look. The Maori valued an object such as a fine greenstone mere or club, not because of its workmanship but because of the mana it bore, this mana being accounted for by its history, its victims in war, the nature and courage of its former owners. One can describe the many attributes of mana. Essentially then mana is a spiritual or mysterious power which is everlasting, which may be inherited or more rarely acquired. When mana is exercised there is a confident expectation that a certain event will occur. One can translate it as authority or control or influence or power or prestige or psychic force but they are all inadequate. Many Maori patients retain full concepts of mana even though they do not always know the word itself.

Europeans have been known historically and currently to suffer illness from the effects of mana.

When the question of the conflict of the Christian faith is raised with the Maori patient, answers such as the following are invariably obtained: "I may be a Christian, underneath I still believe in the powers of the Maori gods. I am a Maori. There is something in me that will not let me forget this."

165   Dr. Laurie K. Gluckman

DUNEDIN

1   FOR A FEW YEARS before the first war, my grandparents used to
take Dr Truby King's house at Karitane each summer. White
and small but of two storeys, the house held only a few of our
large party of family and friends; the rest slept in tents pitched
here and there in the garden.

The house stands on a slope, almost hidden by trees from the
narrow rock-bound promontory behind, to the east. It looks
inland from the apex of a wide flat triangular isthmus whose
sides are beaches and whose base is the hilly mainland. To the
north lies the tidal estuary of the Waikouaiti River, running out
below the promontory; on one bank of it the almost-island of the
sea beach hangs arc-wise from the bold headland of Matanaka,
which closes the view about two miles away; on the other strag-
gles the small fishing and holiday settlement of Karitane.
Northwestward, a steep rounded cone rises above the rough hill
country, Mt Watkin. At the far end of the southern beach untidy
scrubby slopes break to the sea in pale cliffs, and near them tall
stacks rear up waist-deep in swells and running waves. To the
south lies all Blueskin Bay, big Mt Cargill against the sky beyond
it, and then beach on hill-framed beach as far as Otago Harbour
and Taiaroa Head. A world of dry summer greens, cloudy blues,
dun-green, ochre, white.

A little below the house, in front, a tall white flagpole had
been planted, with a platform some feet high round its base.
There my aunts and their friends used to climb and gaze out,
laughing and singing as they dried their long hair in the sun
and wind. Against the house grew big geranium bushes; their
red-flannel flowers were the first I knew and the warm dry scent
of their leaves, sweet and healing, came as if from an open-air

166

linen-press. The garden grew poppies too, the hairy woodland buds of shirleys with their surprised wayward look of wild things never properly tamed.*

These were of the earth and light, and I felt close to them, and to the sweet briar roses I came to know a little later, as to no garden flower since. Yet my favourite flower as a child, I used to be told, was a blue daisy with yellow centre which grew on a small bush at Manono, Grandfather's garden. I cannot remember any feeling for it; it does not make one of my chosen Karitane flowers. Lavender too, I think, grew near the house, and bushes of japonica, and airy elegant columbines; these last in particular seem to belong with poppy and geranium to the very beginning of my life. One morning early Grandfather took me to find small wild strawberries in the dew among their leaves and I tasted that sharp fresh sweetness that was the taste of the world itself, never to be forgotten. On the large white under-leaves of the rangiora bushes the girls of the family used to write letters or messages.

Outside the garden, beyond the pines and macrocarpas which sheltered the south side of the house, the road coming up from the flat passed an old cottage or two and ended in fields. In one of the cottages lived a big old Maori woman, Mrs Harper. In the whaling days, it was said, she used to carry sailors ashore from their boats; we got our milk from her. The promontory grew hilly, all rough grass, broken yellow clay, wild rocky coves, and points and bluffs beaten and shattered by the sea; a little way off-shore, other broken pinnacles of rock stood up out of the waves. A line of Maori earthworks showed plain in the grass; the promontory had been a pa fortified against attack from landward.

On the south beach, walking, gazing over Blueskin Bay towards the Otago heads, we found small rounded shells like shallow bowls with one delicate lip, coral pink or sometimes dark grey, which we called devils' toe-nails; and the more open flatter fan-shells, scalloped, with a wing rather than lip, of a darkish dull purple shade but pale in the grooves. It was often warmer for bathing in the river, but no waves fell there and the tides did not wash its beach so well; seaweed and driftwood might lie longer on its dried roughened sand.

*See poem 'Karitane', No. 2 in 'Otago Landscapes', in *Disputed Ground*.

I was the first grandchild in the family, and at first the only child in those holiday parties; my sister Lel* followed in a little over two years. I know from my mother's sisters and cousins and their friends that everyone played with me, petted me, no doubt spoiled me, but I think I belonged especially to my grandfather, Grandfather (it was a proper name to me, never a mere title), as the first-born of my generation, a man-child, the promise of the family. It is my grandparents and aunts and uncle I remember at Karitane, not my parents, although it may have been my father who carried me up the outside staircase one rainy night to bed, wrapped in a rug, away from the bright fire leaping in the small living-room below, as the raindrops fell cool on my face. It is the young men of the party I remember roasting potatoes in the ashes of an outside fire near the tents beneath the pine-trees, and giving me potatoes to eat, sweet, dry and smoky under their blackened skins; my uncle Harold, and cousin Ben, and the tall red-headed high-spirited Tommy who later married my aunt Kate.

Bathing and playing on the beach, romping in hay and riding to picnics with horse and cart, getting up and going to bed, we were surrounded by the gaiety and affection of three active families, young and intelligent and still in those years almost care-free. Grandfather, Mother's father, Willi Fels, was just over fifty at my birth, and Grandmother four years younger. Mother was the eldest of her family, then came Emily, Kate and Harold. The eldest of their four first cousins, Mary, Dora, Bendix and Esmond de Beer, was some fifteen months older than Harold; Esmond had already been sent to school near London and I did not know him until years later. The four Todds, neighbours and inseparable friends of the other two families, were of almost the same age: Elespie, Bruce, Roland and Ione. Of all twelve, only Mother had yet married, in 1908, six years before any of the others.

My first memories are of a world formed by them, which was made mine as I knew it so closely knit in the small house at Karitane, under my grandparents' care.

*Lesley Brasch (1911–39)

168

In Dunedin the three families, four counting my parents, lived close together in London Street, which climbs the hill obliquely in three sharp spurts from Knox Church to the Boys' High School. You could climb two-thirds of the hill in their four gardens, needing to make only three short crossings of the street to get from one to the next. I could spend my life, it seemed, in those houses and gardens, scarcely running the gauntlet of the world outside.

Lowest down, on the steep rise from Heriot Row to Royal Terrace, lived the de Beers; Aunt Emily, my great-aunt, was Grandmother's next younger sister, her husband Uncle Isidore a first cousin of my father's mother. Their garden went from London Street up to Royal Terrace, cutting off two gardens at the corner where those streets met and taking in a deep gully of bush and ferns with a stream at the bottom from which they got fresh drinking water. From London Street you entered by a short drive and a path off it leading round to the front of the house. I see that drive, shaded I think by macrocarpas where the path left it, as the setting for the opening scene of *King Lear*, but I do not know why.

Directly across London Street from the drive opened the small wooden lower gate of Manono, Grandfather's garden, which higher up on the next terrace of the hill took in the corner of London Street and Victoria Street (now Haddon Place). On the upper corner of those two streets stood the Todds' house. It had been built in the early eighteen-seventies by my great-grandparents Bendix and Mary Hallenstein when they moved from Queenstown to Dunedin; there Grandmother and her sisters lived until they married. Kate remembered that she and Harold and the de Beer children, and probably Emily and Mother too, used to dine every Sunday with their grandparents. Bendix Hallenstein, a genial man whom everyone liked, was very sweet-natured still. He would put a little cream in his glass of red wine, and laugh. While he was alive, my grandparents, Aunt Emily and Uncle Isidore and Mary de Beer with them, used to go to synagogue on feast days; after his death in 1905, all ceased going. His house remained empty then for two or three years, for Great-grandmother went to live with my grandparents, until the Todds bought it. From their upper gate in London Street

169

you could dart in no time up and across the rather stony road to my parents' garden.

This from below looked like a high steep wood inside a small hawthorn hedge; the white house could just be seen above, through the trees. They grew thickly on the banks above the street, sycamore, broadleaf, cherry, ash, ngaio, elm, rowan, alder, southern-beech, and higher up near the house a huge welling-tonia. A narrow drive wound steeply up through them to the level ground of another terrace on which the house stood, between a lawn to the north enclosed by holly and hawthorn hedges, and a roughly triangular rose-garden to the south. Over the garden trees, which were growing steadily and cutting off the view, the house looked down to the harbour in front and across it to Otago Peninsula, and to the right over South Dunedin and out to sea.

Our house, Bankton, had belonged to the first minister of the Otago settlement of 1848, Thomas Burns, a nephew of Robert Burns; he lived there after retiring from his ministry in 1877, but I do not know whether he built it. Later it belonged to Sir Robert Stout before he moved permanently to Wellington and became Chief Justice; later still, to cousins of ours from whom my parents bought it. It was a plain two-storied house of some dignity, brick faced with stone under a grey slate roof.

This was my parents' third house. I was born higher up the hill, in a house in Tweed Street, Littlebourne, which belonged years afterwards to our friends the Skinners and was called Rustat. My earliest memory, if it is properly memory, is of crawling on one of the wide shady balconies of that house, and gazing up at the adults, my mother and a friend, who were standing watching me. They wore light-coloured dresses with long skirts; I think it was summer; from there too you looked out over houses and gardens to the harbour and the peninsula. My parents moved to Bankton before my sister was born.

2 WHEN I WAS about two-and-a-half, a young Miss Darling came to take charge of me in the afternoons. She was one of a small group of girls who once a week read advanced literature with

170

Miss Ross, the principal of Columba College, a Presbyterian girls' school; she was doing kindergarten work (in which she made a great name for herself later), and partly on that account Miss Ross recommended her highly. Wearing a blue poplin suit I met her at the foot of the staircase, put out my hand and said 'Good arternoon, Miss Darling'. She was fair-haired, wide-blue-eyed and ardent, and she fell in love with Mother and with me at once and for good. She continued to think Mother one of the most lovable women she had ever met and me without exception the loveliest child. I think I owe to her something of whatever ardour I am capable of feeling, and my admiration of ardour in other people, in the young and in those whom ardour keeps young.

In her winter holidays in 1914 she took me to Middlemarch, because its high dry air was expected to benefit my weak chest. We stayed with two quiet kindly Miss Dawsons and walked morning and afternoon in the clear cold sunlight. One of our walks took us across the Taieri river, where the fields ended and hilly tussock grazing began, towards a rounded hillock of cropped green, strange sight in that unfettered landscape; in England it might have been a very large prehistoric burial mound. I used to think of it afterwards, from Dunedin, as the 'green hill far away, without a city wall', when I came to know the hymn, but it can have had no such association for me at the time. The picturesque phrase was what struck me, however, and I did not place the Crucifixion there as I was to place other historical or imaginative events in other familiar scenes. Each morning, hard frost scrolled the windows with white arabesques of waving plumed foliage, fantastic flowers and stars; ice formed on the water in our large bedroom jug. I used to whisper to the dog next door 'Taieri be quiet, you'll wake Miss Darling.' The hard stone road outside ran straight towards the wall of the Rock and Pillar range, near above. Eastward, far beyond the Taieri, pale broken hills scarred with black rock rose steadily to the horizon, and somewhere mysteriously on the far side of them, Miss Darling told me, Dunedin lay, so near in thought, so far to reach; road and railway took long miles and hours winding there. It was my first remembered lesson in the strangeness of space and distance.

171

Middlemarch was doing me so much good that shortly before Miss Darling was due to take me home, at the end of her holiday, Mother wrote to say that her friend Agnes Hill-Jack would be coming to look after me there for an extra fortnight. Miss Darling was worried by this. Something kept telling her that she had to take me home. She was so worried that at last she walked to the railway station, some way off, to ring up Bankton; my father, who answered, thought it very peculiar when she said she *must* take me home with her, but she was so urgent that he agreed. The two or three remaining days were a misery to her. She thought that my father would change his mind, and send Miss Hill-Jack the day before we were to leave, but to her great relief this did not happen. He met us at Dunedin station, delighted at my appearance but not at all pleased with Miss Darling. She went home and at once rang up Mother, who was also delighted to see me looking so well and asked her to come not the next day but the following one, for lunch. When Miss Darling returned from kindergarten next day, she found a message to ring my father as soon as possible. He told her that Mother had died suddenly during the night. It was then that Miss Darling knew why she had had to bring me home: if she had not, Mother and I would not have seen each other again.

Mother was expecting a third child. During the night Lel cried, Mother reached out to pull Lel's cot towards her bed, and in doing so brought on a haemorrhage. There are two versions of what followed. One is that my father telephoned the doctor, who failed to come until too late. The other is that the telephone was out of order, so that my father had to walk all the way to Maori Hill in the dark cold of that midwinter night to find doctor or nurse, our staunch downright Scottish cook Jessie staying with Mother while he was away. She died within a few hours. She was not yet thirty-two. The Felses and de Beers, all except Harold and Ben, were in Europe. War broke out six weeks later.

I remember very little of my mother. I cannot hear her voice, but I can hear my father's calling her one evening to dinner as I lay in bed not yet asleep, and the sheer happiness in it that seemed to belong to them both as he called the German syllables of her name so clearly, 'He-*le*-ne!', raising his voice and stressing the second syllable and dropping his voice again on the third. They loved each other almost as soon as they first met, and he adored her.

Mother was small but active and strong, with long black hair thick and waving and parted in the middle, deep blue very bright eyes and dark lashes, pale skin without colour. She was much loved and admired and thought very beautiful; everywhere people used to notice her, my aunts have told me; before she was eighteen the handsome Sikh police in the streets of Hong Kong would turn to stare as she passed. She was also unusually tender as well as happy, even among her affectionate warm-hearted family; she felt deeply and her face was always thoughtful. She lavished her tenderness on her children, I have been told, but all memory of it has gone from me. She played good hockey and was captain of her team, played tennis and golf, walked and rode. When she reached Doubtful Sound with her parents and her sister Emily, old Mr Murrell of Manapouri, who led the party over the rough new track from the lake, gave her name to the big waterfall near the hut, which she was the first woman to see – she was then eighteen. On the maps, the name has been anglicized to 'Helena'.

Two sets of photographs of 1913 and 1914 of Mother, Lel and me show Mother usually grave, almost troubled, even when half smiling. In one set she is standing on the gravel between house and lawn, the holly hedge and garden roller behind in the shade of the wellingtonia. We pose in front of her, Lel small and plump in a white dress showing frilly petticoats, I dressed for a party in black and white pirate costume, black skull-cap, gold ear-ring, skull and cross-bones printed or embroidered on my chest, wide sash. Mother wears a simple dark dress falling to the ground with a row of large flat buttons of the same material down the middle and a narrow black belt at the waist; her sleeves come just below the elbow; two white wings of collar lying broad on the shoulders meet at her throat under a large brooch of enamel and silver. She stands upright, arms hanging at her side, looking down a little at nothing or half smiling at the photographer, detached. So still, so grave with inward serenity, she looks a Greek statue returned to life.

Her death was the first blow to shatter the family. It also, I see looking back, ended my childhood proper, shortly before my fifth birthday. I remember walking with my father and Lel into the side garden, and on the winding paths among the rose-beds. It must have been very soon after she died, when the business of death was clearly over, yet before we tried to begin normal life again. I do not recall that any of us spoke or showed emotion, but my father's silence was heavy as he steered us along the paths, between the low box borders.

3 A FRAGMENT OF very early puzzling over the nature of things has always remained with me. I was lying in bed at night wondering how everything began, trying to go back and back to the origin of existence. Earth, the sun, the stars, the universe itself, God who made it. Was He outside the universe? Then it was not everything, not universal. And if it was not, what existed outside it? Only God? Where and how then did He exist? And did He create Himself? How could He do so? But if that was impossible, either He had always existed, or someone else, something else, had created Him. At that *always*, or that *other*, my mind grew dizzy and was baffled, it drew back, to venture out on the same inquiry another day. I do not think I ever got farther than those vast shadows, or was able to penetrate that beginninglessness. And if existence had no beginning, if it always was and is, how should it come to an end? Must it not continue for ever?

My mother's life on earth had come to an end, she had disappeared, and for ever, as I understood. Was there a time, earlier, when she had not been? Or a time when I had not been? I could not remember or imagine such times. I had a strong sense that everything I knew, and everything that existed now, had always existed, and because it existed must exist always in the future. My mother's death did not necessarily contradict this. It made existence more complex, however, added a dimension to it, and suggested that one should not judge too readily by appearances. That sense of the beginninglessness of things, of their permanence whether they are present or not, and although I cannot tell how they persist, remains with me still.

I do not know whether I dreamed much as a child. Dreams of

houses catching fire and burning frightened me again and again, and I can recall snatches of other dreams, but only one is still with me, because I described it at least once when I was growing up. This was a recurrent dream about a Lady Engine.* I was walking up Royal Terrace with Miss Darling. As we turned the corner into Cobden Street, the Lady Engine steamed slowly from among the houses and gardens on the shady side of the street, passed across it, and disappeared behind the hawthorn hedge that enclosed the garden of the Tower House – the old wooden house with the tower room on top, part of St Hilda's School. We stood quite near, waiting to cross the line. The Lady Engine seemed to turn, as she slowly passed, and looked down at me – to her, clearly, I was alone. It was a kindly look; not because of any smile or movement of the lips, or any tenderness in the eyes, but because she, the Lady Engine, knew I was there and gazed calmly down at me as she passed. Waiting before she came, I had been frightened, my heart beat unnaturally, my head grew tight; but now I had no fear. I stood and watched her, not moving, simply there.

I cannot tell what she was like. Being an engine she was of course dark – blue-black and shiny; and being a lady she must have had eyes and a mouth and hair, but I do not remember them. The loud hissing steam and the muscular pistons that I feared before she came into sight did not frighten me once she was actually there. I did not notice them. So she turned to me – with no movement of the neck and shoulders or inclining of the body – and slowly passed, looking, and was straight again as she disappeared. Her grave expressionless look as she passed by said plainly that she would return, and that I would be there again waiting for her, in fear before and after but impassive in her presence. Not, of course, that this had been her first coming. There was no first. I had always known her.

4 FROM THE TIME my mother died until I left school the real centre of my life was Manono, Grandfather's house. So long as he lived it remained the foundation of my life.

*See poem 'Lady Engine' in *Not Far Off*

In my childhood the family – the world almost – seemed to begin with Grandfather; before him there were only the shadowy figures of my great-grandparents Bendix and Mary Hallenstein, whom our elders again and again mentioned in passing but did not need to talk about. Lel and I continued to live at home, but we must have spent part of nearly every day at Manono and we went often to stay with our grandparents or with the de Beers. Warmth of affection, gaiety and activity, charm, interest, all abounded in their houses. Bankton by contrast was shadowed by our loss. My father, I think, tried his best to be both mother and father to us; a task beyond any man probably, and to him both temperamentally and as a rising lawyer professionally and socially ambitious, beyond his power to keep up for very long; that he kept it up until about the time he sent me to boarding school, more than eight years later, seems remarkable enough.

We stayed with the de Beers not long after Mother's death, at a time when our heads had to be shaved because of some scalp trouble; to make us presentable we wore large white close-fitting cotton caps. One broken half of an aluminium comb that I was given then and continued to use for the best part of half a century served to remind me of the occasion. From then on, if not from earlier still, Mary and Dora de Beer were as close to me almost as my two aunts, and their mother seemed another grandmother. We were as much at home in their house as at Manono. From quite early I recall the rich full-bodied smell of Uncle Isidore's cigars and how it lingered in the heavy smoke-blue velvet or brocade curtains, the red morocco slippers and silk dressing-gown he wore when smoking and talking to us after breakfast, and the fur monkey he would put on like a glove and make wag its head and grimace; his low slow thickish voice seemed another form of the smoke of his Havanas. A stout slow-moving good-humoured indolent hospitable great-uncle, he indulged his taste for good food and cigars and loved company whether of adults or children.

At Manono the years seem to run together, so that I can distinguish only a few landmarks until much later. There was constant coming and going of relatives, friends and visitors in the comfortable large house, where everyone gathered in the sitting-room and in summer on the two verandas. Both my aunts married and left Dunedin, Kate the younger first. While her family were in London she and Tommy Thompson, by now a doctor, were married at St George's, Hanover Square, by the Rev. H. Parata of a Maori family from Dunedin. It was soon after Mother's death, July 1914; for their honeymoon they went to Hanover to see Grandfather's mother, and got back to London before the war broke out. Tommy was soon in the army, and Kate followed her family back to Dunedin. Emily was married in Sydney eighteen months after her to Arthur Forsyth, an Australian engineer who had been working in Dunedin; they settled in Sydney.

I remember Uncle Harold returning home for his final leave and going off to the war; he and Bruce Todd joined the New Zealand forces, while Bendix de Beer and Roland Todd chose to go to England and join the British army in order to remain privates; they had had so much artillery training in the territorials that in the New Zealand army they would have had to become officers, like Bruce. Bendix and Harold were killed in France, Bendix in July 1917 and Harold in October of the same year. The shadow of their deaths must have fallen on me too at the time, but has left no trace I can find. Nearly every young man whom Mary and Dora used to dance with in Dunedin was killed too.

Before peace returned Grandmother died, of cancer, during the influenza epidemic at the end of 1918. Never strong, she was ailing for what must have been a long time before her last illness. I used to stand beside her as she lay back in a deck chair on the front veranda, looking down the green lawns and through the trees, and stroking her forehead to relieve the neuralgia she suffered from. A parasol would be propped up to shade her eyes, of unbleached natural colour on top and cool moss-green underneath; on her hat of fine straw was a tussore silk veil of the same cool green. She wore, in summer, light soft dresses in keeping with her gentleness and sweet nature, light hats with a black ribbon, and I think almost no ornament except a brooch. Even at the end of her life, in her middle fifties, no grey touched her soft light-brown hair; none of us inherited her fine hazel eyes.

My father used to tell me later, in what I thought a brutal manner, that Grandmother need not have died, but starved herself because of some fad or other. Her very small appetite was the extent of her starvation, and the 'fad' described her interest in Indian philosophies and religions. She and Aunt Emily, her sister, who did everything together, had become interested in comparative religion. Their father, Bendix Hallenstein, who kept up a few Jewish observances all his life, had his four daughters given the usual instruction of Jewish girls. Yet their mother was born and remained an Anglican. The girls grew up familiar with the two creeds and observances; and following their own bent and some of the intellectual interests of the time, Grandmother and Aunt Emily came to things Japanese, Chinese, Indian, to Max Müller and Madame Blavatsky and Mrs Besant. With a few Dunedin friends, they taught themselves Sanskrit in order to read the Upanishads and other sacred writings.

Grandmother's interest became centred in theosophy; she used to have strange visiting theosophists to stay, to Grandfather's scorn, and Kate thought some of them probably took her in. Theosophical teaching induced her not to eat meat and other foods, which may possibly have affected her health. I was devoted to Grandmother, drawn by her love and by what I felt to be her goodness and unworldliness, and perhaps feeling her sympathy for my dawning interests; there were books everywhere, all over the house, for she was not methodical like Grandfather. She loved poetry and the arts, read Tennyson and Browning, Yeats, Lionel Johnson, Æ, James Stephens, Tagore, whose books she bought. There were regular Dante evenings at Manono and evenings for Browning and Whitman.

Grandmother was strongly drawn to St Francis, and visiting Assisi once happened to meet the author of a well-known life of the saint, Paul Sabatier, with whom later she had some correspondence. She and Grandfather and my aunts came to know well the setting, the history, the legend, the works of art; a print of Giotto's St Francis preaching to the birds hung in her bedroom, and I grew up seeing the pictures and hearing and reading the stories. Grandmother read and re-read the *Imitation of Christ*, the *Spiritual Exercises* of St Teresa, Molinos's *Spiritual Guide*, William Law's translation of Boehme, St Peter Alcantara's *Pax Animae*, and other such books. Most of her copies were published by or came from the shop of John M. Watkins in Cecil Court,

Charing Cross Road, who specialized in religious, mystical and oriental literature. He had belonged to a London circle which Yeats frequented for a time; I remember him in bent old age as a small, gentle, kindly man peering through thick glasses; he spoke to me warmly of Aunt Emily and Grandmother, whom he had known, then, for thirty years or more.

I fancy Grandmother was more reflective and less inquiring intellectually than Aunt Emily, whose interests leaned towards history; but they shared interests and books and talked of their reading. Both belonged to the Theosophical Society in Dunedin. Grandmother took me or sent me to its Sunday school in Dowling Street for a time. My father must have protested but submitted, thinking it could not do much harm. This was the only formal religious instruction I had as a child and it left no impression on me that I can discern, so he may have been right. The teacher was a Miss Porteous; when I think of her I see curling silver hair, pearls, gauzy veils and dresses, large teeth in a wide mouth, large soulful eyes with lashes widely spaced, and enter again a general mist of sentiment and intensity woven round esoteric doctrines of a colourful, implausible, flimsy, flummery sort, Orders and Aeons and Incarnations; but this impression clearly comes from much later.

I think it was at Easter 1918 that Lel and I stayed with Grandmother at Karitane, not at the Truby Kings' but in the Joachims' cottage beside the river beach. Among the garden flowers at evening I looked for fairies and half believed I saw one. Having heard people speak of them and reading about them in books I was eager to find some and prove what already I felt certain of, that they might exist; Grandmother's attitude I am sure was not disbelieving.

It was my Aunt Kate whom I first remember reading the Bible to me, by lamplight, when I had gone to bed in Uncle Harold's small room at Manono. She was reading the twenty-third psalm, her voice warm with the poetry of it, its pellucid devotion made to glow for me by her charm and fresh gaiety and affection. What it said was both mysterious and reassuring; God was present in the world and yet no less God the creator of the world. The little of the Bible that I knew, and my very hazy notions of religion, which no one told me about while I was

179

always hearing it spoken of in passing, were for years after associated with my passionate devotion to my aunts and their love for me, and with my first images of Biblical figures, formed at Manono from coloured photographs of Michelangelo's prophets in the Sistine Chapel, the angels of Melozzo da Forli and Fra Angelico, and a Madonna and Child with Angels of Botticelli, perhaps mixed up with that of the great Buddha of Kamakura which Grandmother had brought back from Japan in 1900.

It can have been only very gradually that I began to distinguish the assurance which my loving and lovely aunts provided from that given by the twenty-third psalm and other passages of the Bible and a general, quite unformulated sense of the power of God at work in the order of things, although not of his presence. What I knew of Christianity came from the scraps I picked up, and of Judaism I knew nothing at all; no one in our family circle went either to church or to synagogue. I doubt if I knew the difference between the Old and New Testaments until I started to read them as formal subjects at school; then I learned quickly and soon topped my class; but they were taught in a dully mechanical way without insight or feeling. My father had composed a plain short prayer for us to say every night when we had got into bed, and somebody had always to hear us repeat it. Its tone and sentiments were moral rather than religious, although I did not see this until long afterwards; its God was a bare abstract righteousness who bore no resemblance whatever to the good shepherd of the twenty-third psalm.

Gertie and Kitty Geisow came from Queenstown for their Dunedin season; two aged countrywomen as I saw them now, in whose slow quiet kindly voices, patient and humorous, I heard half my own past, and knew again the rock and tussock, the gums and pines and matagouri, the shining pebbles of the lake shore and Queenstown's old limestone schist houses – all Wakatipu almost except the lake water. They loved to talk of the past and especially of our family; they recalled my great-grandparents, dead forty years earlier, as old familiar respected friends who might be living still – 'Mr and Mrs Hallenstein'. Since I had not known them, I thought of them rather as familiar historical characters, Bendix Hallenstein and Mary Mountain.

180

They were much in all our minds, I think; so many places and episodes, so many objects round us at Manono, brought them back to us. As I heard them spoken of and thought of their lives they came to seem almost figures out of mythology, the ancient founders of a line, Abraham and Sarah, or Pelops and Hippodameia.

And yet many people now living still remembered them. In them English and German married, and Jewish and Christian were fused; a marriage of two strong characters that seems to have been notably good and happy. In Bendix and Mary the piety of their time was strong; they were close to the hazards and chances of life in a young country subject to flood, fire, earthquake, hold-ups, bankruptcies, shortages of goods and even food, dangerously dependent on communications by sea with the rest of New Zealand, with Australia and England, at a time when shipwreck was common. The Mountains had been a conventionally pious family of the provincial middle class; this is clearer from her sister's letters than from Mary's, because energy and enterprise took Mary far from her origins, but she too betrays the anxiety and the piety that seemed to belong together. When she and Bendix were leaving England for Australia after their marriage she writes to Tom, 'if we are spared to make the voyage in safety'; and a few years later, telling him of their mother's death, 'Goodbye my dear Tom, may we all meet our dear Parents in heaven is the daily prayer of your loving Sister.' Bendix is more regular in expressions of piety; phrases such as 'I hope this will reach you all well which thank God I can also assure you of ourselves', occur repeatedly in his letters to relatives and friends; although seeming conventional, it is clear that they were really meant.

By what long tortuous path did the Brasches and the Hallensteins come to settle in those obscure northern regions so far from their origin, centuries before, in Palestine? When did they leave Palestine? After Titus captured Jerusalem in A.D. 70, when so many Jews were sold as slaves throughout the Roman Empire? The very old Jewish community in Cologne is said to have been founded when a Roman legion with its camp-followers and slaves was transferred at that time from Jerusalem to the garrison of the Rhine. No record of all that past remains, but I try at times to imagine it; and when travelling I feel some unaccountable sense of having seen a place before, I wonder if it had sunk deeply into the eyes and mind of some ancestor whom I shall never know of.

Charles Brasch

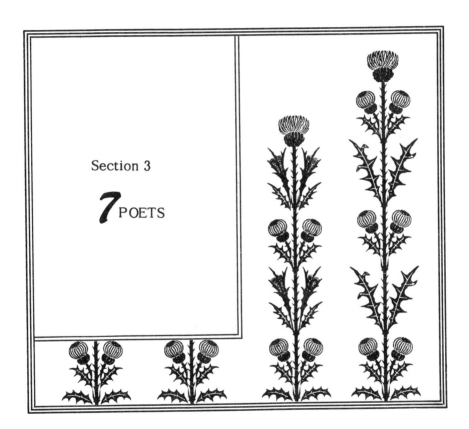

Section 3

7 POETS

CHARLES BRASCH

On Mt. Iron

Red sun, remember
The waterless hills,
Glare of light in
The water-courses.

No milk of cloud
Shall be offered you
From these dried breasts,
To your bronze heaven
No pitying tears.

Thin-skinned the mountains,
And the rocks stained
With crepuscular lichen;
No sap in the thorn,
No voice among shadows.

Red sun, remember
The earth lost in
A shudder of heat.

BY THAT SEA

Cold I lay you beside that bitter sea
Where men have laid their dead since the first flight
From Eden and its everlasting day,
In ground where young grief cast her lot;
No foreign soil to you, who have tried before
The sill of exodus, the farewell shore.

I lay you in the common grave of man
On a bed of earth and under a blanket of stones
To sleep man's sleep in quiet and be gone
With him, leaving no trace among rocks and thorns
But your seed of dust that we tread underfoot
To rebuild the falling mountains, nourish the root.

I take no leave by these waters that turn and return,
Salving grief in their monotony.
You live with me in your death as though reborn,
As if I had not learned, till you came to die,
That in our last role reversing our first one
We must play to the end father and son.

BRED IN THE BONE

I

Once I knew you and did not know
And was almost content.

I heard them speak of you, sing to you,
Praising or loudly crying, my long dead fathers.
I seemed to know you in their words
Which established you, though I could not tell how or where.
From afar off, or from within, in the cleft heart,
You plied them; they lived in your dark and day,
Not to themselves alone, nor of their own will,
Not of choice but by inheritance.
For you created them; even as men they were your children,
Raising cities and cutting down enemies,
Stumbling behind the Ark or prostrated in false groves,
Shepherd among the rocks, judge in the gateway,
Soldier and priest.

All their days you lived unseen among them,
You accompanied their journeys and perils;
At rough birth they moaned for you,
At gratuitous death cried out that you had forsaken them.
If they broke blindly from you
It was always in the knowledge that you waited, everywhere,
Even in anger never shutting up your doors;
So they were free to return in their own time,
To come and go.

And was I not free also
Who did not know you except through them,
Free to breathe of that dark and day,
To tread, without obligation, your chosen land,
To drink of your streams, hearing the songs that sought you,
Count myself of your people?

It seemed you granted me then
The freedom I took for granted,
As if I knew you, almost content.

II

Today I know and know nothing
Living as if you did not exist
Yet in my bones counting on your existence,
Present and infinitely far
Innocent of the world you touch
As it lives in your consent.

I am not of those that have your ear,
I pretend to no creed or party.
I do not know what it means to be with you,
Yet I cannot conceive a world where men did not recall you
Unwittingly, at every turn
And by taking such pains to deny,
A life in which you were not concealed
As a grain of possibility, salty leaven.

I neither believe nor disbelieve,
I expect the rising moon
And the dissolution of empires;
A tree in which the winds nest,
Knowing and knowing nothing.

III

Every land is grown strange
All lands all waters
The songs of Zion are sung on every coast.

Did you not make man to live on earth
Over the length and the breadth of it,
In green valleys among the shade trees and the balm trees
    and the orchards,
On upland pastures, and prairies endless as their winds,
By moonstone lakes suckled at the breasts of mountains
And by the familiar alien sea,
That ocean, the pulse of time, that beats its drum
Hotly against the world's wall—
Did you not say to man, Here and here shall you live,
Mixing your blood with the waters and your bones in the dust?

Tears are our songs today
Sighing and tears
The panting of the runner and the sobbing blood
The heart silence of the homeless,
Affliction that dare not look round the next bend of time
Mistrusting even the day to come;
We who ask the uses of our power
And whose the kingdom we inherit
And where the seat of wisdom.

These are the songs of Zion
Sung in every estranged land.

IV

I am dried up like a stream in summer
Without water, without breath
My life gone down under the stones, or smoke lost in air.
Will you gather me again
For your purposes that I do not know?
Command me, consume me,
That I may live as in my spring days,
But now towards you, and with your will;
Or let me go, cut off your acquiescence
That I may turn my face to the wall
Out of sunlight, and from the sound of waters.
I own myself no longer;
My heart beats without reason
A drum in an empty house.
Why am I prolonged in shame
Profiting neither you nor myself?
Make an end, or a beginning.

V

I have been ashamed, I have drunk humiliation
In my youth and in my middle years; I shall drink it again
As I grow old. Waiting on you
I shall surely drink it, as befits
The callow servant of your office.

To wait on you is to go hungry
When others are satisfied, to thirst day and night
For the bitter waters of understanding,
Bearing poverty and riches with one assent;
To serve is to wait, far from your house,
Where you are not thought of, accepting all conditions
As letters of an inconceivable word
Laid up before you, notes of a song
That is both discord and resolution,
But out of our hearing, beyond our knowledge.

So I shall end my life not knowing
Either myself or you.
Receive my humiliation,
Fulfil this ignorance
In which my words go out
To seek you, heard or unheard,
And never turning back
Denying or confirming,
No trace, no echo and no consequence.

VI

No more words.
No word, except in the bone
In the resurrection bone.
Action is bred there
And praise opened
And repentance fulfilled there.
There is the battlefield
There the seat of judgment.
If I praise in words, do not listen
Nor if I call in words.
Take no account of words
But mark the sentence of the bone
That utters pride or humility
Turns towards or away
Opens or shuts fast.
Hearing and understanding are of the bone
The resurrection bone
That will when time is ripe
Declare without words.

AMBULANDO

i

In middle life when the skin slackens
Its loving clasp of our loose volumes,
When the bone tree stiffens and its well-jointed branches
Begin to creak, to droop a little,
May the spirit hold out no longer for
Old impossible terms, demanding
Rent-free futures where all, all is ripeness,
But cry pax to its equivocal nature and stretch
At ease with wry destiny,
Supple as wind bowing in every reed.

ii

Now that the young with interest no longer
Look on me as one of themselves
Whom they might wish to know or to touch,
Seeing merely another sapless greyhead,
The passport of that disguise conducts me
Through any company unquestioned,
In cool freedom to come and go
With mode and movement, wave and wind.

iii

Communicate with stones, trees, water
If you must vent a heart too full.
Who will hear you now, your words falling
As foreign as bird-tongue
On ears attuned to different vibrations?
Trees, water, stones:
Let these answer a gaze contemplative
Of all things that flow out from them
And back to enter them again.

iv

I do not know the shape of the world.
I cannot set boundaries to experience.

I know it may open out, enlarged suddenly,
In any direction, to unpredictable distance,
Subverting climate and cosmography,
And carrying me far from tried moorings
So that I see myself no more
Under some familiar guise
Resting static as in a photograph,
Nor move as I supposed I was moving
From fixed point to point;
But rock outwards like the last stars that signal
At the frontiers of light,
Fleeing the centre without destination.

Charles Brasch

Halley's Comet

for Hyman Spigl, astronomer: 1911-1962

To see Halley's Comet, far-sent

once-in-a-lifetime faithful
waif of our universe, return
and flaunt her spill of light
kicking her train behind in the curvet
like a flamenco dancer;

to feel an incurious eye cross
worlds, your brow by night,
your sunlit garden, her nearing
slice the blue air of days
till she drops away, shimmering

stream first, light-years backward
in mine-black space, for mantle
distances a lonely child
invokes, and folks out late
crook-necked, a scared delight...

Not to see Halley's Comet...

Judith Rodriguez

Water A Thousand Feet Deep

I stand washing up, the others have gone out walking.
Being at the best, I am homing in on the worst:

to choke in indifferent waves, over ears in ocean--
skim of earth's sweat--what immensities of salt fear
drench us and tighten--with children to save or lose,
the choice, as from old gods, which to consign to destruction:
how to riddle out waste or defiance? what line cast?
what crying hope hold to? for there is no deciding,
it acts itself, the damning sequence secret
as origin and universe, life as an improvisation
on terrors...

the tearaway undertwo. But I never lose grasp on my son
or stop swilling plates and setting them to drain;

till blatantly the door. The boy ran ahead of the rest
and is home. I let him in panting, he trails me insisting
Hey, Mum, so close, there is so much floating known here
between us, have we trod the same waters? Hey, Mum,
is there water a thousand feet deep? Yes, I say,
emptying the sink, and give him figures, the soundings
of ocean trenches, which are after all within measure.
As if in the context of fathoms he'd made a mistake
and it mattered.

Judith Rodriguez

The Nocturnal Citadel

In the snug-warm comfort of our
Nocturnal Citadel we live
and then relive our microcosmic
world of Truth; of joys and fears.

The heart and mind of each of us
gently blend and soothe the senses
that by day are taut, and fraught with pains
inflicted by companion worlds!..

Yet we grope for words with which to weave
this thread of cloth--of daily being--
of kaleidoscopic images
shadowed on our mental screens.

This mass of sensitivity--
of 'Fluctuating Self'--records[1]
both big and small that fly each night
unto the 'Trusted Infinite.'

This constant cord of future times
re-echoes sounds that we have lost[3]
and again presents us with the Truth
of the ever 'Nostalgic Now.'

Thus the relentless nagging of time
is pierced and with the knot of 'now'
we bind the future and the past
and fuse with the Transcendant One.[4]

1. According to the Talmud every soul is an independent
world--the spiritual atomic centre of each self. (A microcosmos.)
2. Rabbinic tradition teaches that each soul leaves it body
nightly and enters heaven where it inscribes its own
actions--good and bad, of the day just past--in the Heavenly ledger.
3. The Talmud reminds us that the soul of every Jew who lived
then, and the souls of all those that were yet to be born, were
present at the 'Giving of the Torah' at Mount Sinai, and thus all
committed themselves with 'Na'aseh ve Nishmah.' (We shall observe
and then it shall be explained to us) to the obligation of the
fulfilment of the Divine Commandments. Hence no Jew ever can
revoke his original oath of allegiance to the Torah.
4. Rabbi Judah Loewe of Prague (commonly known as the MaHaRal of
Prague from his Hebrew acronym) explains in his philosophy that
'past and future' are illusions. Only the 'now' is real. All
time is 'present.' (The Hebrew word עַת time [indefinite] is
etymologically related to the Hebrew word עַתָּה now.) G-d
transcends time and is thus perpetually 'now' (עַתִּי).

Shmuel Gorr

I Am Ready

I am ready to stop right now,
to leave it all at a moment's call...
I think I have lost the tie
of all attachments. This shallow shell
would retire to Eternity.
Strange...There is no attraction even
of what might await...just the urge
to cease, to terminate one's being.

I am ready: Yes, so, dear Lord--
to depart...and feel no loss at that.
The silly cravings will expire
as I slip into Nonentity. Let me go
to where I shall no longer feel
even the soothing sting of Loneliness.
I am surely not the first nor the last
that has felt the urge of no desire.

I am ready, and of old have had
this lack of feeling that gives feelings
of unrelenting emptiness.
They helped me imagine that there is
even in existence, images
that could still the Biting Death of Life...
But these fleeting impulses are false
and I now acquiesce to You.

On The Nature of Fear

Which faculty of man is it that fears;
and why?
Which clumsy crutch of his is this
that is kicked away
and leaves him helpless?

(This screaming silence) of terror
numbs the nerves and mind
and devastates this flimsy structure
we call intellect;
and leaves it helpless.

How Many Times?

How many times to date is it, O G-d,
that I've been broken
and unashamed attune myself
to Your immediacy
to pour out my empty heart
and cease its endless suffering?

How many times, dear G-d,
have I asked of you
to guide my ways,
that this may be the end
of all the causes
that present me here again?

197

The Golden Flight

From her nesting height she first saw
how the eager sun started the day:
Others have sunsets, but she knows
only a long enduring glare.
Her eagle claws are still unblunted
yet her head is not as proudly held
as on her first point of pride.
Though her eyrie is full of bones
she hungers for the eye of day.
Poor bird, seeking the spectre...
the fraud of all attainment.
Fly higher, golden bird,
into the mocking sky of fantasy
that knows no end
until those reddened claws
no longer have their strength
as when the tyrannous glare
first frightened you into flight:
and then... who knows
what then will really hold.

Shmuel Gorr

Waking To Big Stones

waking to big stones
laid one upon another

bullet holes
in thick clusters around Lion Gate

slits for guns, caper plants, and
doves, from the dream

of leaving and returning, of
journeys, packing and unpacking

--now I see the length and breadth and height
of stones,

layers and eras,
the multitude of breachings and repairings

and before the wall
they lay buried in the sides of the mountain
and I

dreaming

Susan Whiting

Tel Aviv Outskirts

rusted 44 gallon drums
scattered in the dunes
and electricity pylons

garbage, carrion birds
in the crowded gas-station snackbar I feel our solidarity--

thorn bush, rusted wire fences
concrete pipes

pipes which flow, and we know
that if one of them would close which should be open

or open, which should be closed
it is impossible to continue in life;

riding the bus into desert--
early morning light exalts the dunes

cuts electricity pylons out of the sky
like never expected understandings
one following another--

this is it, this waste
these pipes, and the light

Susan Whiting

The Wheat Mirrror

Shivers to my waist this morning.
Quick yawns. The green manes of seed shed chestnut light.
Sunbeams scatter through the wheat-stalk water.

Startled grasshoppers graze my ankles,
sandals curling over the dry white stones like tongues.
The ground bristles with lizards and early summer cracks.

Shivering wheat returns light to the olive branches--
the wadi is ripening a river of apricot silk...

Among the stalks poppies float
like wounds,
reminders of the harvest

and I am become like the wheat
growing for the sacrifice,
invoking that ritual moment--

          at my highest, at my heaviest blonde, come--
          cut me back
          back to the litter from last year's celebrations,
          to the shallow graves and broken pots,
          to the burned stubble,
          back to the donkey ploughing--

and I will arch cleanly backwards in culmination.
And my husks will hang on the wind
like a cloud of eyes
to watch the grinding and yeasting and rising
and baking and eating and planting.

                    Clil, Galilee, Israel, '78
                    Susan Whiting

201

In The Cycle of Recurrence

Low cloud imperceptibly moving towards the sea
quiets the farm...
the day suspends no differently at dawn than sunset;
horses' hooves do not quite touch ground--
geese make no sound, the dog does not chase the rabbits;
I am enveloped in natural cocoon, in the embrace of the bush;
enveloped in the process of self-realization,
content to watch from inside luminous skin revolve around me;

 I feel my face turn;
  my flesh thin as a wing--

dreaming chrysalis
tumbles in the cycle of recurrence;
forced by the principle of Spring,

the ornate son
hurls himself
and his sons
into the gold-fire mouth of Jerusalem

Allen Afterman

To Tu Fu in 'To Wei Pa, A Retired Scholar'

I won't meet an old school friend
and still love him and be sad together at our helplessness
and ageing in the 'drunken wildfire' of time;

when my father leans stiffly in my walk,
when I speak with his gestures--
these are powerful, sad reunions;
fire consumes--
other places I could return to are ashen;

I am living myself into my sons,
to be always together;
I will fill them as they grow isolated,
I will console them as my father consoles me

Allen Afterman

Early Morning And A Poem of Kim Yuk[1]

Early morning is creamy with mist,
very Chinese--
birds woke me up:
caws, cracks, grates,
piping mixed with burbling down a sink,
sewing machine chirping,
tsees stitched together with big caw-aaws
(calls like ducks dying of thirst);

Adam is talking to himself in his room;
my wife writes down her dreams, we lie turned aside
bottoms touching;
the peacock walking on the water tank
makes a gaint kettle drum boom
                    Be sure to invite me
              when your good wine is brewed,

now he trumpets
ktree -haw, keeya ow;

suddenly--
only crow caw-aw -aaaws,
the others too busy eating fruit;

ha, finally -roosters;

Sam shakes his long ears by my window, jumps the fence
into rabbit paddocks--
they stop when he stops, Old Sam--
white kitty reclines in the kitchen, playing
with a rabbit's head...

I'm thinking of how to lay the pipe from the high dam
to make a nice shower;
yesterday we hiked to the waterfall --reclined, smoked

...and I'll invite you if blossoms
bloom in my garden;

the baby has five more weeks in the hospital;
we'll see what happens, what happens to our playing

we'll discuss, then, how to live
a hundred years without worry.

Allen Afterman

[1] Kim Yuk, a Korean poet of the 16th century

In The Beginning

"The first act of Ein-Sof, the Infinite Being
is a movement of recoil, of withdrawing
into oneself. Instead of emanation we have
the opposite, contraction." (Gershom Scholem)

Struggling like a body in dream paralysis
this dawn strains to open. My veins
pulse like airpockets in water lines.
In the darkly radiant morning
symbols of creation scream
like long-beaked water-throated birds,
like birds of paradise, ravens,
the first birds...

Cataracts of white mist
curl
in the arms of the hills.
It is said the Eternal One recoiled
from His infinity
in order to give us space. All day
heavy rain upon the fruit trees.

              I walk in
to that stretch of land
which was glimpsed and glimpsed,
which is nevertheless a piece of the earth,
soil, grass.

And beneath are the unbelievable bones
and above are the mounds of ash
and beneath are the miles of bone
like collapsed cattle-yards.

On the surface are the summer-sweet haystacks
the colour of gold teeth
and a farm and children
scouting between old truck tires.

I no longer pray for understanding...
Just give me a space somewhere, some retreat
that is not so mingled and woven
with deception and truth;

a space, God.
A white room
into which I might contract
like light disappearing into an eye
that opens and is always closing...

But, God: your barns, your farm,
children.

[visiting Birkenau]

Marc Radyzner

A Kind Of Accord

I walked around
inside the interior of my childhood
between my bed, my father's sewing-machine
and my chair.

I looked out of the window
at a backyard and an alley
and a sidestreet. Always a backyard
and a back lane and a sidestreet.

I slept in a room where furnace shadows
stumbled against each other on the ceiling.

I was given to drink of the Passover wine,
a taste of "freedom."
Feelings were slipped over me
like clothes too large for me to wear.
The flame my mother called Beauty
was like a street-sign too high for me to read.
I was always sorting things out
but I never chose.

And in the interior of the interior,
and underneath the underneath
a decision shaped itself, no decision.

In the nightly shadow of the cone of light
where my father worked sewing by hand,
and in time with an inner trembling
like a remotely observed fire,
and to the accompaniment of certain recurring
words--Varshe, lahger,
I arrived at a conclusion, no conclusion,
a kind of accord with them all...

I began to understand, this is no game,
              they are serious.
Avoid it; elude it;
do not be...

And memory was always stronger than anticipation.
So much, so quick, so elusive:
I try to remember my childhood
almost as much as my childhood wants to forget itself.

Last night in sleep I saw my father's face,
a squat idol made of stone
[the statues at Easter Island].
'How will you finish all of this?' he asked.
I lifted myself: 'Rung by rung,' I said
and tried to walk to where he crouched
that huge despairing face,

but my arms were forced up
like the legs of a praying mantis,
and my legs began to stamp convulsed in dance.

And everything now is wounding and healing.
Every moment is greeting and leavetaking,
and the more experience the more ignorance,
the more maturity the more bitter memories;

and every level I lift myself up
is the awareness of a level down.

Marc Radyzner

You Who Started All Our Craving

Painful now, almost senseless to say
'God's arm' and 'God's hand,' or 'God's eye,'
'God's light'--

how can we reach?

But Eve, poured directly into ecstasy
purely
like perfume from a root,
Eve, quivering,
already driven--

      when you awoke
from the Nothing you could not remember
perhaps you even glimpsed His eye retracting,
and understood
in what way His hand had touched you...

suffused in pleasure
like a bee in a closed flower
was it from the continual
cycling circles
of consummation without the yearning
that you turned away?

You turned towards the human,
the possibility of rebecoming,
and what you discovered
we know from the inside and long to reverse,
but you chose.

And afterwards the sand between your teeth,
the cistern water,
your flesh breaking into children and original oldness--
you, who started all our craving.

Marc Radyzner

Jerusalem

mooon, moooon--
my son runs over the roof towards it
smiling mother, full and white

          O I glide
separate, so separate from my children

          bomb thud sounds

we sit
in the rubble outside the wall
looking down into Kidron

how fast the sun moves
circling us with shade
               how the lost vision

darkens me, haunts me--
I can no longer grasp it
and I can't give it up

          the city
again and again gives up her walls
opens her gates and dies

how many times dies
like the flower moon
giving her fruit
               and each time her sons
emerge like kings from their domed rooms
and sing her resurrection

                              Susan Whiting

211

Lord, do not turn from me,
I faltered from the fold,
Am I upon your way?
In haste to slip your hold?
I shift and drift and stray.
Who tells me that I am
And am upon your way?

The music of a flute
At evening echoes on,
A fragrance sweet and wan—
But I evoke the word,
I tear apart the weft,
The final threshold broke,
I go—and nothing's left.

What was it that I loved,
And what that now is gone?
Who was my neighbor in
The gaudy tent?
Distorted! Spent!
World cracks like glass. The thin
Shards clink. I only bring
Into that land my ring.

That land? I roamed so far,
Have I the right to come?

THE VOICE:

I watched you long.
I was the hand,
I held the light,
You did not see
Though you were plain in sight!
Upon the way, within my sight.
You are because I Am!
You fared into the land,
I drew you there with me,
I never turned from you.

Karl Wolfskehl

GOD'S WORD
IS MORE ETERNAL THAN ETERNITY

Let the Word stand!
Let the Word stand!
Or your fingers will break.

The Word stands, stands at the gate.
Are you not faint with dread?

The Word has stood through other stress,
Other lightning bounded
Back from the verge of the Word,

And dully drowned
In swelter and swamp.

The Word will not be yours,
Although you make your claim,
The Word is asbestos
And flame.

The Word is rudder,
And keel.

The Word is star and root,
Above all lords, the lord!
What can cage in the Word?

Dig it under—it grows!
Shroud it in night—it glows!
Cast it away—it is your goal.
Only the Word holds!

Without the shaft of the Word
The roof of heaven would fall,
The bright sun would be blurred.

The Word went out before
The furrows stirred and bore.

Before the throngs of heaven chanted
The Word found itself,
Summoned and named itself,
Nothing besides itself it wanted.
The Word unto itself is planned,
Before rise, before close—
Let it stand! Let it stand!

Karl Wolfskehl

215

Yes, I shall walk again
—Although your sloth abounds—
The garden of My word
Which holiness surrounds.

And I shall seek again
—Though not a tear you knew—
The curse begot the cure,
Because I wept for you.

And I shall come again
—Although you would not stand—
To you, the scattered hosts,
Who long have slipped my hand.

And I shall weave again
—Although you have not fulled—
My web of vines. The weeds
Among the stones are pulled.

And I shall call again
—Although you slacked and dozed—
My casks will clear the wine,
I guard the cellar close.

And I shall sign again
—Although you failed to greet—
Until the last of bonds
Fall from your head and feet.

And I shall lead again
—Though laxly you withdrew—
Not one of all my gates
Shall be denied to you.

And I shall storm again
—Although you did not surge—
Inside and out the old-
New gales will blast and scourge.

Shall dwell in you again!
Although you have not white-
Washed it, your heart shall still
Give out a diamond light.

Shall bless again, again,
That I vowed you to Me,
Until we meet at last,
Whole in eternity.

Karl Wolfskehl

CHARLES BRASCH

Poland, October
(from Nineteen Thirty-nine)

Even for the defeated life goes on,
Although the codes, assumptions, purposes
That guided and protected them are gone:
They have become the prey of nothingness.

All that was and was known now only seems,
All seeming changes and all change appals,
As they live out the intolerable dreams
That usurp nature to itself grown false.

They have been used and are not wanted any more,
Not by man; they will not be pitied nor
Remembered. Only to suffer are they still free.
Pain can practise new experiments on them,
Until the fair-spoken world their lives condemn
Dies in each one's death. They are history.

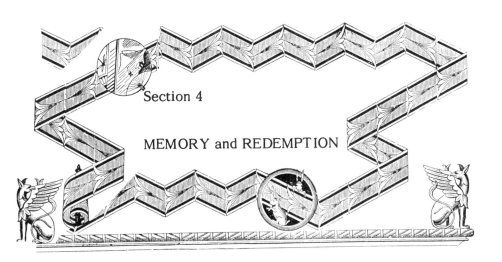

Section 4

MEMORY and REDEMPTION

LILIAN BARNEA

My Grandfather

HE IS RECEDING from me down the corridors of time and it is making me sad—every day he becomes a little more indistinct. The more time passes, the less I am able to separate memory from experience, love from knowledge, so that I cannot help disapproving of some of those very qualities which made me love him so much. I want to try to recapture him on paper, while I am still able to.

For documentary purposes, his name was Jozef. To family and friends he was Eusiej. *Eusiej*: very soft, very Russian. At home, spoken of in my presence, he was always referred to as *dziadzius* (little grandpa). I remember that the mere sound of his name, in whatever form, conveyed reassurance; a pleasant, warm, all-enveloping sense of safety.

In Polish, quite incongruously a language of diminutives, *dziadzius* sounds even more diminutive than does 'little grandpa'. But Grandfather was a tall, imposing man. Whenever I think of him, I see him dressed for the street in an elegant, blackcloth coat with a fur collar. His greying hair is smoothly brushed. He carries a cane. His face seems almost young, his blue eyes are commanding, his whole bearing haughty.

An unlikely picture of a Jew in pre-war Warsaw; in Warsaw at any time, for that matter.

Sometimes I ask myself: was he really like that? How I would like to believe that he was! Or was his bearing merely a façade, a pose sustained out of pride at first, and later out of love; for surely he must have been aware of the sense of security and dignity that we all derived from his behaviour.

220

And, reluctantly, I conclude that it must have been a pose; for though he was born in Kiev, outside the pale, to parents who had been almost totally assimilated, and he went to a good Russian 'Gymnasium' where he was practically the only Jew, yet there must have been barbs, and the fear of insult, and the terrible longing to be the same as the other boys, the deep wish *not* to have been chosen; so that his polite (yes, not arrogant!) self-assurance could not possibly have been the product of such a tortured childhood. And if it was a pose, what an effort it must have cost him, at times, to sustain it!

I never spent as much time with Grandfather as I would have liked. Ours was a formal household, and I was constantly in the care of a governess who adhered to quite a rigid routine. For me, from as far back as I can remember, the day began at eight o'clock. I washed, dressed, and then sat down opposite my governess—a very respectable and mean woman—in the stale stillness of the dining room. She had coffee, while I drank a glass of 'tea'—a drop of tea in a glass of milk, just enough to give it a tinge of pinkness, the degree of that tinge being largely dependent on the mood my governess was in on that particular morning. We each had a sweet bun. Then, weather permitting, out into the courtyard for a ride on my bicycle. The courtyard, enclosed by the house on all sides, was rather like a well; like all Warsaw courtyards it was sunless and gloomy throughout most of the day. In the middle of our courtyard there grew a solitary, pathetic little lilac bush; and round this lilac bush I circled with determination, showing off for the benefit of the little boy on the second floor, until I was called in for my lessons. (Much later it transpired that this little lilac bush had really been very sturdy. Several months after the war, propelled by what I can only very inadequately describe as a feeling of dread-filled anticipation, I went to see the ruins of our house. I was then so awed by the

221

freedom of movement, by the very fact that I was *free* to go back home, that while knowing how utterly impossible it was, I somehow expected my home *to be* there; in spite of this, the bombed-out street, which I found with great difficulty, gave me no particular feeling of shock because of its anonymity—by then all Warsaw streets consisted of identical piles of rubble; I wasn't really sure whether this had been our house, or the one next to it, or the one beyond, so that I had to go to the intersection and start counting: one, two, three, four, five. . . . And then I saw the lilac bush. It was unbearably unchanged and in full bloom. . . .)

Breakfast was at ten o'clock. Grandfather was away in the mornings; my mother, who liked to get up late, was monosyllabic and still wore her dressing-gown. My recollections of my grandmother are very hazy; I vaguely remember her as being dark and petite—there is a photograph imprinted on my mind in which she stands perpetually poised over a huge soup tureen, a ladle in one hand. But I am sure she was there at the breakfast table, as well as the governess who sat inexorably on my right. On nice days the dining room would be filled with the morning sun, which shone on the highly polished parquet floors and the heavy crystals on the sideboard. The yellow of sliced, boiled eggs, the red of tomatoes, the various browns of the herrings looked extremely colourful and appetizing against the snow-white damask tablecloth. Grandmother's meals were a kind of art—she must have attached tremendous importance to food and to the way it was served. When my mother left my father and came to live with her parents, I had been three years old—a thin, pale child, typically revolted by food. Every mouthful had had to be coaxed or forced down my throat. By the age of five—a feat the women never tired talking of—I had developed into a chubby, rather greedy little eater. I savoured breakfast slowly, reluctant to let it end, already looking forward to dinner; not for the sake of food, now

222

that I was full, but because (unless there was some special treat in store) dinner was the focal point of my day: lessons, as well as excursions into an often hostile world, would be over by dinnertime. And Grandfather would be coming home....

Lessons (which I know took place, but do not actually remember having) were interspersed with various other activities, vivid glimpses of some of which have remained with me: I am skating, and I hate it. I am terrified of falling on the slippery ice, I sweat, my hands are clenched; yet I go on skating, clumsily, doggedly. It never occurred to me to ask to be let off, and I never confided my fear to anyone. Like Grandfather, I preserved a stiff upper lip. Unfortunately, sports played a large part in my curriculum—I suppose it was my family's way of saying: look, we are different.

Or my governess takes me to the park. Some children come up: will I play hide-and-seek with them? I don't feel like it, but I say yes, I will. So I play. I run, I hide, I seek, I shout with the best of them; in fact, I lead the game, after several minutes I am the undisputed leader. Why then do I feel such relief when my governess calls: 'Time to go home!'?

About a year before the war, I began learning to play tennis. Tennis held no terrors for me. I knew how pretty I looked in my white, made-to-order tennis dress; little as I was, its social implications were also not quite lost on me— none of my few friends played tennis, and while until now I had envied them their freedom (none, save one, had a governess), I suddenly became rather conscious of my privileged position. Another very vivid glimpse: a huge, sun-filled tennis court. I am sitting on a bench awaiting my turn. I am filled with a sense of luxurious well-being, which seems to have communicated itself to my governess, for even she is less sour than usual. This is my third or fourth lesson, and I enjoy these lessons immensely. On the way back home we will stop at a marvellous pet shop in the heart of the city to get some food for my goldfish. Suddenly a lady sits down next to me. She beams (what a cute little girl!), she is very friendly. She begins to ask me questions, which I answer coyly, guardedly.

Do I like to play tennis?

Yes, I do.

But I am a little young to be playing tennis, aren't I?

Yes.... .

Do I go to school?

No.

?!

Here my governess feels obliged to explain. No, I don't go to school, I learn at home. When I turn ten, I will be sent to a boarding school in England. My family prefer that I have an English education. Yes, to a very good English school, one of the best. That's why I am having tennis lessons already, and English lessons too, of course.

The lady seems suitably impressed, but for me the day is ruined. My feeling of well-being drains away to be replaced with unease. Why don't I go to a Polish school? I have never been told, yet I know. I was born with this latent knowledge, it is ingrained in the very pores of my skin. Being shielded from being Jewish only makes matters worse; I suffer the more, for being told so little. This constant camouflage, which I know is expected of me, also without ever having been told, is extremely trying. (As a result, I was a nervous, oversensitive child, too proud for my age, and proud for the wrong reasons.) I want to go home and stay there. I wish I were sick, not terribly sick, just enough so I could stay in bed. When I am sick, my governess disappears and Mother hovers around me anxiously. She takes my temperature, she reads to me and brings me trays of tempting food. How I want to go home to dinner.... .

In order that we should all be able to get together once

a day (my grandparents and Mother often went out in the evenings), dinner was at the peculiar hour of three. One look at Grandfather; one big, loving hug: 'And how is my little girl today?'; and I would be reassured, I was safe, everything was all right again. And I felt even better when Grandfather started talking. He talked a lot at meals, eating as though the food were incidental, a sort of appendage to conversation. His vibrant talk fascinated and excited me, he rarely spoke of the trivia of everyday life, but liked to discuss world politics, often letting fall names of faraway, exotic places with such intimate ease as though he had just returned from them. He also loved to reminisce and to mention important people: Trotsky, who, he said, had helped him to get out of Russia, when the revolution broke out while Grandfather had been there on business; Pilsudski, Jan Kiepura, Maurice Chevalier; no matter what their political persuasion or their claim to fame, Grandfather had met them all. Indeed, in his study—a small room, almost completely taken up by a piano, two comfortable leather armchairs, and a worn-out sofa on which Grandfather took his after-dinner naps—there was a group photo, taken at the grave of the Unknown Soldier in Paris, in which Pilsudski and Grandfather both stood in the front row, two people apart.

Here I note, with vague disquiet (so that I almost don't write it down, but try to push the memory back into my subconscious), that there were few books in Grandfather's study; and how am I to interpret that? Was he perhaps not very well read, not very studious? I am disturbed by this possibility; somewhere, on the way, I have acquired the notion that there is virtue in studiousness.

After dinner, relaxed, all my unnamed, unspoken fears stilled for the course of the afternoon, I was free to do what I liked during the few hours that remained of my day. Usually I played or read in my room; occasionally I visited or was visited by friends. Grandfather always retired to

225

rest. This routine did not give us a chance to see much of each other; and a visit to Grandfather's room was a rare treat.

I have a peculiar propensity for remembering places. I have retained only the dimmest impression of my father, but I remember well the furnishings of my parents' flat in Sosnowiec, a gloomy Silesian coal town, where I spent the first three years of my life (but where I was *not* born, for my mother made sure that the birth took place in Warsaw).

So now, as in my thoughts I slowly enter my grandparents' bedroom, which was referred to by everyone, including Grandmother, as 'Grandfather's room', I see it before me in vivid detail: the huge, old-fashioned double bed flanked on both sides by marble-topped bedside tables, which matched the marble lamp shade on the ceiling; the enormous wardrobe where, among myriads of other things, Grandmother stored stacks upon meticulously folded stacks of perfumed linen; her dressing table with all its bottles and jars; the blue-green siphon bottle on the window sill; while Grandfather in bed is a dim, obscure figure.

It must have been on this or on a similar occasion, that I perceived on Grandfather's bedside table a set of teeth in a glass of water. It grinned up at me hideously from the depth of the glass; and I was shocked. This was my first encounter with false teeth—an encounter shocking enough in itself; I took a close look at Grandfather: he seemed different, shrunken somehow. A gap yawned when he opened his mouth. His speech sounded funny. I started to cry, and was taken away. This episode, so very clear in my memory, puzzles me. I go over it in my mind, again and again. Grandfather receiving ladies without his teeth in? How utterly unlike him—how improbable! How it disturbs my whole concept of him! I can only surmise that this happened towards the end and that he was feeling (momentarily) defeated.

I say: receiving ladies; for Grandfather treated me like a lady. A little lady, sometimes a naughty little lady, but definitely a lady. He never condescended, never spoke down to me; never demeaned or humiliated me, as the best of grown-ups often did in those pre child-oriented days. In his presence, neither Mother nor Grandmother dared insist that I finish my spinach, or my grated carrots, or the Russian 'spring borsch' which I detested.

Sometimes, Grandfather and I went out together. I have unforgettable memories of the Saxon Gardens or Lazienki on balmy spring days; of sitting on a bench and devouring a large, chocolate 'Eskimo' ice-cream on a stick (strictly against my mother's wishes, because ice-cream in those days in Poland was considered to be a dangerous food; to eat ice-cream was to court a sore throat). In cafés or in restaurants he would hand me the menu, let me choose for myself and abide by my choice. He showed me Marszalkowska at dusk: lights springing up to illuminate the wonders in the windows of Warsaw's finest street; neon signs flashing. He took me to the old city; with him I explored all the beauties of pre-war Warsaw.

I can still hear the measured, rhythmical clip clop of the horses' hooves, as we went by droshky—I, full of joyous anticipation on the way to the city, and sleepy and sated on the way home; Grandfather delighting in my pleasure and conscious, I think, always very conscious of the fine figure he cut. And when we finally got back: 'Here you have a very tired little girl,' he would say. 'But we enjoyed ourselves, didn't we, Lilusia?'

We lived on the ground floor of a large, massive block of flats in the best part of what was later to become a part of the Warsaw ghetto.

The house had been bought by my great-grandfather—my grandmother's father. He had had three daughters; he gave

227

each a flat in the house when he married them off. The remaining flats were also occupied mostly by relatives: uncles, aunts, cousins and their respective families, wealthy or less well off, regardless of their occupation or profession, all lived in the same house. The rooms were large and high-ceilinged, warmed in winter by huge porcelain stoves, which the maids would light very early in the morning; and furnished, for the most part, with solid, dark furniture and heavy crystal and silver objects.

Great-grandfather had invested all the money he had made (he had started out by selling spoons at street corners) in real estate and a lamp factory, one of the largest in Poland. A widower, he left everything to his daughters when he died. It was Grandfather who managed the factory. He had, I understand, brought little into the family except for his good looks and his bearing; and by virtue of these he became the family's spokesman in dealings with the outside world. But not, I think, by unanimous consent. Little as I was, I remember sensing the resentment and jealousy that the other two husbands felt towards him; on one occasion I overheard them talking about 'that *Luft Mensch*' (the then mysterious phrase, or perhaps the derisive intonation of it, went through me like a shaft, and filled me with horror and shame; though no names were mentioned, I knew they were referring to Grandfather).

We also owned a large, sprawling summer villa in Otwock, a holiday resort near Warsaw. Here, the few small children of the family spent their summers accompanied by my governess and a cook. The grown-ups rarely came, preferring, I suppose, more sophisticated places; or perhaps the lack of plumbing had kept them away. It was the magic spot of my childhood—I have never revisited it for fear of spoiling my memories.

The villa was surrounded by a high, wire fence. There was a tall, green iron gate. A path strewn with tiny white stones led up to the first house, in front of which were two well-kept, elaborate flower beds. This was the only 'artificial' part of the villa; the rest was all pine wood. The other two houses were well to the left of the first and hidden from view, as one came in through the gate. Each house consisted of three rooms and a kitchen; there was no running water. We washed our hands and faces in a white enamel bowl, or under the water pump—one child washing, one pumping. Once or twice a week, we were given baths in a large, wooden laundry tub. The place was looked after by a janitor, who lived there all year round with his wife and three children in a small red cottage beside the fruit and vegetable garden in the middle of the wood. They had a fierce, sad, red dog called Canis.

What a blessing those summers were! The vine-covered fence kept out the world; the heady smell of pines and the sounds of the country lulled me to security. Waking early in the morning to the chirping of birds, impatient to start the day, I would lie in bed waiting for the first ray of sunshine to peek through one of the two little hearts in the green shutters. Or, soothed by the patter of rain on the roof, I might drift back into sleep. Later, barefoot, we raced to the lavatory; a wooden shack with a rusty hinge on the door and a heart carved in the wide seat. A fly or two always buzzed around drowsily. I would peer into the smelly depth to frighten myself: what if I fell in? And with a pounding heart I would bounce back into the welcoming safety of the wood.

Day after day we played in that wood, never tiring of it. We climbed trees; we lay on the thick, green moss staring up at the blue sky between the tops of the pines; we tried to catch squirrels; we took turns on the old swing; we picked blueberries off the bushes behind the houses; we ate unwashed, unripe apples from the garden, then pumped water into each other's hands, drank it furtively, and awaited

229

disaster. To drink water, especially unboiled water, after eating unripe apples was certain to result in stomach cramps. But nothing ever happened. About once a week, accompanied by the governess (girdle off—bulges out, and her authority greatly diminished thereby), we ventured out of the villa for a dip in the nearby river.

All the woes of city life were forgotten. Living, as I did, in a state of perpetual contentment, I did not miss Grandfather, nor even pause to think about him; and I can recall only two occasions on which he came down to Otwock. Neither was a happy one. On the first, he was indisposed; he stayed in his room, and Grandmother let none of the children come near him, and I felt very hurt not to be singled out; after all, he was *my* grandfather.

The second time he came, was even less propitious. War broke out on 1 September 1939. Probably because it had been in the air for some time, the family was less scattered than usual. My mother and various aunts and cousins were staying at the villa; in fact, we were quite crowded. The first of September had been a singularly lovely day. The warmth of summer still lingered, but was already merging with the beauty of autumn; and war, though not unexpected, came as a shock in the form of an announcement on the radio. I can see that radio, as I write: a massive, rounded brown box with big knobs, its front covered with rough, beige fabric.

Gas masks were distributed; anti-aircraft ditches were dug; yet, in Otwock, war seemed improbable. But several days later, by some fluke of fate, one of the first bombs of the war fell on the Otwock orphanage, and panic ensued. Everybody, including the janitor and his family, was crowding around the radio when this happened. Magda, the janitor's wife, crossed herself rapidly and with a muttered 'Jesus, Maria, Josef!' gathered her children, dived with them under a bed, and could not be made to come out for some hours. This struck me as extremely funny. In the way of children, I thought the whole thing a lark.

Then Grandfather arrived in a large, black limousine (at that time! when so few people owned cars and transport was being requisitioned by the army!) to take us back to the relative 'safety' of Warsaw, which had not yet been bombed.

I remember the long corridor of our Warsaw flat full of frightened people; the corridor sways; plaster falls from the ceiling; the light goes out. Warsaw is being bombed. I sit on Grandfather's knee. Grandfather holds court. He tells stories of World War I; he encourages; he cracks jokes. Things are bad, but they could be worse. When he was in St Petersburg during the revolution.... The corridor sways. That was a near thing! I am just a little bit frightened, but it is not an unpleasant feeling. It's quite exciting to have my routine disrupted in this unusual manner. I enjoy sitting on Grandfather's knee. Some of his importance, his uniqueness, rubs off on to me—I am his favourite, his only grand-daughter, am I not?

I also remember the morning when I looked out of my bedroom window and saw the green uniforms of the first German soldiers.

All of Warsaw 'knew' him, and he 'knew' all of Warsaw. He wheedled, he cajoled, he persuaded, he humoured, he bluffed, he charmed; he could avert nothing.

I wonder at what point he realized that he should have taken us out of Poland before disaster struck. I hate to think how he must have felt then.

The wall encircled us. There were no more treats, no more excursions with Grandfather. Our world shrank and became very limited; but it was still clean, still warm, there was still food; there was still routine. In my eyes, Grandfather stayed unchanged; he became a little more pensive, perhaps.

231

Increasingly, he talked of his childhood; he quoted poetry. There was a poem by Lermontov that he was especially fond of, a fragment of which has remained with me:

Skazhi-ka dyadya, ved' ne darom
Moskva, spalennaya pozharom,
Frantsuzu oddana....

He still wore the fur-collared coat; he still swung his cane; he still talked big. And he still reassured; he still inspired confidence. In his presence people relaxed; for a brief while the reality seemed unreal. They came to our house in droves to ask his advice: and what did *pan dyrektor* think of the situation? Could *pan dyrektor* help, could he arrange this or that or the other? Here and there, Grandfather was still able to do something for someone; he still had a lot of connections both inside and outside the wall.

I have few coherent memories from that time. An impression persists of utter desolation, in the midst of which Grandfather was the only bright spark. Nothing really bad could happen to us, as long as Grandfather was around. From the blackout, only various shadowy scenes flash on to the screen of my mind.

But I do remember the end véry clearly.

We left the ghetto in the summer of 1942. Blood was flowing in the gutters of one of the streets we passed. 'Borsch,' said my mother unconvincingly, tightening her hold on my hand. And, sheltered as I was from the horrors surrounding us, I almost believed her. We walked with a group of people detailed to work outside the wall. Once out, our ways parted. They went on to whatever their miserable destination may have been; ours was a villa in Konstancin, an Otwock-like resort on the opposite side of Warsaw.

Pines again. And squirrels. And breathtaking smells, and sunshine, and birds, and flowers, and the unbelievable wonder of it all. What were the 'connections', which made

232

this possible? I didn't know. I don't want to know. I loved him very much.

The family we stayed with, spoke Russian. The mother was a big-bosomed, black-haired woman, bursting out of her dress—rather beautiful in a creamy kind of way. The two sons wore moustaches and played the guitar. The father was an indeterminate little man. In exchange for our money, they were supposed to obtain for us forged documents and suitable hiding places. They didn't. Eventually, precarious arrangements for survival were made for my mother and myself—my grandparents had to return to the ghetto. I learned all this much later. During the few weeks we spent there (quiet and inconspicuous as mice), I was merely told to play—and leave the worry to the grown-ups.

My play was pervaded with unease. One evening, at suppertime, as I was playing next to the house behind some bushes, the impossible happened: I caught a squirrel. The squirrel and I were both equally startled; I hadn't wanted to catch it—it had simply walked into my hands. Undecided, I crouched in the dusk. Should I keep the squirrel? Or let it go? I could hear the clink of cutlery—the dinner table was being laid on the verandah. 'Where's Lilusia?' I heard my mother ask in sudden panic. For some reason, I said nothing. I heard my mother come down the steps and look for me in the garden; but I crouched there silently, holding the squirrel by its tail. Keep it? Or let it go? My mother returned to the verandah. There was a mutter of anxious voices. I still crouched, clutching the squirming squirrel with both hands, quite worried now by the concern I was causing, when: 'Lala, Lala!' called Grandfather into the pines in a hesitant, quivering voice.

Lala? Why Lala? But in asking myself that question I was playing for time. Another second. Another split of a second. Because, of course, I knew the answer almost before I had formulated the question. Where Lilusia might hint of

233

Jewishness to any spying ears lurking around, Lala would not. Camouflage, again. A Jewish girl might be called Lilusia. Lala sounded hard, and crystal clear and very Polish.

I felt very humiliated. Cheeks burning, I let the squirrel go.

For the first time I realized, that Grandfather, too, was vulnerable. Grandfather, too, was helpless and afraid. And in the span of that realization, I stopped being a child.

I let the squirrel go and I got up.

Many years after the war, I met a neighbour from our street. He had, he said, seen Grandfather die.

'How?' I wanted to know.

The man hesitated.

'*How?*'

'He was shot.'

'How?'

'On the street.'

'How?!'

'On the street . . . from the back. He knew nothing. I saw him fall. . . . I don't know . . . from the back . . . a stray shot, maybe. . . .'

I let it be. It was the only kind of death to be envisaged for my grandfather, under the circumstances. Nobody would have dared shoot him to his face. And any other kind of death is, of course, unthinkable.

So I asked no more questions. I let it be.

FAY ZWICKY

Hostages

I THINK I BEGAN to hate when I was twelve. Consciously,
I mean. The war was then in its fourth year, there was no
chocolate and my father was still away in Borneo. I barely
knew him. Till then I had learnt to admire what my mother
believed to be admirable. Striving to please with ascetic
rigour, I practised scales and read Greek myths. Morality
hinged on hours of piano practice achieved or neglected. I
knew no evil. The uncommon neutrality of my existence as
a musical child in wartime was secured in a world neither
good nor malevolent. My place among men was given. Did
I have feelings? I was not ready to admit them for there
seemed to be rules governing their revelation which I either
could not or would not grasp. Nameless, passionless, and
without daring I repressed deepest candour. But *tout com-
prendre c'est tout pardonner*; what was once self-indulgence
is now permissible revelation. Why, then, should shame
crimp the edge of my reflection so many years after the
event?

It all started with the weekly visit to our house of a
German refugee piano teacher, Sophie Lindauer-Grunberg.
Poor fat sentimental Sophie, grateful recipient of my
mother's pity. I was to be her first Australian pupil.

'But why me?'

'Because she needs help. She has nothing and you,
thank God, have everything. She's been a very fine musician
in her own country. You have to understand that this is
someone who has lost everything. Yes, you can roll your
eyes. *Everything*, I said. Something I hope, please God,

235

will never happen to you. So you'll be nice to her and pay attention to what she says. I've told Mr Grover he lives too far away for me to go on taking you to lessons twice a week.'

Suddenly dull and bumbling Mr Grover in his music room smelling of tobacco and hair oil seemed like my last contact with the outside world. I was to be corralled into the tight, airless circle of maternal philanthropy.

The day of my first lesson a hot north wind was tearing at the huge gum in front of the house. Blinds and curtains were drawn against the promised heat. The house stood girded like an island under siege. My younger brother and sister had gone swimming. I watched them go, screwing up my eyes with the beginnings of a headache, envying their laughter and the way they tore sprigs off the lantana plants lining the driveway. I awaited my teacher, a recalcitrant hostage. The rooms were generous and high-ceilinged but I prowled about, tight-lipped, seeking yet more room. A deep nerve of anger throbbed in me and I prayed that she would not come. But she came. Slowly up the brick path in the heat. I watched her from the window, measuring her heavy step with my uneasy breath. Then my mother's voice greeting her in the hallway, high-pitched and over-articulated as if her listener were deaf, a standard affectation of hers with foreign visitors. 'Terrible day ... trouble finding the house ... Helen looking forward so much....' I ran to the bathroom and turned on the tap hard. I just let it run, catching sight of my face in the mirror above the basin.

Could I be called pretty? Brown hair hanging long on either side of high cheekbones, the hint of a powerful nose to come, a chin too long, cold grey eyes, wide mouth, fresh colour. No, not pretty. No heroine either. A wave of self-pity compensated me for what I saw and tears filled my eyes. Why me? Because she has to have pupils. Am I such a prize? No, but a Jew who has everything. 'Be thankful you were born in this wonderful country.' My mother's

236

voice sounded loud in my ears. 'They're making them into lampshades over there.' I had laughed but shrank from the grotesque absurdity of the statement. Why the dramatics? All I remember is the enveloping anger directed at everything my life had been and was. I wanted to be left alone but didn't know how or where to begin. 'She has lost her whole family. Taken away and shot before her eyes. . . .' So? Now she has me.

My mother and Miss Grunberg were talking about me as I stood in the doorway. My own hands were clammy as I moved forward to the outstretched unfamiliar gesture. Hers were small, fat and very white, surprisingly small for such a tall, heavily built woman, like soft snuggling grubs. She herself looked like some swollen, pale grub smiling widely and kindly, a spinster of nearly sixty. Her little eyes gleamed through thick, round spectacles. On the skin beneath her eyes tiny bluish vessels spread their nets.

'So here is *unsere liebe Helene*!'

I raised my eyebrows insolently as the girls did at school after one of my own ill-judged observations. It was essential to the code governing the treatment of victims. But this time I had the upper hand and didn't know how to handle my advantage. The cobbles of Köln and Cracow rang hollow under my boots. The light from the pink shaded lamp fell on my new teacher. The wind blew in sharp gusts outside.

'Helen, this is Miss Grunberg.' My mother with a sharp look in my direction. 'I've been telling her about the work you've done so far with Mr Grover. Miss Grunberg would like you to have another book of studies.'

'Perhaps you will play *ein Stück* for me. Liszt perhaps?' She nodded ponderously at our Bechstein grand that suddenly took on the semblance of some monstrous piece of abstract statuary, out of all proportion to the scale of the room. 'Lord no. I've never done him.' I fell into uncharacteristic breeziness. 'I'm not really in practice. Hardly

237

anything going at the moment and I'm pretty stale on the stuff Grover had me on for the exams.' Deliberately fast, consciously idiomatic, enjoying, yes, *enjoying* the strain of comprehension on my victim's round, perpetually smiling face. 'You can *still* play those Debussy "Arabesques",' said my mother, her neck flushed. 'I put the music on the piano,' and she gave me yet another warning look.

I opened the lid noisily and sat down with elaborate movements, shifting the metronome a few inches to the right, altering the position of the stand, bending to examine my feet fumbling between the pedals. The 'Arabesques' moved perfunctorily. I kept my face impassive, looked rigidly ahead at the music which I didn't see. Even during the section I liked in the second piece, a part where normally I would lean back a little and smile. I had begun to learn how not to please. But the process of self-annihilation involved the destruction of others. *Tout pardonner* did I say?

Miss Grunberg arranged with my mother to return the following week at the same time. 'Why are you behaving like this?' asked my mother, red and angry with me after she had left in a taxi. The young blond driver had tapped his foot noisily on the brick path as Miss Grunberg profusely repeated her gratitude to my mother for the privilege of teaching her talented daughter. Moving rapidly away from them I conversed with him, broadening my vowels like sharks' teeth on the subject of the noon temperature. I was desperate that the coveted outside world and its tranquil normality should recognize that I was in no way linked with the heavy foreign accent involved in demonstrative leave-taking on our front lawn.

'Behaving like what?'

'You know what I mean. You behaved abominably to that poor woman.'

'I played for her, didn't I?' She came closer to me with a vengeful mouth.

'You could call it that. I don't know what's got into you lately. You used to be such a good child. Now you know the answers to everything. A walking miracle! What terrible things have we done, your father and I, that you should behave like a pig to a woman like that? We've given you everything. *Everything!* And because I'm good to an unfortunate refugee who needs help wherever she can find it, you have to behave like that! I'm sorry for you, *really* sorry for you!'

'Spare your sympathy for the poor reffos!' The taxi driver's word burst savagely out of my mouth. She flew at me and slapped me across the face with her outstretched hand.

'One thing I do know,' she was trembling with rage, 'the one thing I'm sure of is that I've been too good to you. We've given you too much. You're spoilt rotten! And *one* day, my girl, one day you too may be old and unwanted and. . . .'

'A lampshade perhaps? So what.' I shook with guilt and fear at the enormity of what I'd said, terrified of the holocaust I'd shaken loose and my mother's twisted mouth.

But the revolution didn't get under way either that day or that year. The heroine lacked (should one say it?) courage. Sealed trains are more comforting than the unknown wastes of the steppes. The following week Miss Grunberg toiled up our front path and I sat down to the new course of Moscheles studies and a movement of a Mozart concerto. *Her* music. Scored heavily in red pencil, the loved and hated language dotted with emotional exclamation marks. Her life's work put out for my ruthless inspection. She moved her chair closer to my stool to alter the position of my right hand. 'Finger *rund, Kleine*, always *rund*. Hold always the wrist supple, *liebe Helene*.' I shrank from the alien endearment and her sour breath but curved my fingers, tight and deliberate. Her smell hung over me, a static haze in the dry

239

air. Musty, pungent and stale, the last faint reminder of an airless Munich apartment house. Her dress, of cheap silky fabric, rustled when she moved her heavy body. Breathing laboriously she tried to explain to me what I should do with the Mozart. She couldn't get used to the heat of the new country and was beginning to find walking difficult. But I didn't practise between her visits and gave only spasmodic attention to her gentle directions. I was shutting myself off from words and from music, beginning a long course in alienation. I seldom looked my mother in the eye in those days. I quarrelled bitterly with my sister, ignored my brother.

About six months after my lessons with Miss Grunberg started I was not much further advanced. I spent a lot of time reading in my room or just looking out of the window at the garden which was now bare. Squalls lashed the gum-tree and drove the leaves from the weeping elm skittering across the grass. Miss Grunberg now had several pupils amongst the children of the Jewish community and even one or two gentiles from the neighbouring school. She lived in a very poorly furnished flat in a run-down outer suburb. She still travelled to her pupils' homes. Her breathing had become very short in the last few weeks. Inattentive and isolated as I was, I had noticed that she was even paler than usual.

My mother one day told me with some rancour how well the Lapin girl was doing with the piano. 'She never had your talent but what a worker! She's going to give a recital in the Assembly Hall next month.' I merely shrugged. The boots of the conqueror were no picnic. She was welcome to them. 'And while I'm about it, I've decided to tell Miss Grunberg not to come any more. I don't feel there's much point as you seem quite determined to do as little with music as possible. I've done all *I* can. At least she's on her feet now.' On her feet! Oh God! But I replied, 'That's all right with me' in as neutral a voice as I could summon.

But that night I ground my face into the covers of my bed, no longer a place of warmth and security but a burial trench. At the mercy of my dreams appeared Sophie Lindauer-Grunberg, pale as brick dust. Her face wasting, crumbling to ash, blasted by the force of my terrible youth. And, waking in fright, I mourned for the first time my innocent victim and our shared fate.

How Come The Truckloads?

Somehow the tutorial takes an unplanned direction:
anti-Semitism.
A scholastic devil advances the suggestion
that two sides can be found to every question:

Right.
Now, who's an anti-Semite?
One hand.
Late thirties, in the 1960s. Bland.
Let's see now; tell us, on what texts or Jews
do you base your views?
There was a landlord, from Poland, that I had.
Bad?
A shrug. Well, what did he do?
Pretty mean chasing up rent. Ah. Tough.
And who
else? No-one else. One's enough.

Judith Rodriguez

RUMKOWSKY WAS RIGHT

YVONNE   FEIN

Looking   at   things   logically,   my   parents   should   be
emotional, spiritual and physical wrecks.   Not just because
they have me as a daughter---I have manic-depressive
tendencies as well as a decided talent for carpentry.   And
how many Jewish children grow up to be carpenters?   Well,
there was one, of course.

Anyway, back to the wreckage business of mind and body.
I say this because of what Hitler did to my parents and their
incredible survival with so few, noticeable scars.   I know it
is an old story of suffering and torture that has been told
almost too many times to be retold.   But as it is written in
the Holy Books: for each occasion there is a prayer, so I
write: for each story there is an interpretation.   That is not
stretching the point, for my parents first crossed each
other's paths on a train which was taking them from
Auschwitz to another camp, Goerlitz.

I always found that blackly romantic.   Travel Eurail and
see the corpses.   No courting couple should miss it!   Not
that they were courting then, or even gave one another a
second glance.   Shaven heads and skeletal bodies do not,
after all, a love affair make.   But it was a beginning and
perhaps that is where I should start, albeit that beginnings to
nightmares are sometimes difficult to establish----■-----My
maternal Grandfather, Levi, was clubbed to death before the
eyes of his wife, daughter and baby son, like thousands of
other Jews in '44 in the streets of Hungary.   Admittedly he
spat in the face of a German soldier who was trying to
wrench his skull-cap from his greying locks.   This is not wise
when between you and the soldier is nothing but fear and
hatred on one side and brutally ingrained prejudice on the

other and, in the hands of the soldier, a gun.

In the hands of my Grandfather were those of his family who now waited in shock to be hustled aboard a train with their fellows in criminal birthright. Final destination---and fanfare has been rendered redundant through the passage of years and the cynical jadedness of ears over-assaulted by the name: Auschwitz!

It was in '39 or '40 that the Nazis came to Poland. Dates, though drummed into me at school, are always hazy in my mind because I became so mesmerized by the horror-stories themselves, told in dispassionate tones by my parents at Friday night dinners. So, in one of those years, the Germans took my Father's family in a little town called Vielun. That is, they took his father and mother and two younger brothers of about nine and ten respectively.

My Father, himself, and his younger brother by eighteen months, were in Danzig at the time and when they got the news, my Father rushed to the nearest 'phone-booth to try to reach the Vielun post office. He stood in that booth a helpless fool: no coin, and nobody around to give him one. That episode gave me an understanding of what isolation might be like, and any time you want to open my purse you will always find at least two ten cent pieces there. It is not that I live in fear of a Hitler clone invading Australia with brown-shirted cohorts, but because I am my Father's daughter. I knew him even before his seed struck my Mother's womb.

He was not transported to a camp until '42 or '43, but spent time in the Lodz ghetto in Poland. Two years in fact, when every day hundreds of Jews were rounded up for the death camps, encouraged by bribes of a kilo of bread and a hunk of sausage. They knew they were being fed to die. But they knew, or thought they knew, that one more day of this stinking ghetto would kill them anyway.

Nephew murdered uncle for food. Solidarity was a rare commodity. Survival was the only ethic. Among the few who shared their food were my Father, Jonathan, and his brother, Samuel---my Father often giving his share to Samuel upon whom the pressures were becoming intolerable. They turned white, then yellow, like the rest from this not-so-slow starvation and one day the brothers decided: "Today we will go. We are going to die. We need the food. We have nothing to lose. What does it matter any more?"

But a man called Lefkovic still managed to disagree. He had the enviable post, with his wife, of doling out the soup ration that had kept Jonathan and Samuel alive for weeks. He had been a close friend of my paternal Grandfather, Jehudah, and Lefkovic said no.

"I will help you; steal extra ration-cards for you. You must not go to the round-up platform. From the prison it is on to Treblinka and Treblinka is death. We know that. The stories coming back are true."

The brothers, desperate and weak, ignored him and went. I think it was a Friday. On Saturday, the day of transportation, the Russians cut off Treblinka. No more Jewish smoke to make the air dusky with stench from there. Jonathan and Samuel were rerouted to Auschwitz.

The Polish Jews stood huddled together in the prison yard of Lodz. Rumkowsky, the Jewish lackey, topmost among the hierarchy of informers, "favorite" with the Germans, stood on a platform and dared at last to raise his voice:

"Brothers, you have lived this day to see Treblinka blocked. You have lasted in this hell through guts and luck. It will be years, I know, before these bastards are beaten, but God---not Russia, Britain nor America---God is fighting for us. I know we have years, still, to live like animals, and to be treated like them. But if we have survived the ghetto we can survive anything. Brothers, I know it as surely as I stand here. We--cannot--die !"

My Father remembers his tears at those words and it would have been simple if after this speech a German hand had shot Rumkowsky on the spot. Yet that did not happen. The Jews killed him---either there or in Auschwitz---tearing him limb from limb for his collaboration with the Nazis which had been responsible for countless deaths. At least that was the story.

So the Brothers Lebenzweig arrived at Auschwitz. Still comparatively strong, they were directed to the right hand line: the line of life. Friends, old schoolmates and many others, were sent to the left: death in the ovens.

My Father was called "My Lord." He stole food, blankets and clothing from the German supplies with dreadful caution for his brother and circle. No wonder business in Australia was so easy for him. If you made a mistake in Australia, you didn't die for it.

Camp life was a perpetual fear of death. "Arbeit Macht Frei," it said above the gates of the camp. "Arbeit Macht Tot," would have been more to the point. For if you were not selected for the ovens, you were worked to the point of destruction.

In '44 my Mother, Devorah, came to Auschwitz with her mother and younger brother. She to the right, my green-eyed, long-haired Mother, her family to the left. But she was seventeen; young; for work. Her mother would pine for the little boy who would be killed, so she was useless. But Devorah was not allowed to go with them. She was thrown brutally to the right. Forced to live.

She was to have been a lawyer. Having persuaded her conservative, religious father to let her be educated beyond the age of ten or twelve, unlike most of her Jewish girlfriends, she then badgered him until he bought her a place at the university in Budapest---one of the few places allowed for Jews in that hallowed institution. Now, it was up at dawn, slapped awake by a female humanoid for inspections, roll-calls and "Arbeit!" Punished heavily and often for stealing fresh water for her cousin, she nevertheless persisted in her efforts.

On the white of her forearm she had a number tatooed. I don't know how many numbers there were or what numbers in fact they were. But I have dreamed them on my own arm in dreams of terror and fever, fleeing from an inexorable foe.

Auschwitz became dangerous for the Germans and the survivors had to be moved on. So the cattle were loaded for relocation, my parents travelling in the very same section, a fact they did not discover until they compared notes much later, exchanging long hidden pain as others might gossip. At Goerlitz, the men and women were immediately separated and taken to their quarters: another existence of life-death.

Jonathan was at once selected as a valet to the chief of a large number of prisoners. A criminal in his own right, this man was notorious for having valets who never lasted for more than three weeks or so, after which he would have them shot for some misdemeanour. Jonathan was naturally wary of his appointment. Still, it did give him easy access to the kitchen where the chief's food was prepared. Once more he stole to save the lives of Samuel and friends. "My Lord," he was called with ever-increasing respect and love.

He used to serve the chief his meals, standing rigidly to attention at the side of the room until this creature had finished eating. Then he would efficiently clear the table, taking scraps meant for the German shepherds for his brother and himself. As in Lodz, luck interfered once again. He was in the next room when he heard the chief say to his subordinate:

"You know, I like that Lebenzweig bastard. Everything he does is perfect. But I just can't stand it anymore. The way he watches me as I eat. I feel the hunger in his belly as I swallow my food. Takes all the pleasure out of eating. Soon I will have to have him shot."

At the next meal, my Father placed the dishes in front of the chief, did an about face and left the room at double time. He held down his job.

Now the Germans are an efficient people. Even today they are known for this quality. Those Jews who were strong enough to work were looked after in a fashion, receiving basic medical and dental attention. The dentist's area was the only part of the camp where male and female survivors met. And so it was that my Father and Mother were sitting together in the ante-room waiting to have their teeth checked. This time they looked at one another properly.

My Father was dark-eyed and not too thin owing to his position with the chief. He was tall and lean and cynical, with, as was often told him later, a marked resemblance to Gregory Peck. My Mother's hair was growing back with a vengeance and, being a fanatic for cleanliness, her lithe body, even in its ill fitting uniform, was an unusally beautiful sight. Copper lights gleamed in her recently washed hair and her Atlantic eyes gazed at this man who noticed her aristocratic lines, high cheek-bones and proud bearing. Neither spoke the other's language, so they resorted to

247

German.

"You are 'The Lord,'" she said.

"Yes."

"I have heard much."

"Are you hungry?" Jonathan asked.

"Always."

"Come to the wires, then, at two a.m. How many will you want food for?"

"Three. Two cousins and myself."

And so it began, the German shepherds growing inexplicably thinner, with leftovers and even some delicacies disappearing. But by then the Germans were too concerned with the oncoming Russians to worry about minor food thefts. Once, Devorah was caught on her way to the rendezvous. Jonathan heard a shot and clenched his teeth in terror and hatred. But the next night she was back, badly bruised and smiling through swollen lips.

"I talked my way out of it," she said.

"You should have been a lawyer."

Liberation. World-wide horror and disgust at the slaughter. But it was 1945 and Jonathan, Samuel and Devorah were alive. Now it became another game of survival, living on wits used for smuggling.

First they took a house which had not been too badly damaged by the bombing. They went into shops, taking what they needed to wear. Then Jonathan and Samuel began to teach Devorah Yiddish. To speak German now was dangerous, and they knew they would have to travel across borders which would make the language of Goethe a death warrant. Devorah learned quickly and began to teach Jonathan her mother-tongue. Expeditions into Hungary would be necessary to dig up the family valuables, hastily buried before the Nazis came. The Hungarian border guards would have to be convinced of my Father's 'authentic' origins.

Leaving Samuel to guard the home base, they set off first to Poland. It was a back-breaking trek with avoidance of destruction as its end. At the border, my Mother showed a shapely leg to the guards whom my Father quickly anaesthetised by efficient blows to the backs of their necks. Now they were armed.

Finally, after some hair-raising moments at the Hungarian border with guards who were suspicious of Jonathan, they managed it back to the little village where the house still stood. The treasures were there and speedily retrieved. On their return trip to Germany, while making their way towards the Czech-Hungarian border, Jonathan said:

"We will have to find an alternate route this time."

"I know," Devorah answered. "Though I got you through before, I could do it again."

"No."

"I still say I could do it."

"I told you, you should have been a lawyer."

"Damn you, I would have been. I would have been if not for the Germans. They took everything."

"They gave me you. They gave you me."

"That you call compensation?"

"I suppose not," he said. "But it's all you got now."

"I know."

It was 1948. No country wanted Jews. Jews were desperate to leave Europe. Samuel had met and married a Hungarian Jewess and somehow obtained a ticket and permit to America. The brothers shook hands and hugged one another, crying as though their souls would explode in an agony of blood and separation. They did not see one another again for twelve years.

Morose and empty twenty-four hours later, Jonathan said to Devorah:

"My Great-Uncle, Gary, lives in a village of Melbourne in Australia with his wife and two daughters. They left Europe in '35. He has written. He wants us to come."

With the profits from their black marketeering, they bought two overlocking sewing machines. My Father had been a tailor in Danzig, he would teach my Mother. They would make a living. He went to buy tickets for the journey across the seas and returned many hours later, weary and dis-spirited.

"They would not sell me tickets."

Why not?"

"They are giving priority to families and married couples. We will have to wait months."

They looked at each other for a long and thoughtful moment. Then Jonathan said to Devorah:

"I suppose we had better get married then."

She shrugged. "There is no choice. I must get out of here."

Not exactly from the pages of Jane Austen.

After a trip of six weeks, they arrived at Port Melbourne. Coming through customs and immigration, they caught sight of Jonathan's family who greeted them in Yiddish and with food-laden baskets---Devorah looked at this plenty and shuddered with delight and revulsion combined. Symbolically, Jonathan took a loaf of bread and a roll of sausage and held them aloft in both his hands.

"We live!" he proclaimed. "Rumkowsky was right. We live!"

Seven years later I was born. Already their business was a flourishing concern and it continued to grow. I have a sister who analyses systems for complex computers. I make tables and chairs and sat down at one of my creations, compelled to write by voices which claim it never happened. Compelled by the pain-filled voices of my parents when they fight, cursing the bastard house-painter who brought them together. And they choose to forget the quick-silver adventure of their early years. Sometimes I watch them hide from one another in an inability to admit a mutual need which has never lessened through the years, hide in anger and in hatred, or in love and in fear.

But we live; whether through the force of God, lack of choice, through luck or because of fate, I will never know. But we live.

Bobbeh

morris lurie

A hard woman. On her last day in Poland she buried the silver samovar, to spite the *shkotzim*, the *goyim*, but took the other, the everyday one, the ordinary one, the plated nickel, which she gave – when she came here, on the other side of the world – to my mother, who set aside a morning every month, with polish, with powder, with brushes and rags, and made it shine, made it gleam. Once a month, twelve times a year, a dutiful daughter. But not once did the *bobbeh* ask to see it. Sentiment was not part of her life. Nor was the samovar, really, of ours. It stood in the garage, on a dusty table, shining in the gloom. Why? I asked my mother. My mother frowned, annoyed, my question unworthy of a reply, the fire in her eyes answer enough. The *bobbeh's* samovar! Didn't I understand anything?

A hard woman. She kept chickens. Two in a wire coop in a corner of her hard, concrete yard, and every Friday, Friday morning, the chicken man brought her a third. Handed it to her by the legs at the back gate, the chicken squawking madly, wings beating, hanging uselessly upside down. This chicken went into the coop for next week, or the week after. Its turn would come. Pushing it in, the *bobbeh* would grab for one of the two in there. For *Shabbos*.

251

The *Shabbos* meal. Except what happened, happened every time, was that the moment she opened the coop, the two chickens in there would run out, run into the yard, and then the *bobbeh* would drop the new chicken, so now all three were rushing about, crazed with fear, and the *bobbeh* would swoop and shout and get nowhere and then seize from its hook in the shed either Uncle Hirshel's tennis racket or the carpet beater – that plaited pattern of wicker arabesques on the end of a long handle that she had brought with her from Poland, from Bialystock, where she was born – seize whichever came to hand first, and then, darting, swinging, shouting curses in Yiddish and Polish and Russian, the vilest things, she would whack and thrash all three chickens into either senseless submission or the coop – an old woman, mind you; oh, how slowly she walked – and then, her blood up, muttering, still cursing, shaking her head, no time for a rest now, stuff today's chicken into a string bag and hurry with it to the *shochet*, the ritual slaughterer, who was two blocks away. The *shochet* slit the throat, nothing else. Then the bobbeh would hurry back and sit down on the wooden bench in the yard and pluck out the feathers, the just-dead chicken laid out on the hammock she made of her apron between her spread-apart knees, and then she would come into the house, into the kitchen, and fill it with the foulest smell as she singed off the feather ends over the gas stove, turning the white body, over and over, round and round, slapping it with her hand whenever a flame appeared, her bare hand, immune to pain.

Or gave it to my mother, let her slap and burn.

I didn't want to go there. I never wanted to go. What for? There was nothing there to do. Couldn't I just stay home?

I'll be all right by myself. Really. Please. I whined, I nagged, I sulked: a dreadful child. My mother was outraged.
'The *bobbeh?*' she said. 'You don't want to see the *bobbeh?*'
She was insulted. She couldn't understand me. What was
the matter with me? But enough, enough! She dressed me
in my best clothes, my best coat. Shined my shoes. Pulled
up my socks. Combed my hair. Wetted a corner of her
handkerchief in her mouth to wipe away at my mouth, my
eyes, my ears, a mark on my knee. Buffed me. Polished
me. Tugged and straightened. Made me look nice. And
then, there, the minute we were there, ignored me. Forgot
all about me. She had no time for me now. She was with
the *bobbeh.* Her mother.

And the *bobbeh* would snap, 'Go outside. What are you
standing here for? Go and play.'

Play with what?

The *bobbeh's* yard was concrete, concrete and iron and
brick. Nothing growing, nothing green. Glary in summer,
in winter you froze to death. The high brick side of the
house next door loomed over it. The other side was a
corrugated iron fence. A washing line stretched across,
held up with a long split-ended pole. An open shed. An
outside tap. The chickens. (I was frightened of the chickens.) The back gate was corrugated iron, too. It scraped
on the concrete when you opened it. When you closed it,
the whole length of the fence shook, and clanged like a
coupling train.

'Take the ball,' my mother would suggest. 'Play with
the ball.'

The ball. A bald tennis ball. There was always one
there. I don't know where the *bobbeh* found them. Uncle
Hirshel didn't play tennis any more. He didn't have time.
He worked hard, long hours, selling underwear and socks.
He had not yet married, and lived with the *bobbeh.* (As did
my unmarried Auntie Dora, too.) Uncle Hirshel was a

thin, nervous man with a long nose and sticking-out ears and a stutter, and he was obsessed with fitness. He exercised daily, first thing in the morning, swinging and springing and touching his toes. He rode a bicycle to work. His body didn't have an ounce of fat. 'F-f-f-feel!' he would command me, flexing his arm. And I would touch him there, feel his muscle like frightening iron under his shirt, impossible-to-squeeze steel. 'Ah!' Uncle Hirshel would cry. 'You see? S-s-s-strong!'

But a gentle man, like all the men in the family. Obedient. Quiet. I don't think I ever once heard him raise his voice. And frightened. Once, in Bialystock, he had thrown a stone which had accidentally gone through the window of the house next door. Non-Jewish people. *Shkotzim*. Uncle Hirshel had run crying to the *bobbeh* and then hidden under her bed, and the *bobbeh* had had to order his brother, my Uncle Sam, to go outside in his place and take the beating.

While her husband, the *bobbeh's zaydeh*, sat, said nothing, did nothing.

We called him the *bobbeh's zaydeh*, always that, never anything else, to differentiate him from the other *zaydeh*, my father's father, who was simply *zaydeh*, and who lived with us (his wife was in Israel, or Palestine as it was then), but there was more to the title than that. Look at the ownership it proclaimed! Look at the subservience! He was a small man, made even smaller by the hat he always wore, inside the house and out, the hat casting a shadow on his hollow-cheeked face, the brindley moustache, the vague, faded eyes that looked always wet. He sat and smoked and drank tea – or sometimes a glass of *bromfen*, brandy – and never said a word.

Even on *Pesach*, enthroned on feather pillows at the head of the table, running the *seder*, you felt he was a puppet king, the *bobbeh* in real control. Three days after he died, she took me into his bedroom. On the bed was an old suitcase. She opened it. Inside it was filled with socks and ties. 'From America!' the *bobbeh* said. 'Take!' He had gone there for a year, to make his fortune, believing all the stories, overnight millionaires, streets paved with gold, and a year later had limped back with this, just this, and then sat silent for ever after, smoking, drinking, wet-eyed under his hat. 'Take!' the *bobbeh* cried. 'He never wore them. It's like new.' Grey socks. Grey ties. The *bobbeh's* fingers plucked them from the ancient suitcase, threw them before me onto the bed. I fled.

The *bobbeh* knew everyone and everyone knew her. The back gate clanged with endless visitors. Gossip. News. The kitchen bustled with tea and talk. An engagement. A marriage. Business deals. A death. What did it all mean? I couldn't understand a word. I sat in a corner, flipping through Auntie Dora's movie magazines, and when I couldn't do that any more, I walked through the house. Auntie Dora's room smelled of powder, make-up, cigarettes. There were photographs of movie stars stuck up on her walls, pink pictures of Clark Gable, Van Heflin, Alan Ladd. I stood in the doorway. I didn't dare go in. Uncle Hirshel's room was neat and bare. A bed, a chair, a chest of drawers, a dark wardrobe. No clothes, no pictures, nothing lying about. I didn't go in there either. I tiptoed around the house, shoes creaking on the cold linoleum. Everywhere was dark and cold and smelled of polish. Hard furniture. Locked cabinets. The dining-room table was topped with glass – don't touch. Heavy door handles. Stiff doors.

In the hall a strange blue light fell on the floor through the glass on either side of the front door, the front door that was never opened, no one ever came in that way. I was restless. I was bored. I wanted to go home. When would we go home? I felt the house filled with something more than cold and dark and that smell of polish.

In the kitchen, everyone sat. Talking. Shouting. Drinking tea. Smoking. Eating cake. Except for my mother. She never sat down. She didn't have time to sit down. Whatever the *bobbeh* said, she did. Look in the oven, it must be ready in there! Get more plates! Where's the tea? A knife, a knife, we need a knife for the cake! The back gate clanged. Someone else came in. A chair, a chair! the *bobbeh* ordered. Get a chair! Auntie Dora sat. Uncle Hirshel sat, the *bobbeh's zaydeh* sat, everyone sat and shouted and ate and drank, but not my mother. In the *bobbeh's* house my mother ran like a servant.

My mother was the favourite. Everyone said that. The oldest of three daughters, two sons, she felt the responsibility. It was she who came here first. This was in '33, '34, Hitler already looming. Her visa was for America, passage booked, bags packed, the *bobbeh's zaydeh* already there, walking those gold-paved streets. And then it was discovered that the *bobbeh's* lungs were scarred. Old scars, dead tissue, but scars nevertheless. America, for her, was closed. And my mother? Save yourself! everyone cried. Run! Go! No, my mother said, and came here instead, knowing no one, alone and frightened, sailed to Australia, where there was no law about scars. Found a place to live, found work, saved, saved every penny, saved to bring out her brothers and sisters, but before them, the *bobbeh*. She brought the *bobbeh* out first.

We were kosher because of the *bobbeh*. Bought separate plates for Pesach, finer by far than those we normally used, white plates with a rim of gold that lay hidden under brown paper on the top of the cupboard for the fifty-one ordinary weeks of the year.

For the *bobbeh* we went to *shul*, dressed in clothes we couldn't afford. Then walked with her from *shul*, where she was always the slowest, the last, she couldn't leave until she had spoken to everyone, wished them a *Gut Shabbos*, a *Gut Yomtov*, and then the gossip, the news, the slow walk home, at least an hour it took her to cover that kilometre, a step at a time, until, at last, exhausted, famished, we arrived, and sat. Except for my mother, who became, in the *bobbeh's* kitchen, that rushing servant.

Everyone married, everyone left. She found a wife for Uncle Hirshel, a husband for Auntie Dora, that dreamer of movie stars. A miracle, everyone said. The *bobbeh* moved to another house, a smaller house, she had no need now of all those rooms. The yard here was lawn, and for the first year Uncle Hirshel came weekly and mowed it, and then the idea came to him of concrete, green concrete. 'It looks the s-s-s-same,' he said. In summer the *bobbeh* stood and watered it, the lawnmower slowly rusting in a shed in the back. Then the *bobbeh's zaydeh* died, and this house that had been so small was suddenly too big, empty and echoing wherever you looked, but the *bobbeh* refused to move again. There was a place for her with any of her three daughters, either of her two sons. No. She wouldn't hear of it. No! she shouted, shaking her head. And when the *bobbeh* said no, there was no argument.

So we visited, once a week. On the weekend. *Shabbos.* Sunday. And in between the visits my mother would drop in, as she put it, and clean the *bobbeh's* windows and sweep her yard and polish her floors, arriving home late, tired, exhausted, dark under the eyes. And then, the next day, go again. 'She's alone,' my mother would say. 'How can I not go?'

My mother died before her. Died of exhaustion, worn thin, worn out. Twenty years ago, but I am there now. I stand in my suit, in the *Chevra Kadisha.* I can see the *bobbeh* being led in, supported by my two uncles, Uncle Hirshel and Uncle Sam. Her head is bent, her face is hidden, there is no face there at all. She stands with my uncles. The service begins. And then suddenly she breaks away, she tears herself from her sons, she falls upon the coffin, she screams out my mother's name. She has to be constrained, she has to be pulled up, she has to be pulled away. And now she begins to wail. She wails with a sound I have never heard before. My hair stands on end. I am frightened to look at her, to look at anyone, but especially at her. For I am ashamed. My face burns with shame. A hard woman who made my mother a servant? How could I have ever thought such things? I am a child. I understand nothing.

I stand with my head bowed, made humble by the *bobbeh's* towering love.

Drifting

Serge Liberman

The day I married Rosemary, my father killed me in his heart.

He had threatened, he had warned, had tried with fatherly embrace to dissuade. The skin of his hand was rumpled leather and printer's ink had burrowed under his nails. In his nearness, he smelled of paper and must.

'If you go through with it . . .'

He had never been a religious man, but at fifty-five acquired a reverence for symbol. Entering his home, he touched and kissed now the mezuzah he had earlier ignored. He hung a mizrach on the eastern wall, wore a skull-cap when he ate, and delicately, lovingly even, sipped from the silver kiddush cup that Mother had bought.

I went through with it.

'We finally made it, Bernie, didn't we?', Rosemary whispered when the ring was on her finger and the handshakes and kisses had done their round. On the steps outside the registry, she kissed me on the brow and her black cherry-scented hair brushed against my cheek.

'Are you happy?', I asked, holding her chin.

'Perfectly,' she said. Aren't you?'

'Yes,' I said.

Edward Merrilees, down from Mildura for his daughter's wedding, came up to us. 'You can call me Dad now, Son,' and Cynthia Merrilees, touching my arm, added, 'And I'm Mum.'

The November sun glowed as soft-edged ribbons of light

259

tumbled through the gathering clouds. People walked past and smiled. An elderly woman stopped to watch. Cars passed. A policeman blew his whistle.

My father was in his press, setting type.

On the way to Phillip Island, Rosemary sat close to me, her head upon my shoulder. I spoke about my father, remembering things I had earlier chosen to forget. – Like the number on his arm. Like his heart attack. Like his pain.

If Father ever floundered in his early days in the oceans of either disbelief or faith, he didn't let the slightest ripple betray. He swam in certainty, however far he allowed himself to drift.

Setting out from Europe, he possessed one overcoat, one watch and one book, a slender volume in Yiddish to which he cleaved throughout the voyage. Often he didn't come down for meals and Mother would carp:

'Itzchak, put away Shpinoza and come and eat!'

'But I *am* eating,' he would reply good-naturedly. 'Feasting even, at a banquet that is without end.'

And he would stay on deck to savour, to dine, to gorge again, while the salty sea-breeze flapped the pages and ruffled his hair.

Shpinoza. I liked the sound. It had about it something exotic and strangely musical. I sang it, twisted it with my lips, played quoits with it, said it harshly like my mother, uttered it delicately with Father's reverence for sacred things. Sometimes, he read to Mother as she embroidered her handkerchiefs, and I sat at the foot of his deck-chair, listening without comprehending, if only to hear Father say, 'Yes, yes, that is true,' or 'Shpinoza is a great man, but no, to this I can't agree.'

Father was a clever man.

But sometimes Mother was displeased. Especially when he spoke of God, about whom he and Spinoza disagreed.

'Not in front of the child,' she would admonish, lifting her

260

sea-blue eyes from her embroidery, and then say to me, 'Baruch'l, my precious, maybe you want to go down and get a roll?'

But Father, secure in the certainty in which he swam, would answer, 'Why shouldn't he know the truth? God *is* only an idea, created, nurtured and sustained by the human mind. After Auschwitz . . .'

'Itzchak,' Mother would plead again, more forcefully. 'Please, not in front of the child.'

He would shrug his shoulders, but have the final say. 'One day he will learn it for himself.'

My father's name was Issac, where his father's had been Abraham. And, following ancestral heritage, he might have named me Jacob had he not, at the time of my birth, been full with the spirit of Spinoza. He called me Baruch instead. But where that other Baruch, idol of his veneration, had outside the Law become known as Benedict, on Australian soil his son Baruch was transmuted into Bernard – which he avoided whenever he could.

'My clever Baruch'l,' he would call me, or 'my little Shpinoza' if I had been especially smart. But Bernard he left for the street, for documents, for some later time.

I was eleven then.

That slender Yiddish volume, dog-eared, ragged and stained, retained pride of place among the books with which Father crammed his shelves, long after he had drifted from that anchor that had been Shpinoza. I tried, in later years, to suck its juices and dine at the banquet where Father had feasted, but the lofty Yiddish, the complicated words, the tortuous sentences, all these passed undigested through my boyish brain. I leafed through his other books but these were no less elusive, and I despaired of ever understanding as I watched Father, his hair beginning to grey, reading in his chair, opening one volume and another, extracting, marking, underlining and annotating, through private and unremitting industry gathering sheafs of paper full with his close and spindly script, which he stapled, bound and filed, taking them out when invited to lecture before the Kadimah, the Katzetler or the Lodzer Landsmanschaft.

'What good does all this do you?', Mother said once, bringing a cup of tea from the kitchen. I had followed her in. 'All day in the press, at night with your books. Is that living? You'll ruin your health. So what if, for a change you don't speak at the meetings?'

My father reached out to me and rummaged his fingers through my hair. Rings had appeared around his eyes and the greying bristles of his eyebrows seemed stiff. He had begun to smell of paper and must.

'Well, my little Shpinoza, and what do *you* say?'

He smiled at the helpless shrug of my shoulders.

'Do you know what Shpinoza would say? "The greatest good is the knowledge of the union which the mind has with all of nature." Knowledge, Baruch'l. There is so much to learn and so much to understand.' To Mother, he added, 'After Auschwitz, Rivke, everything that was said and written before has become all wrong.'

After I had turned Bar Mitzvah, Father often took me with him to his lectures. There were never many people present. Fifteen, twenty, on exceptional occasions even thirty. But he held them in thrall as – it seemed to me – he waded through depths mysterious and intriguing, and created ever-widening ripples around words and names that became through repetition increasingly familiar. The fluency with which he spoke about Europe, Israel, Hitler, God, the assurance that stamped each word on Asch and Peretz, Sholom Aleichem and Leivick, stirred in me, less a pride of the man who addressed the gathering – though pride in him was beyond denial – than a resurgent will to taste again of the delicacies that had made that man. It was at sixteen that I began really to read and to absorb those juices that had thus far eluded me.

I began to buy my own books, cheap second-hand copies I discovered at Hall's.

I devoured them eagerly. But Mother was worried.

'It's unnatural,' she said. 'A boy your age should be outside, in the sun, not filling his head with ideas. You're just like your father.'

'Come now, Rivke,' Father said, laughing, letting the creases play at the outer corners of his eyes 'let him be, he's not as bad as all that. A man is nothing but what he knows.'

And as he looked over my expanding shelves of books, taking down Zweig's Spinoza, Dostoievski, Chekhov, Tagore, he nodded with obvious satisfaction and sucked his lips. Only when he came across Russell's Essays did he waver momentarily and say, 'That's a bit radical for a young fellow, isn't it?', but added with his next breath, 'He does make sense just the same.'

Father's endorsement of Russell transformed flirtation into commitment. What Spinoza had been for Father, Russell became for me. In the years that followed, through matriculation and through university, I experimented with Heschel and Buber and Hirsch, and sought sustenance from the Tenach from which they had derived their source, but it was to Russell that I repeatedly returned, as it was towards Ecclasiastes, of all the Scriptures, that my natural inclinations leant, finding in their this-worldly earthiness a resonance that most closely approximated truth.

Father continued to lecture, but to an audience, I noticed, that steadily dwindled. He began to repeat himself and narrowed the scope of his themes to a preoccupation with the War, the Holocaust, and the relation of God to the Holocaust. His conclusion – that God had died in Auschwitz together with His people – was not a popular one; far less the corollary, that survival had no meaning, nor the deaths of the six million, beyond the actual physical facts themselves.

One evening, during a talk, he unbuttoned a sleeve and bared his arm, and pointing at the dull blue number engraved in skin, said, with a vehemence as uncharacteristic as it was fervid,

'God, if He were there, would not have let this be done to a man.'

The outward certainty with which he addressed his audience remained, but the persistence with which he belaboured the same set of themes betrayed – I sensed – the first signs that he might, in fact, be floundering in a swelling tide of self-doubt. People left the meetings unsatisfied. There was talk that Isaac Walshansky was becoming eccentric.

Meanwhile, at university, I had joined the Rationalist Society and, in time, became its chairman.

Mother, when I told her, bit her lips.

'Bernard, you're drifting away from us more and more,' she said. 'Don't you have any Jewish friends?'

'Some,' I answered, not without some truth, 'but we have little in common.'

Father looked up from the tea he was drinking. He seemed tired and ashen, as though he was driving himself too hard.

'Are you sure that the Society's principles are your own, Baruch?', he asked. He had stopped calling me his Spinoza long before.

'As certain as I can be,' I said, in fact totally convinced.

I was studying history and comparative literature at the time and my library, already substantial, continued to grow.

'I see you've relegated our own thinkers to a corner,' Father observed on one occasion.

I had indeed. Where Buber and Heschel and Rosenzweig had been, I had placed Russell and Huxley and Freud, and in place of Peretz and Asch, I had installed Beckett and Camus.

My circle of friends, too, progressively changed. As chairman of the Rationalist Society, my contacts broadened, bringing me to the notice of academics, post-graduate students, editors of journals, research staff. I whirled in a round of university parties, meetings, lectures and debates. I presented papers on 'Determinism and Chance' and 'The Dilemmas of Reason', and published articles, reviews, critiques.

When, in my honours year, I moved out of home, the physical act of moving was a mere formality. Apart from Sunday dinners, I was seldom home in the day. Mother resisted, protested and predicted the worst; while Father, who seemed now to flicker where, once, he had throbbed, relented more easily but, echoing Mother, saw fit to warn,

'You're a grown man, Baruch. Go, if you wish . . . But don't bring home a shikse.'

He didn't laugh on this occasion. Instead, he fixed me with an unfaltering gaze, a gaze that sought out a promise, or some assurance, that I would not stray too far. His hair was prematurely white and a doughy flabbiness had set into his cheeks. He had begun to visit Dr. Benjamin about his sleeplessness.

Only long after I had met Rosemary did it occur to me that Father must have laboured under certain premonitions at the time.

I made no promise.

The following March, I began to tutor in literature and started work towards my Master's degree. In May, I met Rosemary and in August, she moved in with me. She had black hair and delicate lips and wore colours that were bright without being glaring. She brought with her a certain sprightliness and there hung about her the scent of cherries.

One day, Mother asked, 'You're not running around with shikses, are you?'

'I have all kinds of friends,' I answered.

Father merely asked whether I had read Elie Wiesel . . .

Father's health deteriorated. He spent more time before the television set and less with his papers and books. His lectures became infrequent, and in December, Dr. Benjamin discovered he had diabetes.

'There is only one law in this world,' Father said in a mock tone that issued out of his dejection. 'And that is – everything that lives runs to decay.'

Two months later, he suffered a heart attack.

The days he spent in Prince Henry's Hospital were black. Confined to bed, he armoured himself with a solid, inscrutable silence. Mother, thrust suddenly upon the rack of uncertainty, fretted and wept and wrung her hands. She brought Father the 'Jewish News' but it remained on his locker unopened and unread. Even as we sat beside him, he avoided speech, he avoided touch, and turned his grey, melancholy, almost wounded eyes now upon the heart monitor and now upon the King's Domain where the white turret of Government House rose above the green unmoving crests of trees. Sometimes, moved by some inner prompting, he would sigh or raise an eyebrow or shrug a shoulder. But mostly he remained unreachable.

I spent much time looking at the number on his arm . . .

While Father was in hospital, I stayed with Mother. Rosemary minded the apartment to which I returned when Father came home.

Home again, something new, at first barely perceptible, enveloped Father. If he had, in the days following his heart attack, been frightened or bewildered by the glancing touch of death, he now breathed of a calm that plumbed his inner depths. He slept without pills, sat at ease behind his books, and began to glow again.

It was then that he acquired a reverence for symbol and ritual.

'I have been spared twice,' he said. 'And for that I can only be grateful.'

And out of gratitude, he nailed a mezuza to every door, made benedictions over the Sabbath wine, wore his skull-cap when he ate and walked to the synagogue on the Sabbath.

One Sunday, upon visiting my parents for dinner, I found him incinerating papers in the back-yard. It was early April. There were apples on the trees and the first issue of lemons was ripening. Father stood beside the incinerator feeding the flames, every so often bending back as a puff of wind blew thick smoke into his face. I started as I recognised the papers full with Father's close and spindly script.

Moving forward to salvage the files not yet consigned to fire, I exclaimed, 'But that's your life!'

Father grabbed my shoulder. He smiled, wryly, as he fed another sheaf of papers to the flames.

'Yes, Baruch. Wasted, wasn't it?'

Some six weeks into his convalescence, it occurred to him to visit my flat. I was at a Rationalist meeting and Rosemary who had stayed behind to complete an essay, opened the door. He didn't stay. Instead, he turned on his heels, and without a second glance at Rosemary, hurried, almost stumbled down the stairs.

When I visited my parents again on the following Sunday, Mother greeted me first.

'You can still show your face? Do you know what you are doing to your father? Have you thought for one moment . . .?'

Father restrained her with an upraised palm.

'Don't shout,' he said to her as he turned to me. 'Baruch, tell me, is this what I lived through Auschwitz for? Is it? For my sake, give her up.'

His skin which had begun to shine again resumed the matted dullness of leather.

'But she's a lovely girl,' I said. 'You have only to meet her, to talk to her to see . . .'

'Apikoros!', Mother exclaimed, 'I knew this would happen!'

Father again motioned her not to shout.

'No, I will not meet her,' he said. 'Some things are more important. You must know at all times what you are and what *they* are.'

'But I don't *believe*.'

'It isn't a question of belief, but if nothing else, then of respect.'

'I can't give her up now,' I said. 'It's too late. I wanted to bring her home. I wanted to tell you. We are planning to marry in November.'

'Aren't you ashamed?', Mother remonstrated.

Father fixed me with his gaze 'If you go through with it . . .' he began, but didn't finish. He adjusted his skull-cap and repeated, 'For my sake, Bernard.'

Where he had long before stopped calling me his Spinoza, he now disowned Baruch as well.

'They'll adjust,' I said to Rosemary. 'We're not the first in this situation.'

But my parents didn't adjust. Sunday dinners became more

strained and recriminatory. I invented excuses for avoiding them.

I continued to whirl in my own orbit. Rosemary and I prepared for the wedding. Despite my pleadings, my parents refused to meet her.

'Perhaps we *are* doing the wrong thing, Bernie,' Rosemary said.

'Whatever we do now will be the wrong thing,' I answered. 'They won't be reconciled.'

In the end, we made peace with facts. Ours would be a registry wedding, without a reception, without white dresses or flowers or bridesmaids. The Merrilees would drive down from Mildura; my parents would come if they changed their mind. A single photographer would take pictures and a party for friends would follow our return from Phillip Island.

'Hardly the wedding a girl dreams about, is it?', Rosemary said, brushing her lips against my cheek.

Mother still tried to change my mind, pleading at every opportunity. But Father, his eyes averted, said, 'I don't want to talk about it. He's a grown man. He knows his obligations.'

Neither wavered. On the evening before the wedding, I telephoned them.

Father answered.

'There is nothing to talk about,' he said. 'Until now you've been our son. If you go through with it . . .'

On the way to Phillip Island, Father's dry unemotional tone haunted, more tenaciously than Mother's heated shriller plaints. I stared at the road ahead and found it hard to speak.

'You don't regret it now, do you, Bernie?', Rosemary said, touching my cheek. With her hair drawn back by a crimson ribbon, she looked more alive, open, gay.

'Things might have been different, that's all.'

'If we had been accepted?'

'If we had been accepted. And yet the paradox is that, in a way, things couldn't have been different. It's being too harsh to expect them to accept.'

'That's an unexpected change.'

'It's just another way of looking at things. One would have to go back to some different beginning to understand, to a beginning starting not with us, Rosemary, nor even with my parents' coming to Australia, but further back still, generations, to a distant encounter of the Jew with Europe. And even then, the story is only a fraction told.'

Rosemary's gaze upon me, open and exploring, compelled me to continue.

'For the chairman of the Rationalist Society, this is an unusual admission to make, I know, but the truth is this: the history of the Jew is a chain and each generation a link along it. Do you realise what our marriage means, Rosemary? With me, one specific chain has come to an end, its continuity has been disrupted. And in a way it's . . . it's awesome.'

Rosemary kissed me on the ear, but I doubted if she really understood.

When we returned to Melbourne, I swallowed my pride and took Rosemary to my parents' home. She thought it unwise. But I had resolved to force them to meet her, something I should have done long before, but had repeatedly deferred.

It was Sunday afternoon and the weather was mild and faintly sunny.

Mother opened the door.

She had evidently considered such an encounter, for she visibly took control of herself, set her jaw firm and knotted her brow with a forced determination. Her hair lay in careless grey tangles, her eyes hardened to flint.

'Mother, this is Rosemary.'

'You may as well come in,' she said, sizing up Rosemary with one scanning glace.

'Was this the right time to come?', Rosemary whispered, nervously, as we entered the lounge-room.

'And when is the right time?', I asked in return, smiling and squeezing her hand.

There were fruit and nuts on the coffee-table and one of

Father's books in a chair. The room smelled of polish and, strangely, of aniseed. On the dinner table lay Father's open Tenach.

'Your father's out walking,' Mother said, intercepting my gaze.

'How is he?'

'God protects.'

She wore a chequered apron and her hands were moist and white and wrinkled from laundering clothes. Following us into the lounge-room, she made minimal fuss over her appearance. She merely dried her hands, brushed away some recalcitrant strands of hair and with a corner of her damp apron wiped her brow, asserting, although without words, that whatever happened in her household, the daily chores of living had to go on. Yielding to the habits of hospitality, she pushed towards us the bowl of fruit and nuts.

'Here, take some,' she said, sitting down opposite Rosemary who, hands in lap and faintly smiling, let herself be lapped by Mother's scrutiny.

We scraped about for conversation but stuck to the ordinary, the inoffensive, the commonplace – Father's health, Rosemary's Fine Arts, my Master's thesis. Rosemary, to her credit, did not try to impress. In her own buoyant but unobtrusive way, she added her bit and let her quaint and vivid turns of phrase and her poise, more than any exaggeratd deference or misplaced brusqueness, reach across to Mother who, I saw, or sensed, in the nest of irrevocability, was not wholly displeased.

We stayed a mere forty minutes.

In the doorway, with Rosemary already outside waiting on the steps, Mother took my arm and riveted me with eyes that were grey and deep and probing.

'You've made your peace with me, Bernard,' she said. 'What else can a mother do, but your father, may his years be many, won't be so easy.'

Father came to me in many forms, though not in the form that mattered most. It was the memory he revisited time and again, that store and labyrinth in which he remained perpetually preserved and most tenderly revered – as a younger, pulsating man exulting over Spinoza, as the eager scholar gathering notes, as the fluent speaker holding audiences in thrall, as the printer in his press, smelling of paper and must. But he, the man, my father, of the flesh and blood now kept apart, neither reaching out to me nor letting himself be reached.

I telephoned each week. Mother always answered.

'God protects,' she said whenever I asked after him. 'May his years be many, your father is keeping well.'

In May, Rosemary, bounding in, bag over shoulder, buoyantly announced she was pregnant.

'May it be in a good hour,' Mother said flatly when I broke the news, and added as though it were an afterthought, 'Your father's out.'

When I hung up the receiver, I felt suddenly, inexplicably, afraid. 'The greatest good' Father had once said quoting Spinoza, 'is the knowledge of the union which the mind has with the whole of nature.' – I had never felt myself so separate, so adrift. In silence I went in to Rosemary who was studying at the desk, pressed her shoulders, bent over her, kissed her and smelled the cherries in her hair.

And ever thinking of my father I continued to drift in the months that followed, berthing nowhere, in my reading flitting between Russell and Wiesel in a bid to reconcile the world of reason with the world of madness that both Wiesel and my father had known. Time and again I saw him roll up his sleeve before his audience, saw him expose that blue number engraved on his arm, and I realised, with a jolting abruptness, that if any man had the right to believe or the privilege to doubt, it was he, my father, who had suffered that madness, and not myself who, nurtured in the security of unbeleaguered theory, had learnt of life from mere dabbling in books. And I wanted to run to him often, and lay this new awareness before him, but each time I fell short of action enervated before the image of his wounded eyes, his distance, his silence . . .

The semesters passed. I resigned as Chairman of the Rationalist Society and left it altogether. Soon after I gave up the round of parties, meetings, lectures and debates, and near the end of the year submitted my thesis. Its subject, that of manners and morals in eighteenth-century French and English fiction, had become utterly banal, irrelevant and trivial. Rosemary, well into the last phase of her pregnancy, showed signs of swelling. She put on weight, her rings became tight on her finger and in the middle of December, Dr. Ritter admitted her into hospital for rest.

'Well, this is it, Bernie,' she said with a sparkle, sitting up in her bed. 'We can start thinking of names now, can't we?'

'What about Joshua for a boy and Rachel for a girl?'

'I'll sleep on it,' she said with a lively toss of her head. 'Now hold my hand and wish me luck.'

In the corridor, I met Dr. Ritter. Tall, broad-shouldered and greying, he stooped over me as he spoke. His voice was deep and gravelly.

'There is no real cause for alarm, my young man. Your lady's pelvis is a little small and she has a little too much fluid on board, but we shall manage . . . You look worried, my young man.'

It was less worry than destitution that he saw . . .

The academic year over and the campus closed for the summer break, I wandered aimlessly about the streets of Carlton, escaping from the premature heat in a succession of bookstores, record shops and coffee-bars, while back home, alone in my flat without Rosemary's ever-reassuring presence, I watched television indiscriminately, listened to music without enjoyment, and opened and shut a succession of books for which all patience had been drained. I often thought of Father, alone in the press, setting type.

Three days after entering hospital, a Friday, Rosemary went into labour. It was arduous and painful and continued through the night. I sat in the hospital foyer, drinking coffee from the cafe-bar. The subdued light, the dark brown carpets, the lack-lustre prints hanging on the bone-coloured walls depressed me. I felt encompassed by a brittle shell with only Rosemary remaining to fill the aching hollow within. Dr. Ritter's remarks about her pelvis and the fluid troubled me incessantly, and, in the silent solitude of waiting, grew into proportions that made me tremble as I sat thinking, remembering, reliving, and mulling over again and again how different things might have been. 'Wish me luck,' Rosemary had said. Luck alone was insufficient. In that night of waiting, aware of the imminence of the birth of my child, I sensed the burgeoning of something grander, something more fervid, more profound, that another might have recognised more certainly as prayer.

And when Dr. Ritter came at seven in the morning to deliver the child, and I saw Rosemary again soon after, weary but quietly content, the baby cradled in her arm, its black eyes blinking, its lips sucking, and its nose quaintly flattened, that unspoken fervid reverberation swelled still more grandly and more profoundly and burst into the flush of ecstasy and the exultation of thanksgiving.

'He's ours, Bernie,' Rosemary said.

'He's us,' I answered, barely able to answer.

'May you both have an easy upbringing,' Mother said when I telephoned her. 'Where is your Rosemary? I'd like to send her flowers.'

'And Father?'

'It's Saturday,' Mother reminded me. 'He's gone to the synagogue.'

It was half-past nine. I shaved, showered and dressed, put on a suit I seldom wore. I found a skull-cap in a drawer and put it in my pocket. Outside, the sun shone calmly, the air smelled of acorns, and a breeze ruffled my hair as I drove across the city to St. Kilda where my father had gone to pray. It was with a lightness of spirit born of resolve that I entered the synagogue.

Slightly stooped, and swaying to the cantor's musical chant, Father seemed at one with the serenity of the place. Above, the dome rose high and dust-laden beams of yellow light tumbled through the windows, converging on the rostrum where the cantor sang. Father, in an undertone, sang with him. Before the Ark covered in velvet, above which arched the legend

273

'Know Before Whom Thou Standest', the congregation prayed, bound in a solidarity from which I felt myself apart. But in my own way, in the way of inner ecstasy for which I lacked appropriate words, I reached out, whole-heartedly, to offer thanks to Whoever it was before Whom I stood. And I felt for Father then and understood his pain and, with my gaze, clung to him through the remainder of the service, awaiting that moment when I could approach him to deliver the news and be received in turn.

The service over, I watched him as, lovingly, he removed his prayer-shawl, folded it, and with his prayer book, which he kissed, placed it in the locker beneath his seat. His features – the brow, the cheeks, the chin, and more than these his hands – had acquired a certain heaviness, or solidity, that told, I thought, of inner certainty. I wanted to approach him and to greet him. But the congregation began to disperse and I moved with the murmuring current towards the outer steps where, full with the birth of my child and alive with the aura of worship, I stopped to wait for him

Coming out, he saw me, hesitated, looked me up and down, held his breath. There were deep creases beside his eyes. He wore his summer suit.

'Father,' I said, approaching, reaching with words across the physical space between us. 'I have a son . . . You are a grandfather . . .'

I reached out, but the fingers of my reaching met with steel. He brushed past me and descended the steps. There were people still about. I ran after him.

'I know it's been hard, but listen to me. For one moment.'

'What is there to say?', he asked, in that crusty unemotional tone that haunted.

'I came to tell you, as soon as I could. Rosemary . . . this morning . . . she gave birth to a son. That's what there is to say. I have a son . . .'

'Then you have more than I have.'

Nearing the gate, I tried to reach him once more.

'I can't believe it. That you can so totally give us up. *This* is what you survived for.'

'For this I survived? Apikoros! *You* can talk about survival, when you haven't learnt yet to wipe your nose.'

'Father, don't turn away. Not now. I need you. If there is a God, don't be so hard. Father!'

Turning into Charnwood Crescent, he drew away, walking in the shadows of buildings thrown upon him by the sun; while, left alone and standing at the gate, poised between the synagogue and the street, my private universe tottered about me. Without foothold and without anchor, I floundered, and stood amidst the rubble in the aching emptiness of ruins which, I felt, I knew, not even Rosemary nor my newborn child could ever adequately restore.

ALL THE STORMS and SUN-SETS

MARIA LEWITT

'Israel,' my mother would say, 'our poor, tiny Israel.' And whenever she did, it reminded me of a day long past, when as a young boy, I brought home a kitten---all scrawny, frightened, with dull coat and sad eyes. Mother fed it on milk and while it slurped voraciously, she looked at her freshly scratched arms and mumbled, 'kitten, you poor, little kitten.'

There is something about my mother I can't quite understand. Her constant moaning, sighing, shuddering---her emotional overflows. Her very mixture of contempt, yet consideration towards people, even issues.

My childhood, when I think of it, was crowded with images. 'Horror stories,' as my father called them. 'Stop it,' he would urge. But my mother would look at him in her specific mournful way.

'My son has to know,' she would insist. 'I was told of pogroms, he has to know of Hitler and Our War.'

For she always referred to the Second World War as 'Her War.'

The pieces of jig-saw kept sinking into my mind. Wretched people, hunger, army boots, finality of death, unheard of brutality, squalid streets.

'And what's more, we were having Literary Evening---You know where?---In Warsaw Ghetto ----What do you say now, you Ober Huhem?'

Fragments of a puzzle which was my parents' past.

On a day I told my parents I'll visit Israel, mother stopped in the middle of whatever she was doing, like a horse would stop suddenly when sensing danger. It took her a while before she set herself in motion again.

'It is all Israel needs. If it hasn't had enough trouble without you. All it needs is you.'

'Mama,' I tried to explain.

But she became a torrent. Pouring out her views of girls who couldn't find themselves husbands, of all drop-outs, of all the heart-broken, spoiled, selfish, pigheaded, who belonged to my generation. Israel, the remedy, Israel the answer for everyone. An escape route.

So when I arrived in Israel, I sent my parents a letter.

'That thumping of the heart,' I wrote, 'the tears in the eyes and the urge to kiss the ground you told me so much about, didn't happen.

'The Israeli custom officer radiated just about the same amount of warmth as any other officer at any other international airport. Sure, it felt good to be let out of the claustrophobic capsule after being cooped up in it for what seemed to be an eternity.

'As for my luggage, no problem. My rucksack proved to be not too heavy. The only item which weighs on me is the address book with names of your friends you instructed me to visit.

277

'I promise nothing. Will see how many I'll manage.

'It rained on arrival. Was met by your cousin Bertha. She fed me on chicken soup in the middle of the night. Her flat is stale and gloomy---like herself.'

I posted the letter and on the way to Jerusalem regretted sending it.

Tree covered hills. Mile after mile. Planted as a memorial to Six Million Martyrs of my mother's War. 'Coniferous ones symbolize children,' explained our guide.

Mixed trees, like a mixed crowd. Strong next to weak, tall next to short, notable next to ordinary. Some reaching to the sun, others pointing their arms down.

That willowy one would be my mother's cousin Janka, who managed to matriculate and worried because her feet grew too large. . .And that one on the side would be my grandfather who never trusted big crowds. So after all, he had set his roots down in Jewish Soil. A loner, not alone any more.

The faces, the episodes, the world which was, emerges.

Fragments, pieces, as always puzzling.

Shouldn't have sent that letter. I wished I hadn't. And I also wished for the day when family groups will bring laughter to those tree-covered hills.

A new life in the shade of the forest, in the shade of their people. For now those hills seemed so very quiet and dark and dense and solemn.

Jerusalem was all I expected; gold and white, fascinating, interesting, intriguing, oriental and modern.

What I didn't like were TV antennas out of place in the Old City. And burning eyes looking at you from flat roofs.

Following you, following you.

What I loved were old olive-trees. Remembering King Solomon and the Temple. Still there. The trunks curved with furrows, dry, twisted.

Who leaned on you before, who sought your fruit, who dreamed in your shade, who plotted?

All the storms and sun-sets.
All the armies who passed you with a song, with guns.
All the prayers whispered by ardent lips, prayers of
love, of concern, of revenge.

Those trees stirred my mind like mother's literary evenings.

I visited places. I visited my parents' cousins, friends. I kept looking them up because my parents wanted me to meet them, or wanted them to meet me, or for whatever reason.

'You promise, you call on Borys? Is he handsome! I nearly fell in love with him myself---Good man, good friend. I hope Israel is kind to him.'---My mother's voice always in the background.

Borys lived in an old part of Tel-Aviv, far from sophisticated new quarters, far from the noise and glitter of Dizengoff.

Small groups of men talking, gesticulating.
the streets, the houses---not always clean.

279

And old people, so many old ones; carrying
almost empty string bags.
And shops, as if transplanted from Eastern Europe.
Some locked due to the owners' military commitments.
The displayed goods sprinkled with dead insects and dust.
The note already curling at the corners,
as if stained with nicotine.

Borys' flat was small. He himself a head shorter than
me. An old, greyish-bald man. His eyes alive, but just.
Luckily his English was passable.

We sipped tea from tall glasses. He asked me if mother is
still so beautiful, if father is still so head strong? 'What are
your plans? If you want to settle here----'

'I don't. I simply came to see. That's all.'

'Pity,' he said, his hands shaking. 'Yes, Ghetto. I often
think of those days, when we were together, your mother,
little David----' he pounced it at me.

'Who is little David?'

Borys picked up a cigarette. 'I should not be smoking,' he
apologized. 'So they never told you? Typical of them,
dreamers, as always----I have to tell you now, no? In few
words, your mother's first husband and their son,
were----how you say it? e-x-t-e-r-m-i-n-a-t-e-d? By
Hitler's men.'

'Oh that. I knew it. Except for the name,' I lied.

'Sure?'

'Sure.' I drank my tea.

'We had our dreams, you heard about our dreams? Like
the end of the War. To settle in Palestine, among our
people----Not many lived to see this miracle happen.'

280

'You believe in miracles?' I felt numb, like when hit hard. Bruises and pain were still to come.

His wife set the table. A tactful woman, but impossible to remember. She served some food. I wasn't hungry. I told them I failed my exams.'

'Big deal. I heard of bigger tragedies.' Borys offered his sincere condolence.

'Funny, so have I.'

'You should see our young people. They have their studies disrupted by conscription all the time. It is much harder for them and somehow they manage.'

'I'll manage too.'

'I am sure you will. You are your mother's son, after all. And your father's.'

A few days later, Negev. Whisked through in a comfortable bus. Sand, sand, sand. Crazy rock formations. Stones---big and small, huge and tiny, but stones everywhere. A few acres of cultivated land. Green, as I have never seen green before. Even greener, because the whole area around was so dull and hostile.

Kibutzniks. Growing eucalyptuses in the sand of the Negev.

I welcomed the gum trees and suddenly wanted to go home.

But I stayed. I kept my eyes open. I made myself see all. I wanted to chase away the image of my mother and her little son. I wandered through the deeply buried alleys of my labyrinthic self.

So when my parents argue, then stop when I arrive, is my mother's first life the cause? And when she cries because of me, is her little boy the true reason?

Jerusalem again. Military Cemetery. Rows of uniform graves, as if ready for inspection. Little variation in ages. From late teens to early twenties.

My contemporaries. Never to be heard from, never to be known. Only in the minds of their people and mine.

Visiting friends, relatives. Constantly urged to come back again. Endless cups of tea, endless advice, endless hospitality. Greater in their small flats than in our spacious houses. The tea always in tall glasses. A custom which must have been initiated during Polish, or Russian, winters, where a glass of tea meant to thaw frozen insides and hands at the same time. How typical of my parents' friends, to carry on the tea ceremony in the blasting climate of Israel. Why not beer instead?

Sonia with a wrinkled face, a dull husband, a funny girlish smile, two sons in the army and the best honey cake.

'I believe you knew my parents in the Ghetto?'

'Oh, yes. Your mother was the soul of our Literary Evenings. She told you about it? You know?'

'Yes, I was well briefed.'

No reference to little David.

'Some people like going back to their past. I don't. I rather look to the future. Unless you prefer to speak of your parents as they were----painful recollections. Who needs them? You better tell me of them as they are.'

No reference to mother's first marriage.

The husband came to life only when I was leaving. He wished me Shalom. Sonia insisted on walking me to the bus stop, so we went down together.

'You want to see my roses? I want to show them to you. Come, follow me.'

Tiny patch of dry sand and a few half dead bushes.

'My husband wanted me to grow egg-plants. Practical. Maybe he was right. But once in a lifetime, I wanted to do something----unpredictable, foolish, beautiful----You like them?'

'Sure I do.'

'It took me a long time. Look, buds. If the hamsin leaves them alone, I will have my first flowers this year.'

'And if not?'

She stood there, looking from her roses to me, smiling her funny smile. 'I will start all over again. It's the only way, no? For me the whole Israel is like my garden. Hard to blossom, yet coming to bloom.'

Back on the plane. After stringent customs search. All my trinkets turned inside out and then repacked efficiently by a pretty apologetic girl.

Shalom, Shalom

Tomorrow, home, tomorrow, my parents, and facing the future.

The roaring of jets. The stewardess serving food on plastic plates, smiling her plastic smile. People queueing in front of toilets, or already stretched on empty seats. Some listening to the piped music, or drinking.

The view from my window is obstructed by a wing, can't see much. I lean in my seat, images crowding my solitude, as always. Keeping check on wing.

Clouds shift, like the mist over Kinnereth. Unearthly light where everything might be possible. Quiet, only water rippling the surface. Sun penetrating, sending rays, sharpening lights, confusing shades.

Rounded Judean Hills, overlapping each other. Bedouins in their keffiyehs, followed by women, all in black and scores of children. One moment in full view, next nowhere to be seen.

Sometimes a man on a donkey and a herd neither of goats nor of sheep. Must have been left by mistake by Noah.

The empty wilderness.

And in the Negev I have seen shapes, ruins, openings, nobody else has seen, for my eyes have been open.

The mystic wilderness.

Had my parents settled in Israel, where would I have been? On the frosty slopes of the Golan Heights, on the sandy banks of the Suez Canal, or another name and age in the Military Cemetery?

Would I have walked hand in hand with my girl through Jerusalem Museum, or rushed home for Sabbath with a bunch of flowers for my mother?

Would I have taken the windscreen wipers off my car, just as a precaution, because at long last we were a nation with all kinds of people, standing on our own feet, looking forward, so we must have our own thieves too.

I slept again, ate again, thought again. Crossed a dangerous zone between reality, reflections and dreams. I dreamed of my mother's shining knights turned into greying shaky old men.

Let the weather be kind to Sonia's sons and the guns remain silent forever, so the boys will return to their mother's roses.

Let the old people's string bags never be empty.

And may there always be samovars next to Yemenite hookahs.

Let the new projects grow, even if every door must bear the name of the donor.

And let little David's memory stay alive in the archives of Yad Vashem as a proof to those who dare to doubt the mass genocide which took place in my Mother's War.

The plane started to descend. The wing is active again, the jets screaming, or was it my inner voice?

I greeted the little boxes, the network of streets, even the traffic, all growing in size. Closer, closer to the ground.

We land on stable Australian soil. Home.

Customs, sliding doors opening, then slamming shut. I catch sight of my beautiful mother and my strong-headed father.

All clear. Going through.

'Good to have you back, son,' father's voice vibrating. Mother all over me. Kissing, hugging. 'Hi mama.'

'My son, my Ober Huhem,' she heaves. 'And how was Israel?'

'It was O.K.'

I, TONGUE OF ALL

I suffer your
I utter your
Dismay, and sin, and hoping.
I, tongue of all,
To all I call:
Take heart! The gates are open!

As I, you wooed,
As I, pursued
Those whom this land has bred:
Ignore the signs!
We are the same,
Alike the lives we lead.

And this was done,
And this went on
Until the scales were full,
Over-full, of wrong
To which we clung—
And then He took the toll!

And now the thread,
The mesh, the web
Are ravelled, slit and torn.
In our own land
We are the banned,
The slandered, hated, scorned.

The gravest lot,
The greatest lot
Dissolves the frothy pledge.
Your country doomed
You, so assume
Your fathers' heritage.

In rack and stress
He promises
Through gentle gusts of storm:
Be unafraid,
The choice is made:
I bid you journey home.

Karl Wolfskehl

BIOGRAPHIES

Allen Afterman was born in 1941 in Los Angeles. His mother was an internationally known gypsy singer and his father a worker in the garment industry. He graduated from UCLA and Harvard Law School, has lived in New Zealand, Singapore and Australia, and has done cattle ranching in New South Wales. In 1981 he moved to Israel with the poet Susan Whiting. They have three sons and grow olives in the Western Galilee.

Herz Bergner was born in Poland in 1907 and was the uncle of the artist, Yosl Bergner. He wrote and published many Yiddish titles, two of which have been translated into English: Light and Shadow and Between Sky and Sea. He died in Australia in 1970.

Lilian Barnea was born in Poland, where she survived the war on 'Aryan papers.' She has subsequently lived in England, Israel and America, and in Australia since 1966. Her novel, Reported Missing, based on the Yom Kippur War, was published by Collins in London in 1979.

Charles Brasch, 1909-73, born in New Zealand, was a major literary figure, both as the founding editor of the literary journal Landfall, and as a poet of renown. His books include The Land and The People, 1939; Disputed Ground, 1948; Ambulando, 1964, among others, as well as several volumes of prose. A selection of his critical work, The Dance of Life will be published by the University of Otago Press.

Alan Collins' family on his father's side arrived in Australia from England in 1844; his mother's family are Sephardic Jews from Amsterdam. He has spent his life in the printing and newspaper industry, and edited a Jewish newspaper for many years. His hour length play, based on the life of Shabbatai

Zvi, was broadcast on Australia's ethnic radio network.

Yvonne Fein is currently a student at Melbourne University. In 1978 she won an award in the F.A.W. competition and has had two stories published in the Melbourne Chronicle. She is married and has two children.

Dr. Laurie Gluckman was born in Auckland, New Zealand in 1920, and graduated from the Medical School, Dunedin, and was a foundation member of the Auckland Medical Historical Society. His research interests center on disorders in cultural and racial minorities. His wife, Ann Jocelyn, who is currently principal of Nga Tapuwae College, shares his interests in Polynesian history. Dr. Gluckman knew and was instructed, in early life, by many elderly Maoris.

Shmuel Gorr was born in Australia of Russian-Jewish parents, and educated in the United States, in England, and at the University of Melbourne. He inherited an 18th century English printing press from a friend and has printed five of his own books of poetry on it. He is a Lubavitcher Hassid, a poet, printer, bookmaker, and Jewish geneologist of great note, owning what is possibly the largest collection of portraits of rabbis.

Nancy Keesing's range of literary activities are inexhaustible. She has written books on Australian slang, six collections of Australian folk verse in collaboration with Douglas Stewart; four volumes of poetry, literary criticism including Australian Postwar Novelists, children's books; and has edited numerous anthologies including History of the Australian Gold Rush, and Shalom, an anthology of Australian Jewish Short Stories. She was a member of The Literature Board of The Australian Council from 1973 to 1977, and its Chair from 1974 to 1977; and is currently the Chair of the New South Wales Committee of the National Book Council. In 1979, she was honored with the award of Membership of The Order of Australia (A.M.). Born in Sydney in 1923 to parents who had been established in New Zealand since 1843 and in

Australia since 1851, she is married to Dr. A. Mark Hertzberg and has two children.

Maria Lewitt was born in Lodz, Poland in 1924, and attended underground schools and evening classes after the war. She arrived in Australia in January, 1949, and supported herself by such jobs as sewing and running a milk bar. Her autobiographical novel, Come Spring was published in paperback by Scribe Publications Pty Ltd., 1980; by Reader's Digest Condensed Books in 1981, and in hardback by St. Martin's Press in the United States in 1982. She is married, has two sons, two daughters-in-law, and three grandchildren.

Dr. Serge Liberman was born in Russia and came to Australia in 1951. He has been the editor of the English section of the Melbourne Chronicle since 1977; and a recipient of the Alan Marshall Award on two successive occasions, 1980 and 1981. He has been widely published in quarterlies, and two of his stories appeared in Ethnic Australia, edited by Manfred Jurgensen. His collections of stories, On Firmer Shores, Globe Press and A Universe of Clowns, Phoenix Publications Brisbane, deal with such themes as migrants, the conflict between generations; obsessed artists, rootless philosophers; and communities doomed by time or their own natures.

Morris Lurie was born in Melbourne in 1938, and has lived in England, Greece, Denmark and Morocco. A frequent visitor to the United States, his stories have appeared in the New Yorker, Antaeus, and Punch, and many of his stories have been broadcast on the B.B.C. He has written four novels, three collections of short stories, and several children's books, one with the delightful title, The 27th Annual African Hippopotamus Race.

Michele Nayman was born in London in 1956, but grew up in Melbourne. In addition to stories and poetry, she has written scripts for film and television, and in 1980 won the Bronze Award at the London Video Festival for a training video she co-wrote. She has worked as a journalist in Melbourne and in Hong Kong for Asian Business Press, and as a business development consultant in Singapore and has travelled widely in this region.

Marc Radyzner was born in Switzerland in 1944, of Polish Jewish parents who had migrated to Belgium before the war, and then to Australia in 1950. He and his wife lived in Jerusalem from 1980 to 1982, returned to Australia to live on bush property, and recently relocated again to the Galilee.

Judith Green Rodriguez was born in Perth in 1936, and has lived and taught in England and Jamaica, where she met and maried Fabio Rodriguez from Columbia. Her later books of poetry contain her linocuts. Water Life was the recipient of the inaugural South Australian Biennial Prize for Literature; and Mudcrab at Gambaro's of the PEN International/Peter Stuyvesant Prize for Poetry in 1981. She was poetry editor of Meanjin from 1979 to 1982; and is currently editing an anthology of Australian women poets.

Judah Waten was born in Odessa, but his family migrated to western Australia while he was still an infant, just before the First World War. He has worked in England, and has travelled throughout Australia, India, Europe, and the U.S.S.R. A prolific writer, his work has been widely anthologized and translated into German, Russian, Chinese, Hebrew and Spanish.

Susan Whiting was born in Melbourne in 1947, and graduated from Melbourne University with a degree in architecture. Her poems, Rites was published by Angus & Robertson in 1978, and she was awarded a Writer's Fellowship from the Australian Council in 1981. She is married to the poet, Allen Afterman. They live on a small farm in the Western Galilee with their three sons.

Karl Wolfskehl (1869-1948) claimed descent from the Kalonymus family, which had been settled in Mainz for a thousand years before his birth. He was influenced by the work of Stefan George and collaborated with him in a three volume publication. Very much involved with the "George Circle," his Munich home was its meeting place from 1899-1932. He left Germany in 1934, lived in Italy and Switzerland until 1938, when he left for New Zealand. The experiences during these years turned him from a poet in the German lyrical tradition of Greco-Roman themes into a poet of Jewish themes.

Fay Zwicky was born in Melbourne in 1933, and began writing and publishing as an undergraduate at Melbourne University. She divides her time between two careers as a concert pianist and as a teacher of literature. She has lived in Indonesia, America and Europe, and is currently a Senior Lecturer at the University of Western Australia. In addition to her own books, she has edited two anthologies, Quarry: A Selection of Western Australian Poetry and Journeys: Four Australian Women Poets.